Labour's Utopias

The collapse of communist rule in Eastern Europe has led to a widespread view that socialism is a dead, or at least a dying, force. *Labour's Utopias* argues that this assumption is based on the popular conception that socialism's various traditions are simply different means to a common end. Peter Beilharz looks at three strands of socialism – Bolshevism, Fabianism and German Social Democracy – in order to assess whether this argument is justified, concluding that in fact each has a distinct vision of an ideal future.

Peter Beilharz argues that as we approach the millennium there is still a strong need for utopian vision, a vision that Bolshevism was never really equipped to provide. Instead, Beilharz sees the reformist traditions as the most viable alternatives to capitalism. Fabianism is introduced as a substantial independent alternative, albeit one that ultimately succcumbed to Stalinism, whilst Social Democracy is revealed as an even richer source of inspiration for the future. The important question posed in this book is not how Bolshevism failed us, but how socialism is to survive the triumphant but ethically bankrupt capitalism of the 1990s.

Labour's Utopias will appeal to scholars and students of politics, history and sociology, and to all those with an interest in the alternatives to capitalism.

Peter Beilharz is a Lecturer in Sociology at La Trobe University.

Labour's Utopias
Bolshevism, Fabianism, Social Democracy

Peter Beilharz

London and New York

First published 1992
by Routledge
11 New Fetter Lane, London EC4P 4EE

Simultaneously published in the USA and Canada
by Routledge
a division of Routledge, Chapman and Hall, Inc.
29 West 35th Street, New York, NY 10001

© 1992 Peter Beilharz

Printed and bound in Great Britain by Biddles Ltd, Guildford and King's Lynn.

British Library Cataloguing in Publication Data
Beilharz, Peter
  Labour's utopias: Bolshevism, Fabianism, Social Democracy.
  1. Socialism, history
  I. Title
  335.009

  ISBN 0–415–06616–6

Library of Congress Cataloging in Publication Data
Beilharz, Peter
  Labour's utopias: Bolshevism, Fabianism, Social Democracy/Peter Beilharz
  p. cm.
  Includes bibliographical references and index.
  ISBN 0–415–06616–6
  1. Socialism. 2. Utopias. 3. Socialism – Soviet Union – History.
  4. Socialism – Great Britain – History. 5. Socialism – Germany
  – History. I. Title.
HX44.B3726 1991
335 – dc20   91-9729
                                                                     CIP

Contents

Preface

In 1987 I published my first book, *Trotsky, Trotskyism and the Transition
to Socialism*. By the time of its appearance – before then – I had come to
the conclusion that my generation had expended enough energy in the
critique of the revolutionary tradition; the time had come to turn attention
to reformism, not least of all given its political centrality. At that time I took
leave of the Department of Sociology and Politics at Phillip Institute in
order to take up a research fellowship in the School of History at the
University of Melbourne. My project at Melbourne was to be entitled
'Bolshevism and Reformism'. The intention was to spend a few weeks,
perhaps a month surveying other national traditions in order to understand
the *differentia specifica* of reformism before dedicating the bulk of my time
to the analysis of Australian labourism. This book is the pretext which
turned into a text, as it became clear to me that clarifying the problems of
central traditions such as Bolshevism, Fabianism and Social Democracy
constituted a major project in its own right. Of the many people I need to
thank, then, first of all I should thank my colleagues at Phillip and at
Melbourne, without whom the project would not have been possible. Two
individuals warrant special mention – Stuart Macintyre and Ian Britain,
both world leaders in their fields, which I was trying to straddle. In 1988 I
left Melbourne to take up my present position teaching social theory in the
Department of Sociology at La Trobe University. Again, my colleagues and
students here have proved invaluable. The La Trobe School of Social
Sciences funded research conducted at Amsterdam, London and Oxford.
The staff at the International Institute for Social History were especially
helpful; my special thanks to Mieke Yzermans and Kies Roedinger. I used
the Passfield Papers at the London School of Economics thanks to Dr
Angela Raspin, and consulted the Fabian and Cole Papers at Nuffield
thanks to Mrs Eleanor Vallis. The letters of Bernard Shaw are quoted
thanks to the Society of Authors on behalf of the Bernard Shaw Estate.

In Amsterdam I enjoyed the help and friendship of Guglielmo Carchedi, and in London, of Michèle Barrett. Paul Hirst was enormously helpful with materials and advice, as was Wolfgang Lubitz in Berlin, and Michael Taveira in Melbourne. Agnes Heller and Ferenc Fehér consistently offered advice and encouragement, as have my close friends in and around *Thesis Eleven*. Many others offered abundant advice, critical comments and help – Alan McBriar, José Harris, Trevor Hogan, Terry Irving, Ian Britain, Stuart Macintyre, Roger Fletcher and Johann P. Arnason. Julian Triado and Peter Murphy have taught me more than they know. Peter Sowden at Routledge (née Croom Helm) has consistently done the things that model editors do, in the most friendly of ways, as has Sue Joshua. The manuscript was typed with more patience and tolerance than I have a right to expect, by Therese Lennox, Glenis Massey, Beth Robertson, and Elaine Young. I am very grateful for their unflinching support. Finally, Lindsey Brake performed a superb job as copy-editor.

For a very long time it has been my blessing to love, and to be loved, by Dor. Our children Nikolai and Rhea, actual doodlers on drafts, aspirant illustrators of manuscripts have always helped to keep us smiling. Finally, as I have grown older, I have come more fully to understand Goethe's words, *Was Du erlebt von Deinen Vätern hast, erwirb es, um es zu besitzen.* I have had the good fortune to be well taught. I dedicate this book to my teachers - N. W. Saffin, Colin Duncan, Zawar Hanfi, and Alastair Davidson. Saffin bid me read Bellamy when I was seventeen; it was an experience from which I have never looked back. Duncan taught me about ethics and about morality. Hanfi taught me to read Marx and Weber, and helped me to re-engage my own native tradition. Davidson introduced me to Gramsci, still the most inspiring of Marxists, and helped me journey through Trotskyism. Each did much else besides. My teachers are not responsible for the conclusions to which I have come, but without them I could not have set out on this path at all.

Peter Beilharz

Introduction

Oscar Wilde once wrote that there was no decent map which did not somewhere have a place for utopia upon it. The global events of the past few years would seem to vote against his judgement. Wedged between the dissolution of tyrannical communism in the east and economically triumphant but ethically decadent capitalism in the west, what then is the future of socialism? The argument of this book is that socialism remains a vital tradition, more vital than we have been prepared to recognise. It is also that socialism has more futures than are conventionally recognised. Indeed, there is a widespread, but thoroughly misleading sense that the varying socialist traditions are merely differing roads to the same end. Thus Paul Mattick:

> Between Lenin and social democracy there were no differences so far as concerned socialist construction and its organisational problems. The only difference had reference to the manner in which control over production was to be acquired: by parliamentary or by revolutionary means.[1]

This is by no means the singular view of a marginal council communist. G.D.H. Cole argued the same proposition in the thirties, when he put it that between Bolshevism and Fabianism the 'differences, indeed, concern mainly the means of bringing about socialism, and not its character when the Socialists have attained power'.[2] This is not a minority view, indeed it has become more widely popularised than ever in the west as the media glorify the events in Eastern and Central Europe, not as the collapse of communism, but as the death of socialism. As Pierre Bourdieu has pointed out, the claim that some thing or other is 'dead' is a wish-desire – 'I wish it were dead!' Thus we are treated in the nineties to all kinds of morbid death-wishes – 'the death of the subject', the end of modernity, the 'end of history', the death of 'metanarratives', the death, now, of socialism.[3]

The premise of this study is that socialism remains a necessary current in modern culture, not least of all because it is home to a good deal of argument about the nature of the good society. The idea of utopia provides a central symbol with which we can make sense of society and sociology – this is a view which unites such apparently disparate thinkers as Karl Mannheim and H.G. Wells. This is because utopia is ubiquitous: all social and political theories contain more or less explicit images of the good society, the society of the future. The massive literature which has been generated on utopianism already attests to this. Yet that field of analysis still tends to focus upon work which is literally or openly utopian in form. The premise of this study is that utopias need often rather to be read out of texts or arguments, especially those which are not so self-evidently utopian as the Rip Van Winkle genre typically associated with the term. This is especially so in the case of modern socialism, because its leading thinkers have often been bashful about owning up to the images of society to which they have nevertheless been prepared to dedicate their lives.

This study concentrates on three leading traditions – Bolshevism, Fabianism and Social Democracy. The primary concerns of this book are political and theoretical. For this reason I eschew the chronology which would immediately be suggested by the conventional historiography of ideas. Bolshevism is placed first because it becomes the ether of our age, bathing all other traditions in its light. The Fabianism of the Webbs, which precedes Bolshevism, nevertheless succumbs to Stalinism. Social Democracy, which survives Bolshevism, leads best into the future. There are many other thinkers who could be included – Sorel, for example, or Gramsci, or de Man. This study does not, however, seek to be exhaustive, nor to offer an encyclopedic typology of thinkers. Its purpose rather is to explain three major labour traditions which originate in Marxism or in local socialist traditions. Without claiming that the three traditions are exhaustive or representative, it can nevertheless be asserted that they raise most of the problems and themes pertinent to socialism in its heyday. It might of course be objected that these were not ethnic labour traditions, so much as middle-class intellectual creations which were forced on unwilling and more sensible local labour movements, that the 'real' utopias of labour are to be located in trade union newspapers and minutes, and so on. Such an argument would reflect a legitimate case for a certain kind of labour or social history. The concern of this book, however, is rather to establish the theoretical and political profiles and coordinates of these socialisms and in the process to throw light on the relationship between ideas, intellectuals and socialisms.

History informs this study, but its main purpose is to address the question: do the revolutionary and reformist traditions merely represent different roads to the same utopia, or do they in fact aspire to different images of the future? The argument is put that they do indeed embody very different conceptions of socialism as such. In the terms of social theory, these differences can be expressed as follows. Bolshevism is in essence a labour utopia, Fabianism is a utopia governed by the principle of social function, while Social Democracy contains an image of the future closer to that of the ideals of the French Revolution or 'new liberalism'. In terms of political economy, this distinction is appropriately suggestive of the real differences between the traditions: Bolshevism represents a foggy-headed attempt to escape from or to transcend modernity and especially capitalism, while also bearing precapitalist and futurist components; Fabianism makes its peace with modernity and capitalism, but apes its early dreams of functional differentiation; and Social Democracy affirms the industrial fundament of modernity while seeking the pursuit of social self-development within the spaces which modernity offers. National traditions here weigh heavily. Viewed historically, the Soviet utopia vacillates between populism and futurism, the British between medievalism and constitutionalism, the German between romanticism and modernity. Viewed open-endedly, each offers endless prospect for the discussion of politics and society – from the aestheticised sexuality of Morris to the public puritanism of Lenin, from the liberal feminism of Mill to the modern feminist utopia of in vitro fertilisation, beyond the scope of analysis here but nevertheless related to it, from the small nuclear family to the image of society as family, from the image of domestic technology to that of collective laundries and cookhouses – all these debates intersect directly with those raised again by Green politics in Western Europe.

The idea of utopia thus offers an extremely fruitful device through which to discuss the question of the good society and, in tandem, to survey the socialist tradition as the critique of existing society. To read *Labour's Utopias* in this way is to raise the possibility of better understanding both the commonalities and differences between the traditions, and to reopen the question of the discursive pertinence of these traditions today, when capitalism more than ever is in need of criticism and reform.

1   Socialism, utopia, social theory

The map of socialism is as complex and variegated as any other. Its different traditions take quite different paths, some to Olympus, others to the dirty water of the Thames. In order to contextualise these traditions we need first to address their sources, first of all, in the work of Marx. But while the work of Marx is central to socialism, it is not exhaustive of its breadth and depth across various national traditions.

Marx, of course, was neither the first socialist nor the last. It is, however, necessary to begin from this fact because it is so often and so easily forgotten. In the first instance, the intellectual hegemony of Marxism within the socialist traditions has frequently led to a sense that Marx in fact somehow created socialism out of nothing. Marxism did eventually become the dominant trend within socialism, but this was later, and it was arguably bound up with its scientific pretensions, its claims to truth unparalleled in other traditions. Where Marx appealed to the value of *Wissenschaft*, knowledge viewed as a human science, Lenin and others in the west seized upon the claim to scientificity in order powerfully to legitimate Marxism as a positivist science. Marx had railed against weaker, earlier socialisms as utopian, and did seem content with the sense that the worldview developed by the firm of Marx and Engels was the real thing. Thus while Marx did not create socialism, he did place it onto a new foundation and open the way to the construction of so-called scientific socialism. Utopia, in this view, was a thing of the past; but as I will argue, this characteristically nineteenth century view merely rested on a new definition of terms – Marx's work remained replete with images of the future, as do other competing social theories and socialisms.

In the last instance, Marx was not the final moment in the history of socialism. Bolshevism became intellectually ascendant after 1917, and is only now finally losing its historic claims to hegemony. Fabianism, often the *de facto* consciousness of Anglo labour movements, itself had little generic relationship to Marxism at all. Social Democracy, the European hegemony within socialism before the Red October, has been buffeted and beaten and yet still emerges as the most potentially fruitful of labour's utopias. And there are other trends which are not here analysed in any detail – the traditions following Tawney in England, Gramsci in Italy, Lefebvre or Castoriadis in France, and there are also other significant national traditions such as Austro-Marxism. Yet the figure of Marx rightly remains central to modern socialism. He was – is? – its most powerful thinker. He speaks to us as a contemporary, as Marshall Berman has so brilliantly shown in his study *All That Is Solid Melts Into Air*.[1] At the same time, there is no justification any longer for viewing Marx as the master thinker of socialism. When it comes to making sense of the Webbs' utopia, say, we need to think of Owen, Bentham and of John Stuart Mill; for Cole, it is Morris, Rousseau and Ruskin who matter, and when we think of socialist utopia at all we cannot help address the towering figure of Saint-Simon.

SOCIALISM, ANCIENT AND MODERN

As we begin to open up the optic in this way, to take seriously the diversity of socialist traditions, to acknowledge the plurality of actors and thinkers given to proposals regarding the socialist future, however, we also begin to risk crowding out the stage. As leading analysts of utopia such as the Manuels have shown, utopia is a ubiquitous figure in western culture.[2] The contrary protest, made by J.C. Davis, is equally profound – if everything is utopic, how ought we distinguish one set of claims from another? Davis' protest concerns mainly the transhistorical nature of the Manuels' view – their study begins with the ancients and ends with 'Freudo-Marxism'.[3] The scope of analysis in the present study is more easily circumscribed. The immediate source of distinction is not Marx, but Durkheim. Durkheim's lectures on *Socialism and Saint-Simon* establish an essential distinction between modern and premodern utopias – in our context, between socialism and communism. In effect Durkheim extended Marx's early critique of primitive communism in the *Paris Manuscripts* into a general proposition – all communist utopias were primitive, as they alike rested upon a preindustrial and moral ethos, viewing economic life as less than central and thus viewing social levelling and generalised asceticism as the telos or goal. This made both the distant Plato and the recent More communists. But Marx was a modernist. Socialism differs from communism in that it is modern and future-oriented, and while this orientation does not allow it to escape tradition, it means that socialism offers in effect a realisable utopia, a plan for the reconstruction of utopias. While communism is primarily a moral utopia the logic of which is that private property is bad for you, socialism – however millenarian – is concerned with more expedient matters concerning the construction of the good society, or at the least a better society.⁴)

Durkheim's text on socialism is one of the most important documents establishing some of the specific differences generated by the field, for Saint-Simon and Fourier remain far more significant utopian thinkers for modernity than, say, Plato or More. In order to establish the field for this study and to contextualise a whole series of debates such as those between Bellamy and Morris, we need to begin with Saint-Simon and Fourier, for while they are both modern utopians, their differences cast light on a whole series of pertinent issues and debates about the possible good society. If we go to the outer limit of the debates on modern utopia, then a great deal of subsequent argument becomes more clear.

Saint-Simon was the founder of corporatism, or at least of technocracy. It is in Saint-Simon that we find the identification of the categories life, or society, with *industry*. Saint-Simon helps to generate a theme which subsequently pervades all socialist traditions, for he raises the issue of status or legitimacy of citizenship with reference to productivity. Saint-Simon's hoped-for world is not only one where those who do not work shall not eat; it is also a place where they absolutely shall not rule.⁵ As Paul Ricoeur points out, Saint-Simon leaves a legacy which affects all socialisms, for he introduces into social theory the theme of idleness and parasitism as social problems consequent on the evasion of the central social responsibility ascribed to citizens: the duty to be *productive*. Saint-Simon then adds his second profound message - that the elimination of the social problem of parasitism can finally lead to the disappearance of the state.⁶ For the logic of Saint-Simon is that the only legitimate social functions are those of production, and those of the scholarship which aids production.⁷ It is no accident that this corporatist utopia is today defended by western labour movements, for it exhausts the contemporary utopic vision of citizenship – good citizens are those who either boost Gross National Product or who conduct *Wissenschaft* as part of that process.⁸ For Saint-Simon was indeed to argue that 'Politics is the science of production'; here there is a politics of economic interests, but no other politics.⁹ Thus the second legacy – for where there is no politics, there need be no state, or at least no state conventionally defined.¹⁰ Saint-Simon proposes that there ought henceforth to be three chambers of government, functionally defined and solely directed to the national productive task.¹¹ Politics would thus become administration, society would become a technocratic utopia untroubled by the routine vicissitudes of everyday life as encountered by the 'unproductive' masses. Bourgeoisie and proletariat would be locked into perpetual embrace, while parasites rich and poor alike would wither and government along with them. For the new society would only have hands, head and heart, and the parasites would be expelled by the body corporate.

Fourier's fantasy was rather different. His utopia was romantic and anti-industrial, privileging the image of the body in an erotic rather than physiological way. Where Saint-Simon saw insufficient industrialisation as the problem, Fourier already viewed factory civilization as a culture of degradation. But like Saint-Simon Fourier had a Plan, and like Saint-Simon his was a plan which was envisaged as realisable. For there was also something of the technocratic planner in Fourier, even if his utopia was rural rather than industrial as was Saint-Simon's. Fourier's belief was that the perfect harmony of humanity would lie in groups of somewhere between 1,500 and 1,800 souls. Each individual, in Fourier's view, was the receptacle of no less than twelve distinct passions; the challenge was to organise a social form which was harmonious and yet encouraged difference. The solution was as follows: individuals ought to change jobs eight times daily; in each occupation they would share their work with other members of a 'passionate industrial series'.[12]

Evidently Fourier's was a libertarian utopia, Saint-Simon's something more authoritarian. While Saint-Simon's influence can be felt throughout Bolshevism and Fabianism, the utopia of Fourier has nevertheless been deeply influential; certainly echoes of Fourier, along with Schiller, can be found in as central a recent thinker as Herbert Marcuse. But Fourier also influenced Marx, in his romantic phase, as had Rousseau. Rousseau, too, lurks perpetually behind the romantic advocates of utopia. For much of modern radical sociology is altogether too happy to take on Rousseau's institution-blaming individualism, for which all evil is social and all responsibility is external. While some, such as Lafargue, are then attracted to the construct of the 'noble savage', others, such as Cole, are more directly influenced by the latent attack in Rousseau on representation, and others again, like the Bolsheviks, are attracted to the idea of the general will which they themselves claim to represent.

With Robert Owen, we return to a different world. While the French utopians stand at the outer perimeter of modernity, Saint-Simon sensing the future in the present and beckoning it forth, Fourier reeling back from industrialism, wanting to go forward to the new idyll, Owen stands firmly planted in the soil of English ethnic ruralism. Where Saint-Simon's utopia is technocratic and Fourier's licentious, Owen's utopia is paternalistic. The authorised, preferably rural environs can return us to a better state, for Owen. Like Carlyle, he believed in work for its own sake; like Cobbett, he identified the old traditions as the new avenue to utopia. Like Carlyle and Cobbett, Owen believed that workers produced too much and consumed too little. Owen's citizens would then live in small societies, of 300 to 2,000 souls, all of whom would, however, not frolic together like Fourier's butterflies, but would rather dig the furrows of the earth, to be edified by spade cultivation.[13] Adorned in Roman or highland garb they would live communal lives in parallelogram houses. Thus Owen's utopia is a spartan, or certainly a *communist* version of Fourier's phalanxes, in Durkheim's sense of the word.

Yet Owen's utopia was enormously influential on the British, if we are to accept their own testimonial. Perhaps this reflects the widespread enthusiasm for the educative bias in Owen's work, the vulgar materialism for which the good boy or girl taken out of nasty circumstances could then become the fine and upstanding citizen. Certainly Owenism gave a practical impulse to feminist utopias, as Barbara Taylor has shown in her splendid study *Eve and the New Jerusalem*, for if boys could be changed, then so could girls be – gender roles could be shown to be the social constructions which they were and could thus be contested.[14] Similarly, Owen provided a fillip for the already existing emphasis on the central value of co-operation for socialists.

After Owen the greatest event in English-speaking utopias of the nineteenth century was arguably the publication of Edward Bellamy's *Looking Backward* (1888). As Kumar points out, after *Uncle Tom's Cabin* Bellamy's was the biggest selling nineteenth century novel.[15] Itself an Americanised utopia, a mechanical institution feeding and housing apparently fulfilled human needs and compacting individuals together in one big 'happy' family, Bellamy's work also elicited the most powerful of late Victorian idylls. William Morris was driven near apoplectic by Bellamy's dark and militarised scenario; in return, he penned the beautiful narrative of *News From Nowhere*. Morris' is an idyll anticipating *Wind in the Willows*, a peaceful pastoral world where machines are conspicuous only by their absence and parliament is made useful, as a storage house for vegetables and manure. The popularity of Morris' volume frequently leads people to dismiss his utopianism as too thoroughly distant and medieval. Medievalism certainly meant a great deal to Morris, though he also made his pact with modernity – and with machinery. Indeed, as Paul Meier has shown, like Edward Thompson before him, Morris' image of the future was closer to Marx's than is often thought – Morris was prepared, like Marx in *Capital*, to reject the capitalist application of technology rather than to snub technology as such.[16]

Today, since the rise of the Greens, Morris becomes more and more influential as the progenitor of romantic socialism, a legacy passing back through Ruskin to Carlyle, and forward to G.D.H. Cole, a homespun English equivalent to the fascinating but obscure utopianism of Ernst Bloch, whose monumental *Principle of Hope* only recently became available to English socialists in their own language.[17] Less scintillating, but equally significant in the context of labour's utopias, is the influence of John Stuart Mill. Viewed in the light of conventional political theory, Mill would likely be viewed as something of an oddity when it comes to utopia. Yet his thought was deeply influential upon the likes of the Webbs, for whom utilitarianism was not the 'pig philosophy' lambasted by Carlyle but a legitimate general social principle leading not to individualism but rather to collectivism, as the state could now act as guarantor of the greater happiness. More, Mill too had himself voted against socialism but for co-operation, and unlike many of his peers was prepared both to countenance and even to advocate the idea of the steady-state economy.[18] In effect, then, Mill had strayed somewhat from the path established by his father and by their shared hero and teacher, Jeremy Bentham, who in any case today is generally viewed with disdain, thanks largely to Foucault's *Discipline and Punish*, as dystopian, father of the evil eye of the Panopticon, master of all that it sees, or is capable of seeing.[19]

Like Mill, Herbert Spencer might at first seem odd company for the thinkers of labour's utopias. Yet Spencer, too, is a vital figure in this setting, for all the socialisms discussed here have a teleological basis. Evolutionary thinking permeates all of labour's utopias, and so too does the organic metaphor visible in Comte and alive and well still with the Webbs. Classical socialists usually believed history to be on their side, in one way or another. So did Spencer, even if he was mortified by young Beatrice Potter's determination to follow his own principles through to the socialist conclusions which could equally well be drawn from them as could the utopia of laissez-faire.[20] More generally, it ought also to be observed that Spencer's most central contribution to sociology – the concept of differentiation – itself became widely influential for socialists, both through his own work and via Durkheim's *Division of Labour in Society*. The issue that was to divide reformers, setting, say Marx against Durkheim, Cole and Morris against the Webbs, arose over the question whether specialisation was enabling for the individual, or disabling. Relatively rare were the voices, such as those of Marx and Richard Tawney, who were to defend the idea of the social individual, refusing to privilege either the individual or the social organism.

If no one today any longer reads Spencer, if Morris and Bloch are some of the reasons why people still read utopias, then Bentham is one reason why utopianism has in some quarters fallen into disrepute. Those who would pose as legislators are frequently taken to be aspirant totalitarians. Yet the problems of capitalist civilization face us yet, and will face us more brutally given the likely extension of capitalism into an even more extensive world system than has hitherto been possible. One similarity shared by

Item Issued

Andrew Stevenson

Student

Due 03/12/2010 23:59

Labour's utopias :
Bolshevism,Fabianism, social
democracy / Peter Beilharz.
Beilharz, Peter.
335 BEI

the otherwise disparate classics of social theory - Marx, Weber and Durkheim – is that they all actually set themselves against utilitarianism, which for them in different ways is itself dystopic. To turn to each in order to explain their relevant views will help to explain the relationship between social theory, socialism and the utopian disposition.

MARX: ONE, TWO ... MANY UTOPIAS

Engels did his damnedest to drive away the spectre of utopia in *Socialism – Utopian and Scientific*. It was Engels, too, who tried to link Marx with Darwin as the siamese twins of Victorian science. Yet behind these claims and denials, images of utopia lurk ubiquitously in Marx's life-work. Marx's work contains at least five distinct utopias – these are to be found in the *Paris Manuscripts*, *The German Ideology*, the *Grundrisse* and *Capital* volume III, as well as scattered in the writings on the 'Russian road'. Further fragments which throw light on the utopic impulses in Marx's theory, and which also deserve mention, can be found in *The Communist Manifesto*, *The Civil War in France* and in the *Critique of the Gotha Program*.

In the *Paris Manuscripts* we find Marx at his most romantic and most redemptive moment. Here Marx establishes a labour ontology – labour is the defining attribute of human being, and so his utopic image is that of a craft labouring society. It is as though Marx was an unwitting guild socialist. As he writes in criticism of James Mill, the good society would be that where, in contrast to present society, 'my labour would be the *free expression* and hence the *enjoyment of life*', whereas in the framework of present society 'it is the *alienation of life* since I work *in order to live*... My labour *is not* life'.[21] In the *Paris Manuscripts* themselves two distinct themes emerge with reference to the future society. First, Marx makes a strong case against the alienation of labour which precedes private property. Though Marx leaves the premises of his case implicit, it immediately becomes clear that his critique of political economy rests on the counterfactual of *unalienated* labour, a preexisting form of activity in which control over the process and the product of labour signal a precapitalist condition which must now be redeemed. If the essence of humanity is its capacity and need creatively to labour, then the image of socialism in the *Manuscripts* is that of the society where this integrity is regained. Second, Marx extends this case in his fulmination against 'primitive communism'. Like Durkheim, Marx rejects the ascetic, levelling communism which we might associate with premodern utopia from Plato to More.[22] The object of socialism ought rather to be a humanity rich in needs.[23]

Beside this implicit utopia of the craft society, written in 1844, we find the far more widely recognised utopia in *The German Ideology* of 1845. Here Marx outlines the future in terms directly aligned to Fourier's utopia. Marx criticises the capitalist division of labour, and in this context proposes that

> man's own deed [i.e. the division of labour] becomes an alien power opposed to him, which enslaves instead of being controlled by him. For as soon as the division of labour comes into being, each man has a particular, exclusive sphere of activity, which is forced upon him and from which he cannot escape. He is a hunter, a fisherman, a shepherd, or a critical critic, and must remain so if he does not want to lose his means of livelihood; whereas in communist society, where nobody has one exclusive sphere of activity but each can become accomplished in any branch he wishes, society regulates the general production and thus makes it possible for me to do one thing today and another tomorrow, to hunt in the morning, fish in the afternoon, rear cattle in the evening, criticise after dinner, just as I have a mind, without ever becoming hunter, fisherman, shepherd or critic.[24]

Two observations are appropriate here. The first is that, while the terms of Marx's discourse are continuous with those of the *Paris Manuscripts*, the general frame of reference is more historical than philosophical. Within this frame the image of utopia is rural rather than urban, but is evocative of the Renaissance rather than of the medieval guild. The issue of terms of historical comparison becomes fascinating, because while Marx is, like Durkheim, Weber, Tönnies, Maine and Spencer, given to a major focus of division between modernity and premodernity, Marx's work is also over-determined by the currents of German Enlightenment, for which antiquity and modernity provide the contrast, and by those of nineteenth century ethnology, for which the great divide is that between the modern and the 'primitive'. The second observation elicited by Marx's text is its relation to Fourier's utopia. Marx's utopia is a paraphrase, or a parody, of Fourier's schedule for 'Mondor's Day'. While Marx rejected the mentality of the blueprinter, and happily scorned writers of receipts for Comtist cook-shops,[25] he did actually mimic Fourier's detailed fantasy in this way. Fourier offers schedules for two Harmonians, Lucas, a poor man, and Mondor, who is rich. Lucas' day is a gentle frenzy of horticultures. Mondor's day has more civilised moments interspersed with horticulture – lunch with newspapers (one hour), mass (thirty minutes), library time (one and a half hours), art, concert, dance, theatre before bed.[26] Marx's utopia in *The German Ideology* seems at first to be Fourier's, if with a carnivorous and cerebral twist. Yet there is more to Marx's utopia than this. Later in the text Marx returns to Fourier, now proposing that Fourier's own work best be viewed as parody, in the same way as we today might say that Morris' *News From Nowhere* ought, more as a tease than as a political program. As Marx puts it, in criticism of Karl Grün, there is no obvious reason why we should read Fourier literally; Fourier is not necessarily gargantuan, but may rather simply be inverting images of the society which he rejects.[27] As for Marx, he also modifies the image of the new world in Mondor's Day by returning directly to the Renaissance, proposing that the new society would not be one where each should be Raphael, but rather a place where anyone in whom there is a potential Raphael should be able to develop without hindrance.[28]

By the *Grundrisse* (1857–58) Marx has in effect developed both these earlier utopias, the utopia of creative labour and the utopia of creation itself. Now he returns to the theme of labour so central to his philosophical anthropology. He criticises Adam Smith, with his Augustinian biblical curse theme itself so influential among premodern utopias such as Cokaigne, and revived later by hedonists such as Lafargue. Marx's view is different. Humans need work, and, we might add, so does the society of the future. Labour, for Marx, is self-realisation; it is therefore neither play nor fun or mere amusement in the way which Fourier suggests. 'Really free working, e.g. composing, is at the same time the most damned seriousness, the most intense exertion.'[29] Here we see Marx as Raphael, but more, for Marx proposes that the work of material production can also be like this, when it has a social character and a character that is scientific (cultural) and general. This theme leads to a further utopic theme of the *Grundrisse*, where Marx unveils the possibility of a technological and automated economy outside which humans might seek their fullest development. To the degree that large industry develops, the creation of real wealth comes to depend less on labour time than on the general advance of science and technology. 'Labour no longer appears so much to be included within the production process; rather, the human being comes to relate more as watchman and regulator to the production process itself.' The worker now 'steps to the side of the production process instead of being its chief actor'.[30] Freedom now seems to consist in a realm beyond the craft utopia of the early writings: its substance is less creative labour in everyday life than the free time beyond that labour. The free development of individualities now depends on the general reduction of necessary social labour time, which corresponds to the artistic, scientific (cultural) development of social individuals in the time thus set free. Wealthy is the society which demands less necessary labour time, where the working day is six hours rather than twelve.[31] Plainly it is the prospect of automation which makes this utopia visible to Marx.

In terms of philosophical anthropology, then, the transition from the *Paris Manuscripts* to the *Grundrisse* is a shift from a labour ontology to an ontology of creation. The young Marx identifies real labour, socialist labour, as creative labour, yet it is labour which remains the vital constituent term. Via *The German Ideology*, into the *Grundrisse*, it is the conceptually broader term – creation – which takes its place. By the third volume of *Capital* Marx has made his peace with the economic culture of modernity; labour has become more to be of the realm of necessity than of freedom. In the first volume of *Capital*, Marx offers the sense that the defining attribute of humanity, and thus of socialism, is in fact the *imagination*: comparing architect with bee, the *differentia specifica* emerges that only the human imagines before acting.[32] By the third volume, imagination may still be viewed as the premise of socialist construction, but work looks more like work.

> Freedom in this field [of economy] can only consist in socialised man, the associated producers, rationally regulating their interchange with nature, bringing it under their common control, instead of being ruled by it... but it nonetheless remains a realm of necessity. Beyond that there begins the development of human energy which is an end in itself, the true realm of freedom, which, however, can blossom forth only with this realm of necessity as its basis. The shortening of the working day is its basic prerequisite.[33]

Freedom is now located beyond labour. Socialism is built upon the fundament of socialised and minimised labour, but its real achievement is to be found in the expanding moments of free time which the new economy facilitates.

These four glimpses of utopia provide some sense of Marx's images of socialism in the west. As will be seen in this study, they rattle and echo throughout later arguments; Morris and Cole strike up an affinity with the early Marx, while Kautsky and some Fabians, especially Bernard Shaw, develop affinities with the later case. The utopia of Marx-Mondor in *The German Ideology* evaporates, in part perhaps because modernity demands so much diversity of its citizens that they develop something of a taste for tradition rather than a demand for ongoing change in a world which seems in any case perpetually to be changing. The fifth image, to which we now turn, is an image closer to the Soviet path. For while city versus countryside is a debate which divides many utopias, the extent of the debate between moderns is less embattled than that between modern and premodern utopias. While many modern utopias contain preferences for, say, the garden city, the central focus remains that on city life.

Slavic political culture of the nineteenth century was deeply divided between westernisers and slavophiles.[34] Marx's own views were clear even before he forged his pact with industrialism, for modernity thankfully brought with it the transcendence of the idiocy of village life.[35] This view is probably less arrogant than has sometimes been thought. Marx uses idiocy in its technical, know-nothing sense, and while Kant may never have left Königsberg he would certainly have agreed: for the age of modernity is also the age of cosmopolitanism. As we shall see in the analysis of Bolshevism which follows, Russian Marxism was torn between these extremes. In shorthand, the struggle between Trotsky and Stalin can be portrayed as a manifestation of this rupture – for Trotsky was indeed the cosmopolitan and westerniser, while Stalin's tastes were decidedly parochial, both Georgian and, by adoption, Great Russian. Lenin's own life and work represent something of a compromise or alternation between these alternative courses, for he vacillated between populism and modernism. Marx helped to make this vacillation possible by giving countenance and apparent approval to a possible and distinct Russian road to socialism. The textual basis for this narodnik utopia, based on the rural *mir* or *obschina* in Marx's work is slim, centring on his correspondence to Vera Zasulich. Zasulich, like many other petitioners, had asked the Old Man whether it was absolutely necessary that Russia follow the long and arduous path of capitalist and bourgeois development taken by Western Europe before socialism would come onto the agenda. Most Russian followers of Marx took this for a fact; Marx, after all, had viewed socialism as the necessary development of an equally necessary capitalist stage of development. England led; others would follow. Yet in the case of Russia, Marx was prepared to allow a hypothetical dispensation: Russia might indeed be an exceptional case.[36] The impact of this thinking into the twentieth century was untoward: first the backward Russians, then the Chinese would do their worst in pursuit of the primitive communism which Marx rejected, all in the name of Marxism itself. Yet the idea of rural utopia remains powerful, both among socialists and beyond, especially since the heightened sense of ecological disaster attendant upon late twentieth century factory civilization.

Marx's stronger utopias, however, are governed to an increasing extent by the sense of industrialism as a human fate, if not to be mastered then at least to be put to good advantage in the pursuit of free time. Alongside these social images of the future, however, there also exist in Marx three fragments of political utopia which warrant discussion. The first is in *The Communist Manifesto*. At the foot of the *Manifesto* we find a list of certain minimalist demands which help to anticipate the reformism of Eduard

Bernstein. Marx and Engels here make a series of demands which sound lukewarm by the standards of postwar capitalism – a progressive income tax, state centralisation of credit, communication and transport, free education for children in public schools. Some of their demands are less meek – the abolition of property in land, of inheritance, equal liability of all to labour. Like Saint-Simon, the *Manifesto* suggests that once production has been concentrated in the hands of a vast association of the whole nation (NB), 'public power will lose its political character'.[37]

Marx's well-acknowledged tendency to eschew a theory of politics is of no small consequence in the history of Marxism. The likes of Bernstein filled the political lacuna in Marx by extrapolating the *Manifesto*'s ten point program into the minimum program of social democracy. Marxism became reformism. This was a plausible enough extrapolation, for despite Marx's apocalyptic vision of socialism arriving by rupture from the heart of capitalism in the penultimate chapter of *Capital* volume I, Marx had in the same work allowed the possibility of real legislative advances in the interests of the working classes in the chapter on 'The Working Day'. But Marx was also a lifelong revolutionary, and the likes of Lenin then found it altogether too tempting to 'smash in the face' of revisionism, and to substitute the vanguard party of hardened professional revolutionaries for Marx's sense of a self-activating proletarian mass. Lenin in this sense simply took Marx at his word when he spoke of the disappearance of the state and politics. Marx's refusal to elaborate an emancipatory theory of politics or citizenship was thus an open invitation to the Jacobin upstart who could simply pencil in his own utopia in *State and Revolution* as though it were Marx's. If only Marx had been more inclined to blueprint, the Bolshevik hawk could less likely have come home to roost.

Only in Marx's very early writings did he pursue a politics of citizenship.[38] By the *Paris Manuscripts* the proletariat had already been universalised as the subject of world history: 'Citizen' now was replaced by 'Comrade', effectively rendering the real subject of capitalism and socialism as the figure of the proletarian.[39] This tendency was confirmed in Marx's later dismissal of matters to do with the state in *The Civil War in France* (1871), and then expanded through Bolshevism in terms of the 'new socialist man', finally found incarnate in the person of the coalminer Stakhanov, hero of Soviet economic life and model of the new producer. Saint-Simon would have been pleased, if not Marx.

The Civil War in France displays something of Marx's reluctance to develop a theory of politics. Here Marx simply refuses the state as a 'parasitic excrescence', necessarily aligned with capital and against labour. The working class cannot simply lay hold of this ready-made state machinery and wield it for its own purposes. The Paris Commune offers an alternative model, a utopia of direct democracy, as it is a working, rather than a parliamentary body.[40] Marx clearly already bears the hostility toward parliament which was to become a general motif in the twenties. As Dahrendorf has remarked, anti-parliamentarianism had almost become a fashion by the later Weimar Republic.[41] German, Russian and Italian radicals ever since Marx have chosen to scoff at parliament as a bourgeois talking-shop; consequently their political utopias have tended to skirt both the question of the state and the question of parliamentary democracy. With the British, given their own constitutional traditions, this is another matter, though Fabians such as Cole, too, sympathised with William Morris' manure-house proposal, itself part of a tradition of cynicism toward (corrupt) government reaching back to Cobbett and Carlyle, while the sillier side of Shaw also deemed parliament to be an unfunny joke, an insult to (his own) intelligence. But where Marx enthused for direct democracy, Shaw was eventually prepared to dispense with democracy altogether.

The question of the state appears again in Marx's *Critique of the Gotha Program*. Marx begins by outlining a transitional utopia, a society which is formed by the capitalist society from which it emerges. Consequently labour here is rewarded in terms of its direct contribution. The state form which corresponds to this newly established society is the revolutionary dictatorship of the proletariat. Real communism, to each, from each, in a utopia of abundance, this would follow.[42] This implicit division into stages of development, between a merely socialist utopia and a fully fledged communism was later to become extremely useful to the Bolsheviks, who could blame all kinds of exigencies and measures on their incomplete level of development while still holding before the masses cornucopian carrots of 'full communism'. It was only in this latter phase of history, as Engels had advised in *Socialism: Utopian and Scientific*, that the state would wither away.[43]

Engels' text brings us full circle, for in it he returns formally to the analysis of the question of utopianism in a way without parallel in their project since the young Marx and Engels lampooned utopian socialism in *The Communist Manifesto*. Engels notes the effective origin of utopian thinking in Sparta, and then turns to the great 'modern' utopians – Saint-Simon, Fourier, Owen. Like Durkheim, Engels rightly views Saint-Simon as the greatest early thinker, the political defender of the third estate who becomes the enthusiast of a new project of class harmony and advocate of the end of the state.[44] Engels' mistake, however, is to drive too firm a wedge between utopian and scientific socialism, as for example when he claims that the solution of social problems which lay hidden in underdeveloped economic conditions to be exposed by Marx, was misunderstood by the utopians, who attempted rather to evolve the future out of the human brain.[44] To accept this formula would be both to deny that Saint-Simon had a sociology, and to let Marx off the hook as a 'scientist', whereas he too, as we have seen, was a utopian, a man of many utopias, a theorist whose image of utopia transforms like litmus with the increasing domination of the nineteenth century by industrialism itself. Science, of course, is also part of this process; but contra Engels the next phase, after Marx, is that of scientific utopia, not the replacement of utopia by science. Science becomes the tool of utopia, a theme already indicated in advance by Bacon in *The New Atlantis* and by Goethe in *Faust* and further extended into our own times by H.G. Wells and by Leon Trotsky.

DURKHEIM, WEBER AND UTOPIA

Durkheim's relationship to socialism is less than controversial. His enthusiasm for meritocracy and professional guilds, his hostility towards inheritance is well recognised. Strong parallels emerge, as will be shown, between Durkheim and the Webbs, via the mediating principles of Spencer. Once we recognise the contribution of Marx both to socialism and to social theory, we need also to recognise the extraordinary significance of figures such as Durkheim and the Webbs, for their unexotic species of socialism have been deeply influential in national cultures less given to rupture than, say, the Russian after 1917.

To make of Weber a socialist would be altogether more radical a challenge. And yet there is a major textile of continuity between, say, Marx and Weber which largely goes unrecognised because scholars have been content to accept the image of Marxism as a self-sufficient science and, at the same time, have been happy to view Weber either as the father of American sociology or else as a secret Nietzschean. The influence of Nietzsche on Weber is undeniable, and it is gratifying now to see it recognised in the English-language Weber reception. As Alan Sica observes, however, the shared centrality of Goethe to Marx and Weber may be even more intriguing an affinity.[46]

As for Weber and socialism, there can be little doubt that Weber shared Nietzsche's terror that socialism would confirm the nastiest tendencies already made manifest by insipid liberalism and stupid utilitarianism. Yet it is altogether too easy a slide to deduce from his public distance from socialism manifest in the theory of bureaucracy, in the lecture on socialism or latent in the apparently negative philosophy of history in *The Protestant Ethic and the Spirit of Capitalism* that Weber's social theory contains no utopia or lessons for socialism itself. It is clear that unlike Marx and Saint-Simon, Weber understood socialism as meaning more administration rather than less. But the theoretical objection here is to the concentration of power in a single, central source. It follows that Weber would not necessarily resile from 'market socialism', any more than he would out of hand reject the social democratic welfare state, provided that it did not diminish either individual responsibility or the principle of the sovereign nation state (an argument with which Bernstein, for example, would agree). For contrary to the sense that Weber's utopia was either America or the dystopia of 'the iron cage', Weber's final message, borne in the lectures on science and politics and in *The Protestant Ethic*, is that modernity offers spheres of existence within which we can aspire neither to Faustian/Marxian fullness, nor to limited specialisation à la Durkheim or the Webbs, but to an ethic of responsibility which nevertheless encourages individual autonomy and social plurality. Alongside the 'radical Durkheim', there may then also be placed a radical Weber, or at the least a Weber who contributes to the recasting of socialism in the face of the new century.[47]

It was Weber, after all, who warned his excessively romantic young friend Georg Lukács that the October Revolution would set back socialism for one hundred years. As Fehér, Heller and Markus remind us, this period is now coming to a close, even more emphatically given the recent path of developments in the Soviet Union and throughout Eastern and Central Europe.[48] There must, of course, now be debate over the future of socialism or the project which takes up the baton after socialism. But in this process, it must also be recognised that the tradition called socialism has to this point been a necessary and perpetual alter ego to capitalism. This is so in at least two senses. First, socialism is a necessary historical response to capitalist civilization. Inasmuch as the 1990s signal an opening period of expansion of capitalism, to the extent that it now finally becomes a complete world system unobstructed by the earlier and partly independent Soviet bloc, the necessity of the critique of capitalism initiated by others but most emphatically announced by Marx and Engels in *The Communist Manifesto* becomes even more emphatic than before. Second, and this is to return to a theme which is common to Marx, Weber and Durkheim, socialism is one constitutive term of modernity itself, it is a social form or utopia which is bound up with and to industrialism and which knows itself to be so. So long as there is any discussion of markets or market/state mixes there will be an ongoing need to draw on the traditions of socialism: it still provides some of the terms of discourse for interpreting and making modernity.

The significance of Weber in this context is that he still offers friendly critical advice to young socialists, but now in a broader theoretical sense, and in at least two different ways. One general lesson to be taken from Weber here is that, notwithstanding the gushing effluvia of critics right, left and centre, there is no necessary historical relationship between the capitalist economy and democratic forms of social and political activity.

Unlike his American followers, Weber was unable to extend his thesis of elective affinity between protestantism and capitalism into a world-historic proposal that there was a similar affinity between capitalism and democracy.[49] In Weber's sociology this stance reflects the premise that power is always better when it is disaggregated rather than concentrated. This premise, in turn, reflects another, anthropological principle. Weber managed to run a line between Marx and Durkheim on the question of philosophical anthropology, and this in turn is suggestive of his image of the good society. Marx, as we have seen, earlier embraced a view of the developed individual as a Renaissance or craft figure; in his later work, the image is modified by the sense of capitalism as fate, so that the individual now seeks 'wholeness' or fulfilment beyond labour rather than through it, in the realm of freedom now located beyond necessity. Durkheim's view was, by comparison, relentlessly modernist – for Durkheim the good individual took his or her place in the division of labour less as fate than as a happy interpellation into a specific place with specific tasks conferring specific and specialised social identities upon citizens.[50] For Marx, the image of Renaissance fullness was sadly lost; for Durkheim, the rupture was a happy one. For Weber, the loss of Faustian universality was also, in some ways, dreary; but the prospect of the calling or vocation still remained, however compromised by specialisation, so that individuals might aspire towards a limited kind of diversity, competence and responsibility within the interstices of the division of labour.

Neither Faustian universality, nor the pathetic options of hedonism or overspecialisation would do, for Weber. Yet Weber, for his own part, argued in 'Politics as a Vocation' as though there was a fixed distinction between an ethics of responsibility, which he advocated, and an ethic of ultimate ends, which he renounced as dangerously chiliastic.[51] Weber clearly understood the limits of orthodox Marxism and revolutionary politics; just as he had counselled the young Lukács regarding the consequences of the Russian Revolution, so here he insisted that if 'one chases after the ultimate good in a war of beliefs, following a pure ethic of absolute ends, then the goals may be damaged and discredited for generations'.[52] And so it has been with socialism. At the same time, however, Weber offers inspiration for the way forward, for he returns to the question 'how ought we to live?' 'Which of the warring gods should we serve?' Weber then closes this kindred lecture, 'Science as a Vocation', with the plain and simple imperative that we each of us find and work with the demon (god) which holds the fibres of one's life.[53] Our gods today then are personal gods, offering ethics which we choose to follow in life. Socialism remains one such god, but in this specific sense, as a metaphor which refers to the values of a project which rests within traditions such as those clarified by

Marx. Notwithstanding the cultural pessimism which oozes from the metaphorical flourish mistranslated by Talcott Parsons as the 'iron cage', Weber produces rather a strong response to what presents itself to us as the face of modernity – 'here I stand, I can do no other'.[54] There is thus a Promethean moment in the social theory of Max Weber, as well, for his work combines a sense of integrity and independence along with a sense of commitment to fully human values, with the hope that humanity might flourish as it may within the constraints and limits of modernity.

With Weber, then, we are a long way away from the innocent hopes and subtle parodies of Fourier, a cultural universe away from Owen and the practice of spade-husbandry. We are even some good way from Marx's theory, with its barely hidden hopes for the reflowering of Athenian antiquity. Yet we stand still in the flow of culture for which ethics remains primary, choices remain our responsibility, and socialism remains one of the choices. Neither Marx nor Weber is less than ambivalent about modernity. Neither Marx nor Weber offer anything like the 'unmixed modernism' which Morris howled down in Bellamy.[55] Morris remains in this regard as much a contemporary as does Marx or Weber, for his work too was governed by the question of how we live and how we might live, and he again took seriously the interconnection of past and future. For Morris understood that history was a process where people struggled and lost the battle, and yet the thing that they fought for came about in spite of their defeat, and when it came turned out to be not what they meant, and others had to fight anew for what they meant under another name.[56] And perhaps more than the others surveyed here, Morris too understood how central democracy was to this process called history. The modern utopian imagination has been far too commonly obsessed with the organisation of economic life, revealing its predisposition to view the realm of 'necessity' as the vital premise of all civilised life. Social democracy is the tradition least completely dominated by this socialism of the stomach. Fabianism falls somewhere in between. Bolshevism, with which we begin, of course had its libertarian dreams, but when it had failed to satisfy either stomachs or hearts then it set upon heads. As socialism through the twentieth century has lived in the shadow of October, so we depart from the most influential of recent labour traditions, from the Bolshevik utopia.

2 Bolshevism

The Bolshevik utopia exercised an extraordinary influence over socialist thinking. For here were to be found not only the hopes and dreams of Marxists and radicals, but also their clumsy, halting yet inspirational attempts to realise these hopes and dreams historically. To speak of the early Bolshevik utopia in practice is to summon up images of the crucible of the avant-garde, of Rodchenko, of Mayakovsky and Tatlin, of the 'new socialist man', new socialist art and fashion, and the hope of a new, liberated sexuality for men and women alike. Yet to speak in this way is also to raise the other utopian voices of October – the puritanism of Lenin, the various hopes of the populists to extend or to return to the past rather than to break with it, the hopes that the legacy of the February Revolution and before it, the 1905 Revolution might be to install now a bourgeois democracy, with a liberal utopia as its guiding star. Plainly the Soviet Union was a mess of competing utopian hopes, and even when some of these visions were finally silenced by the course of events in the twenties the authorised Bolshevik utopia still shifted, from syndicalism to populism, in Lenin's case, and finally into the dystopian project of totalitarianism embodied in Stalin's strategies of forced industrialisation and collectivisation.

Lenin and Trotsky provide the authoritative views of the Bolshevik utopia; our focus here will remain on their work. But as in the other traditions, they were not the only figures who discussed utopia or who offered implicit utopian visions. Four other figures also demand attention – Bogdanov, Lunacharsky, and Bukharin and Preobrazhensky. Bukharin and Preobrazhensky were finally obliged to succumb to Stalinism. Bogdanov and Lunacharsky's visions belong rather to the earlier period, where they jostled with Lenin's for influence over the members of the Russian socialist movement.

LUNACHARSKY AND BOGDANOV

Lunacharsky has aptly been christened Bolshevik Commissar of Enlighten-ment.[1] He was the self-styled philosopher-poet of the Revolution. Before the Revolution his reputation had more to do with religion than with Enlightenment. Like Bogdanov he viewed religion and Marxism as more than compatible. He argued this case in the two volumes of *Religion and Socialism* (1908, 1911). Religious bonding helped to provide the ethical basis of socialism. Marxism should be an anthropocentric religion where God was Man, and Revolution should be the greatest act in the process of 'God-building'. Together with the ideas of Bogdanov, these views were sufficient to bring Lenin out in a rash: *Materialism and Empiriocriticism* was the cudgel with which Lenin then proceeded to beat such idealists into conformity with the mechanical materialism which he viewed as a party item of faith.

Lunacharsky's commitment to a new philosophy brought with it an enthusiasm for a new proletarian culture, another view associated with Bogdanov which Lenin and Trotsky were to reject. At the same time, the Bolshevik leaders shared with Lunacharsky the commitment to education, if not to the sense of Enlightenment which believed that even in the religious sense, socialism should let there be light. Lenin regarded Luna-charsky positively, as a fish who had been caught up in Bogdanov's net, and who could yet be extricated from it by a more ambitious fisher of men. Bogdanov was another matter.

Bogdanov was one of those thinkers for whom knowledge must be invented afresh, a natural candidate for the genre of utopia.[2] Thus Bog-danov lived as he died, finally, engaged in experimental blood transfusion, victim of his own Faustian project to remake the world. For our purposes, however, the most significant feature of Bogdanov's work is that he wrote what has been called the first Bolshevik utopia, *Red Star* (1907). In 1912 he published a second utopian novel, *Engineer Menni: A Martian Stranded on Earth*. Utopias located on Mars were a generalised phenomenon of this period; one bibliography, for example, lists an 1889 work by Joseph Fraser published by E.W. Cole, *Melbourne and Mars: My Mysterious Life on Two Planets*.[3] Richard Stites explains that Mars was a vogue planet at the turn of the century, for there was a popular argument that its canals had been built by Faustian (or Suezian) men.[4] In entering this field Bogdanov was adopt-ing and manifesting the hallmarks of Soviet modernism – constructivism, space rockets, gadgetry, and so on. Mars, as Stites relates, has in Bog-danov's novel become a communist utopia, blessed with a homogeneous population all of whom work, but voluntarily. There is no state or politics but there are clothes of synthetic material, three dimensional movies and a death ray. Consumption is unlimited. It ought to be little surprise that Bogdanov is recognised as the founder of Soviet science fiction, and not just as the Machist adversary of Lenin or colleague of Gorki – for he was the first writer of Russian science fiction to combine a well-written technological utopia with the appropriately scientific Marxist views on communism, not something Zamyatin achieved in his dystopian novel *We*.[5] Mars after all was the Red Star, itself offering a symbolic linguistic pun on Marx's name. It was Marx's planet, planet of the future, heavenly inspiration for earthlings.

In all this Bogdanov was no mere monomaniac. He took on himself not only the responsibilities of medical science and science fiction, but also those of constructing a theory and program of proletarian culture, together with a science of organisation elicited by the development of automation and the rise of the proletariat. Thus Bogdanov is now viewed not only as a pioneer in science fiction but also as an innovator in Russian cybernetics. Truly he was a figure of his time, and a symbol of the maelstrom forces unleashed by the October Revolution.[6]

Bogdanov remains, however, a minor if still fascinating figure in the story of the Bolshevik utopia. The major actors are Lenin and Trotsky. Lenin's work contains at least two distinct images of utopia – the syndicalist utopia outlined in *State and Revolution*, and the populist utopia implicit in the theory and practice of the New Economic Policy, a multi-class Russian utopia. The syndicalist utopia is in theoretical terms far more clearly advocated than the New Economic Policy utopia, which is later taken on by Nikolai Bukharin, himself earlier an enthusiast for the utopia of war communism – the end of money, the end of commodity economy – which is also associated with Trotsky's dystopia, the socialism of militarised labour.

LENIN'S 'UTOPIAS'

Lenin wrote no novels, neither Marxian nor martian tracts in science fiction. And yet despite the general refusal of utopianism among the ranks of scientific socialists, Lenin did offer up a blueprint, a wilfully utopian gesture embodied in *State and Revolution*. The result was likely more fictional than Lenin ever understood, and yet despite this the book has taken on authoritative status for Marxists, and is even touted as proof of the libertarian current which it has been alleged is part of Lenin's theory, if not practice. Before we turn to the task of determining the existence or non-existence of this secret libertarianism, however, it is appropriate to take up Robert Tucker's recent suggestion that Lenin's original utopia was rather different. Tucker reminds us in his essay on Lenin and Bolshevik culture that Lenin's proletarian credentials – so much to the fore in *State and Revolution*, where there are no citizens, only proletarians – were actually late acquisitions. In the leading text of early Leninism, *What Is to Be Done?*, utopia is conceived rather in terms of a union of all non-exploiting classes. Here Lenin refuses the call, 'To go among the workers', as too limited a slogan, the slogan of Economism. His own solution is somewhat broader – 'To bring political consciousness to the *workers*, the Social Democrats must *go among all classes of the population*; they must dispatch units of their army in *all directions.*'[7] Thus while Lenin's conception of the party of professional revolutionaries was truly elitist, it was nevertheless accompanied by a sociological populism. Lenin admitted that this project was at best a dream, but he invoked the authority of Pisarev for the idea that

> the rift between dream and reality causes no harm if only the person dreaming believes seriously in his dream, if he attentively observes life, compares his observations with his castles in the air, and if, generally speaking, he works conscientiously for the achievement of his fantasies.[8]

The Lenin of 1902 was not only the one-eyed advocate of the vanguard party; his own intellectual culture obliged him, simultaneously, to be a populist, for alongside his elitist conception of politics we find a populist image of society, and in this sense we also find in Lenin a populist utopia, as well as the party-utopia, the small band of heroes which leads the popular alliance against Tsarism.

The image of a populist, or multi-class utopia then revives in Lenin's last years. The text which is most frequently associated with Lenin's utopianism, however, offers a rather different sense of the future, one which owes a good deal more to 'castles in the air' than to the attentive observation of everyday life. *State and Revolution* coincides with 1917, with the symbolic year zero of Bolshevism. In a certain sense it expresses both the hopes and fears of that tumultuous year, for as Tony Polan argues, it emits a 'libertarian' image of proletarian dictatorship but at the same time it rests upon a deeper message, that of 'police socialism'.[9] For Lenin's utopia in *State and Revolution* offers an image of the end of the state, the end of classes and implicitly of politics. Meanwhile, the highly steeled staff of the secret police are entering this utopia by the back door.

The utopia of *State and Revolution* is one of direct democracy. The political system, such as it is, is reminiscent of Marx's comments in *The Civil War in France*. Workers are to rule, subject to the three R's of socialist democracy, rota, recall, and relativity of income. Lenin here betrays an administrative conception of politics, which can be traced to Saint-Simon but is more severe even than that of the Webbs. For Lenin identifies matters of state and bureaucracy as *administrative* problems,

problems of registration, filing and checking, which any fool among hundreds can do. These administrative practices represent the substance of the new 'politics' which is to replace the smashed bourgeois state. Who is to initiate this process? The people, the sociological actor in Lenin's early picture has by this stage textually disappeared, pending its later, actual disappearance. The agent of the new political and economic process is now a single actor, the proletariat. According to Lenin '*We ourselves*, the workers, will organise large-scale production on the basis of what capitalism has already created.'[10] The implications are clear. Within the confines of an imagined nation-state (for Lenin's theory of imperialism is simply not here brought to bear) the workers themselves will become the universal citizen, running both the economy and the polity. This is a productivist utopia, the like of which would have seen Saint-Simon grinning. But more, and worse, it replaces Saint-Simon's *les industriels* with a one-class society, it offers a falsely homogenised cosmos in which each is a 'worker' and the workers are the people. And worse still, the ventriloquist use of the '"we" the workers' already announces the heavy tramp of administrative footsteps entering this utopia via the rear.

Lenin, ever the good teacher, proceeds to explain his utopia by use of example. His specific model of utopia is the post office. 'To organise the *whole* national economy on the lines of the postal service... this is our immediate aim.' Here all technicians, foremen, bookkeepers and all officials will receive no more than a workman's wage, all under the control and leadership of the armed proletariat.[11] The state will 'wither away', Lenin assures his readers, leading now to the creation of an order 'without quotation marks', no longer a so-called proletarian state but real socialism. Parasites, the enemies of the people will be swept away, and each will take turn with the broom of proletarian dictatorship.[12] The form of organisation to be adopted by the new society will be centralist, according to Lenin, but not from above (presumably centralist with 'quotation marks').[13] Certainly Lenin views the post office as a model without quotation marks, for his concept of socialism is that where the 'whole of society will... become a single office and a single factory, with equality of labour and equality of pay'. More, all 'citizens are transformed into hired employees of the state, which consists of armed workers. *All* citizens become employees and workers of a *single* nationwide state "syndicate" '. Accounting and 'control', these are the main practices necessary to arranging the smooth working and correct functioning of the first phase of communist society.[14] The convenient distinction between the first and second phases of communist development now enables Lenin to propose that the image of society as a massive factory 'is by no means our ideal, or our ultimate goal'. Rather it is 'but a *step* for the purpose of thoroughly purging society of all the infamies and abominations of capitalist exploitation, *and for further* progress'. For once the members of society have learned how to work the post office, the need for government of any kind begins to disappear altogether.[15] Those who disrupt the system will be dealt with by rough justice. 'And then the door will be wide open for the transition from the first phase of communist society to its higher phase, and with it to the complete withering away of the state.'[16]

Lenin uses the conjuring devices of dialectical materialism in order to present his case as apparently hermetic. Thus, for example, he proposes that the political initiatives taken by the Paris Commune signify a situation where quantity is transformed into quality.[17] Trotsky was later to offer a similar travesty of thinking in his kindred proposition that like a lamp which shoots up in a brilliant flame before going out, so the state, before disappearing, assumes the most ruthless form – the dictatorship of the proletariat.[18] Yet despite all these tricks, Lenin also delivers the firm judgement in implicit praise of his own work, that there 'is no trace of an attempt on Marx's part to conjure up a utopia, to make idle guesses about what cannot be known'. This, of course, is because Marxism is a science, if now of distinct positivist and materialist provenance in contrast to those of Marx's own commitment to *Wissenschaft*. Following and extending the cue provided by Engels, Lenin guarantees it that 'Marx treats the question of Communism in the same way as a naturalist would treat the question of the development, say, of a new biological variety, once he knew that such and such was its origin and such and such the exact direction in which it was changing.'[19] Like Durkheim, like the Webbs and Kautsky, and like Marx, Lenin saw socialism as a process heading his way. Unlike the Webbs, Kautsky and Bernstein, he imagined the future as one beyond bureaucracy. Beyond politics, there is only administration. Beyond capitalism, there is syndicalism, a society composed of workers and only workers, a productivist utopia, a workers' state without obvious political forms beyond the state.

Lenin's fantasy seems to have no apparent relation at all to the Russian conjuncture in 1917. It is as though his head were in Britain, where syndicalism was actually on the march, and capitalism was an effective reality and not an unevenly developed economic form, as it was in Russia. Lenin had understood this when he wrote his earlier study, *The Development of Capitalism in Russia*. At the turn of the century, his own personal scenario had not differed dramatically from that of Menshevism; he harboured no strong hopes that Russia might constitute an exception to the general pattern of development which social democrats expected throughout Europe, if not across the globe. What then had happened to the populist utopia, to the image of a society run by the self-appointed political representatives of the proletariat but actually populated by a variety of classes, including the rural masses?

The answer to this puzzle can be found in a contemporaneous text, 'Left Wing Childishness and the Petty-Bourgeois Mentality', published in May 1918. In this text it becomes evident that Lenin's head and his utopia were now neither in Britain nor in Russia, but rather in Germany. Read with *State and Revolution*, this text reveals that Lenin's imaginary future is German, and this literally: for the proletarian subject of the Russian Revolution exists, but is to be found in Germany. The idea of imperialism thus returns here, but in a teleological manner. For in *Left Wing Childishness* Lenin identifies Russian socialism as Soviet state-forms built upon the economic forms of German state capitalism. This is his hope because

> Socialism is inconceivable without large-scale capitalist engineering based on the latest discoveries of modern science. It is inconceivable without planned state organisation, which keeps tens of millions of people to the strictest observance of a unified standard in production and distribution.[20]

The problem, for Lenin, is that history has played a wicked trick on the Bolsheviks:

> History... has taken such a peculiar course that it *has given birth* in 1918 to two unconnected halves of socialism, existing side by side like two future chickens in the single shell of international imperialism... While the revolution in Germany is still slow in 'coming forth', our task is to study the state capitalism of the Germans, to spare *no effort* in copying it and not shrink from adopting *dictatorial* methods to hasten the copying of it.[21]

So eggs must be broken in order to make an omelette, still even if the ingredients are dispersed across the continent. The case is not only suggestive of Lenin's convenient reading of history, but also of the fundamentally capitalist nature of his image of socialism. For as Lenin finally concludes

> At present petty-bourgeois capitalism prevails in Russia, and it is *one and the same road* that leads from it to *both* large-scale state capitalism and to socialism, *through one and the same* intermediary station called 'national accounting and control of production and distribution'.[22]

Here we see the source of Mattick's view, that revolution and reform are merely differing routes to the same conception of industrialised paradise. The automotive power of capitalism drives all civilisation into modernity, or some variation on its theme.

The problem raised opaquely by Lenin needs rather openly to be confronted: what is the relationship between the utopia of capitalism and the utopia of socialism? Mattick and other critics of so-called state capitalism score too easy a critical victory in their equation of capitalism and 'state capitalism' or collectivism. There is no obvious political or theoretical gain in the empty juxtaposition of the utopia of a 'really free' society (Fourier, Marx in *The German Ideology*) to the differing forms of domination offered by eastern and western modernity in the twentieth century. If we take seriously the arguments of Weber, or Durkheim, and if we are able to acknowledge the distinctly industrial drift in Marx's own concept of socialism, then it becomes something less than obvious that 'socialism' is the qualitative negation of 'capitalism'. It then becomes a matter of definition and debate, for example, whether the capitalist utopia is actually best understood as a market utopia, and what the proper place of markets in socialism might be. In this regard the obvious flaw in Lenin's defence of 'state capitalism' as 'socialism' is not that it is 'capitalist', but that it completely eliminates democracy and the question of democratic forms as a bourgeois class relic. The state capitalist school would then at the very least be obliged to acknowledge that its complaint has its origins in Marx's own insistence, throughout the economic writings, that socialism was the immanent product of capitalism's own evolution and laws of development. For as R.N. Berki puts it, without specific reference to Lenin, the logic of chicken and egg is actually to be found within Marx's own work. Communism and capitalism are united not in that they represent two identical (or different) eggs, or one egg in two forms. They are actually chicken and egg, or more precisely egg and chicken.[23] So here the chickens come home to roost, but these are not the garlic fowls of old Cokaigne, begging please to be eaten. The outcome is that Lenin's utopia stands as a capitalist economic reading of modernity which claims to represent socialism. Lenin's concept of socialism here joins that of Bellamy, and equally receives from Morris a kicking. For Lenin's utopia too represents in this sense 'unmixed modernism', an enthusiasm for capitalist industry as though it were modernity. At the same time, ironically, it also in another sense emerges as a distinctly premodern, or communist utopia in Durkheim's sense – for it remains, in the shadow of *State and Revolution*, a one-class utopia, a society not only without politics but a society unmarked by difference or by differentiation. The point of connection upon which these odd utopic partners – capitalist/industrial, but also undifferentiated – rest is the early utopia of developing liberalism itself, with its idea of a one-class society of citizen-producers,[24] an idea which itself resonates throughout rural tradition in the form of the ideal of the independent yeomanry.

Into 1918, then, Lenin's utopia is that of a westernising, industrialising ideal, one aspiring towards modernisation in the narrower sense. Lenin's future society is one populated conspicuously by male proletarians, who happen, coincidentally, to be Germans. The collapse of the German Revolutions and the practical rediscovery by Lenin of imperialism bring a return of focus to the realms of the Soviet Union itself. Notwithstanding revolutionary common non-sense, the utopia implicit within the experience of the New Economic Policy is likely the authentic Leninist utopia. The utopia of *State and Revolution* cannot be dismissed as a bizarre fantasy; it captures symbolically part of the Bolshevik imagination, and echoes throughout the arguments of Trotsky, Bukharin, Preobrazhensky and other Bolsheviks for whom the period of War Communism itself offered some sense of utopic sustenance. But if Lenin was briefly a metaphorical Trotskyist in 1917, by the New Economic Policy he was, in quotation marks, rather something of a Maoist, espousing the idea of class coalition and defending the idea of a positive collaboration or *smychka* between workers and peasants. The consequences of this shift are clear in the 1923 document 'On Co-operation'.

'On Co-operation' is a significant text in at least four related ways. First, it indicates a revived or even novel interest in the practice of co-operation itself. Lenin, for his own part, had earlier rejected co-operation in 'The Tax in Kind' (1921). Co-operation was a central practical value in the British labour movement, but it represents a rather erratic refrain in the history of Russian social democracy. Lenin proposes that the idea of co-operation may have been a mere fantasy in the past, but that it now moves to centre stage – 'the only task that remains for us is to organise the population in co-operative societies.' Indeed, once the population is organised into co-operatives, socialism will achieve its aim automatically.[25] In this context Lenin refers to Robert Owen, who understood the economic problem well enough, if not the problem of the class nature of the state and the necessity of revolution.[26] But the prospect of reformist co-operation is not the same as the prospect of co-operation after the revolution. Co-operatives under capitalism are necessarily capitalist; after the revolution, they become socialist.[27] Second, co-operation offers itself as a principle of class harmony among the toilers now freed of their exploiters. The New Economic Policy, the partial legalisation of capitalist economic relations initiated in 1921, now relies upon co-operation, for co-operation now offers a non-capitalist form of economic organisation. Co-operation is thus also politically expedient, for co-operatives are the simplest, easiest economic forms, which are also the most acceptable to the peasant. The utopia of *State and Revolution* slips silently into the quagmire, for as Lenin now declares:

It is one thing to draw up fantastic plans for building socialism through all sorts of workers' associations, and quite another to learn to build socialism in practice in such a way that *every* small peasant could take part in it.[28]

Co-operation is thus also strategically vital to the Bolshevik project, as it appeals economically to the peasants and bridges gaps in the economy which might otherwise be filled by conventionally capitalist forms of activity. For as Lenin confesses, a new 'social system emerges only if it has the financial backing of a definite class', which co-operation can assist to secure.[29]

Third, co-operation now comes into play as the centrality of culture begins to dawn on the Bolsheviks, even those who like Lenin have spurned the idea of a new and innovative proletarian culture. Lenin's view of socialism here is that the revolution was the easy part; seizing state power, after all, may not be a tea party but nor is it an especially complicated or elongated process. But now the entire people must go through a period of cultural development, a veritable 'cultural revolution'.[30] Here again Lenin counselled sobriety – the new rule for good socialists was 'as little philosophising and as few acrobatics as possible'; the New Economic Policy (NEP) was an advance (on *State and Revolution*?) because it could be adjusted to the level of the most ordinary peasant and did not demand anything higher of him. Socialism in any case now referred not to the 'classless', one-class, politics-free society of *State and Revolution* but to the system of civilised co-operators which emerged from the class victory of the proletariat over the bourgeoisie.[31] In this vista the image of a higher phase of communism becomes sublimated into the process of cultural revolution itself; the first stage of the new society seems rather to be that which emerges from the seizure of state power, while the cultural revolution would now be seen as sufficient to make the country completely socialist.[32]

There is a fourth level of significance in Lenin's 'On Co-operation'. Whether or not the argument represents a return, say, to the views of *What Is to Be Done?*, it does, for all its populist sentiments, nevertheless follow one particular component of Marx's own thought. Marx's economic writings are all characterised by differing types of automatic and teleological forces. In the first volume of *Capital* Marx, even though himself no co-operator in the British sense, nevertheless waxes lyrical about the positive effects of the process of co-operation in the labour process. Co-operation, according to Marx, constitutes both the historical and logical starting point of capitalist production.[33] It is in the act of co-operation that the egg of capitalism/communism is hatched. For with co-operation we have an increase not only in the productive power of the individual, but also the creation of a new power – the collective power of masses. Marx uses here as authorities not only John Bellers but also Aristotle – in co-operation, he says, we see the essential sociality of the human being.[34] It is not obvious that Lenin's concept of culture is also related to Aristotle's; the primary need of the fledgling Soviet economy is rather that of an economic culture of work in the manner of Weber's *Protestant Ethic*. In any case, the difficulties involved are more substantial than either Lenin or Marx will allow, for while Marx for his part praises co-operation as the site where the fetters of individuality give way to the capacities of the species[35] he does not in this context address the necessary and converse consequence of complex co-operation in a highly differentiated division of labour. Leaving these particulars aside, it at the least becomes clear that Lenin's later utopia not only connects with Marx's idea of a possible exceptional 'Russian road'; it also plumbs other substantive themes from within the depths of Marx's utopianism. For Marx had argued that capitalism was proto-socialism, the ground or bed of socialism. Lenin's revisionism of the 'first capitalism, then socialism' schema of orthodox Marxism is thus a less dramatic departure from the classics than it might at first appear.

FAUSTIAN BOLSHEVISM: TROTSKY'S UTOPIAS

The legacy of Lenin's later utopia is eventually taken up and developed by Bukharin, in the Soviet Union, and by Mao Zedong in the People's Republic of China, where 'cultural revolution' becomes as compulsory as was the forced march into economic 'modernity' ordered by Stalin. The spirit of the hypermodernist utopia partly represented in *State and Revolution* is carried on by Leon Trotsky. Trotsky remains still a source of great fascination. Classical Marxist and cosmopolitan intellectual, early critic of Jacobinism and Leninism, Trotsky also became Commissar of the Revolution, fighting at the front while reading French novels and never letting go of his Promethean hopes, however modified they were by strategic defences of the *smychka* or the limitedly local experience of the Russian Revolution.

Trotsky's deep commitment to classical Marxism already gives the lie to his own utopia – it is the utopia of futurism, of hyperindustrialisation with such few pragmatic twists as necessity demanded. In some regards Trotsky remained throughout his life a 'Department One' Marxist, one for whom socialism without massive heavy industry simply made no sense. Yet while his Marxism was always marked by the thinking of the Second International, his utopianism was also deeply influenced by the experience of the Russian Civil War and War Communism. The point of connection with

Lenin's later utopia here is evident: while Lenin was prepared to accept and eventually to enthuse for co-operation as a gradualist means to the consolidation of socialism, Trotsky's hope was to see the process compacted by a greater emphasis on the process of industrial development and primitive accumulation. If, as Marx had insisted, and as Weber and Durkheim had agreed, socialism was itself a variation on capitalist development, then that development had to be assured. All his mature life Trotsky clung to the hope of the immanence of this process mediated through world revolution. Everywhere socialism itself was incipient, bourgeois civilisation rotten-ripe, the time for the storming of heaven always near. The idea of Permanent Revolution itself expresses this idea of an accelerated, radicalised modernity.

There are two main sources of utopia in Trotsky's work. One is in his Americanism, the second is in two central works, *Terrorism and Communism* and *Literature and Revolution*. Trotsky's enthusiasm for the American image of utopia is more enduring than is Lenin's passing attachment to the utopia of German state capitalism. In this regard Trotsky is an emblem of Bolshevik modernism. Krishan Kumar, among others, has shown in his magisterial study *Utopia and Anti-Utopia in Modern Times* just how vital is the image of America to *fin-de-siécle* utopianism. This is not just a question of enthusiasm for Bellamy, extensive though that was. Chicago, New York, the garden cities... the brash, the adventurous, the experimentalist, the bold, all these signs were taken to be part of the idea of America itself.[36] Unfortunately Kumar chooses not to pursue the equally significant connection between the Soviet and the American imagery of utopia. As W.H.G. Armytage argues, Bolshevism is deeply indebted to Americanism. Bolshevism often constructs its worldview in the imagery of American technology and enthuses for an everyday life which runs at *Amerikanski tempo*.[37] As with Lenin's German utopia, the sense of surprise which we might experience in response to such an enthusiasm is understandable, but misleading. Trotsky, too, worshipped at the alter ego of the chicken of capitalism.

Trotsky's interest, however, was less in the cultural or political attachments of American society than in its technology and productive forces. Together with Lenin and most other revolutionary Marxists, with exceptions such as Mattick and Bogdanov, Trotsky was fundamentally attracted to Taylorism, to the principles of 'scientific' management. For Lenin, the attraction was in the smell of efficiency, planning and discipline. For Trotsky, the source of magnetism seems rather to have been in the dynamics of growth themselves. Thus:

To have Bolshevism shod in the American way – there is our task! We must get shod technologically with American nails... Americanised Bolshevism will crush and conquer imperialist Americanism.[38]

Trotsky details his Americanism later, in *The Revolution Betrayed*, where Americanism becomes the essential nucleus or embryo of Soviet socialism:

Soviet forms of property on a basis of the most modern achievements of American technique transplanted into all branches of economic life – that indeed would be the first stage of socialism.[39]

Bolshevism in Detroit, Trotsky astride the Empire State Building; here we see still in the thirties the power of high Bolshevism's early hopes – the 'new socialist man', social engineering... genetic engineering, no limits, anything possible.

The 'utopia' in Trotsky's *Terrorism and Communism* comes directly out of this earlier set of circumstances. Written in 1920, it is a document symptomatic of heroic Bolshevism – besieged, misanthropic and at the same time wildly optimistic for the chances of remodelling men, women and society. Trotsky's argument rests on a pernicious rendition of the philosophical anthropology which Marx criticised in Adam Smith. Trotsky's premise is the following:

As a general rule, man strives to avoid labour. Love for work is not at all an inborn characteristic: it is created by economic pressure and social education. One may even say that man is a fairly lazy animal.[40]

If the Soviet peoples are lazy, then they must be coerced. This conclusion follows immediately, for Trotsky: 'The only way to attract [!] the labor-power necessary for our economic problems is to introduce *compulsory labor service.*' Where Lenin's utopia in *State and Revolution* is one big post office, Trotsky's in Terrorism and Communism is one big military barracks. Trotsky does not shy away from his own implicit, now explicit logic, for he is a good Commissar, well attuned to the policy implications of political views:

How are we practically to begin the utilization of labor-power on the basis of compulsory military service?

Hitherto only the War Department has had any experience in the sphere of registration, mobilization, formation, and transference from one place to another of large masses.[41]

Where Lenin's image of efficiency is derived from the administrative realm of the postal services, Trotsky's comes from the god of Mars in his most recent Russian incarnation. The new society is based, without shame or even apology, upon the *militarisation of labour*.[42] Trotsky is putting a view of society which is essentially identical to that which Marx criticises as 'primitive communism'. Coercion is the fundament, the glue which holds society together. Freedom means nothing, nor creative labour, in this universe.

Commissar Trotsky denies his own past in *Terrorism and Communism*, just as Lenin had in *State and Revolution*, and with similarly dismaying effects. The young Trotsky had agreed with Rosa Luxemburg that socialism was the realm of freedom, that the barracks was no model for its utopia at all. In *Our Political Tasks* (1904) he had poured vitriol on Lenin for just this implicit crime. Trotsky maintained his critique of Leninism, and his distance from Lenin to greater or lesser degree until 1917. Trotsky's Marxism throughout this period represented the spontaneous democratic spirit of the 1905 Revolution. For Trotsky, the experience of 1905 was transformative. Not only did it show the possibility of socialist revolution, as he argued in his study *1905*, it also thereby took the floor out from under the feet of Lenin and his professional vanguard of aspirant Jacobins.[43] In 1911 Trotsky was still collaborating with the Menshevik Pavel Axelrod, to whom he had dedicated *Our Political Tasks*, and this despite his 'independent' stance, critical as it was of Bolshevism and Menshevism alike. Trotsky understood that Lenin was a shrewd operator, a businessman of the Revolution.[44] He had long ago anticipated the possibility that Bolshevism was incipient totalitarianism.

Leon Trotsky exchanged his conscience for the mantle of power in 1917. He now rejected his old ethics and his positive anthropology decisively. The new contingent utopia became that of militarised labour. But the longer view, and the more captivating image of utopia he divulged only in his 1924 work, *Literature and Revolution*. In these pages we find the expression of the most extraordinary of Bolshevik hopes, producing an abundance of contemporary fears. Trotsky departs from the proposition consonant with Marx, that a new society which fed, housed and even made literate its people would not yet fully deserve the nomenclature of socialism. Only the emergence of a new culture, a new science and art would signify such an historic breakthrough. The possibility of such a development, Trotsky explains, would rest upon the combination of mental and manual labour.[45] On this basis Trotsky rejects the slogan of *proletcult*.

It is fundamentally incorrect to contrast bourgeois culture and bourgeois art with proletarian culture and proletarian art. The latter will never exist, because the proletarian regime is temporary and transient. The historic significance and the moral grandeur of the proletarian revolution consist in the fact that it is laying the foundations of a culture which is above classes and which will be the first culture that is truly human.

Trotsky did not refuse the new art, only its world-historic claims. As to the immediate initiatives of the avant-garde, these he supported as 'realistic, active, vitally collectivist, and filled with a limitless creative faith in the future',[46] i.e. highly compatible with his own rendition of Bolshevism. For his own emphasis was not on the small beer of dealing between proletarian and peasant; his view was the long view, which saw the revolutionary art of the period as transitional in exactly the same way as the revolutionary dictatorship of the proletariat and peasantry was transitional.[47] If the NEP became the general framework for Lenin's utopia, Trotsky's view was that the NEP was never more than a phase; however necessary itself, the stuff of socialism was something more totalising and thoroughgoing than the pact with the peasants could allow.

Trotsky is at home in the world of literature and art, as *Literature and Revolution* well attests. His sociology of art offers some striking insights, for example, into futurism as a manifestation of the avant-garde: the story is by our times a familiar one, where the *enfants terrible* stamp their feet, smoke and fume until they are accepted into the house of art, whereupon revolutionary intentions rather quickly subside.[48] This is bound to happen, Trotsky argues, because futurism embodies a Bohemian nihilism. It denies any sense of the past. Marxism, by comparison, is a tradition which knows itself to be a tradition. The vision of socialism is its tradition.[49] At this point Trotsky's own case catches up with him, however, for the status of tradition is something which is scarcely capable of coexisting with the Faustian hymn for change in which *Literature and Revolution* culminates.

Trotsky's utopia is that of the fullest development of the modern impulse, with classical trappings complete. He begins to express this theme when he suggests that already in the new elementary schools across the Soviet Union the proletarian Shakespeares and Goethes are running about barefoot, but their culture will not be that of the proletariat – it will be that of socialism.[50] Unlike the social democrats who argued similarly, however, Trotsky's conception of socialism was gargantuan. While Lenin narrows the image of socialist culture to a fairly pragmatic definition of what the regime actually produces and no more, Trotsky lifts the optic to the heavens. Trotsky's utopia rests on the idea of a quantum leap from the realm of necessity to the realm of freedom.[51] He addresses the possible Nietzschean objection, that his own view is that of the herd, sentimental and passive. This view he rejects, because competition will not disappear under socialism, it will be sublimated into culture. To the extent that political struggles will be eliminated under socialism, the liberated passions will be canalised into technique, into construction and into art. Art will only then become more general and mature, only then will it become the most perfect method of the progressive building of life in every field.[52] Trotsky's 'political' world harks back to Saint-Simon – no longer will citizens squabble over the immediate conditions of life, rather they will henceforth divide into 'parties' over the question of a new gigantic canal, or the distribution of oases in the Sahara, over the regulation of the weather and the climate, over a new theatre, over chemical hypotheses, over two competing tendencies in music, over the best system in sport.[53] Clearly this is not the utopia of Marx or Lenin. Rather its constituent terms are reminiscent of H.G. Wells' utopian science fiction, with the difference that we are spared the fictional form – for this utopia of Trotsky is a real fantasy, neither a literary device nor an intellectual goad but the symbol of a real imagined future.

Socialism, for Trotsky, is veritably the new paradise. In art, and implicitly in everyday life its achievement signals the end of tragedy. Why? Because tragedy for Trotsky is a medieval form, and fate a medieval mentality. Trotsky's is a universe without doubts; his new world is a world which decisively rejects both the fact and the idea of the human condition. Tragedy seems to Trotsky to reflect the problem of scarcity, or the limits placed upon humanity by the realm of necessity.[54] The logic is direct – once we collectively enter the realm of freedom, tragedy dissolves, for tragedy represents the childhood of humanity which now approaches its maturity. But this is not the maturity spoken of by Kant in *What is Enlightenment?* It is not the maturity of moral autonomy and the responsibility of judgement within the constraints of morality and of tradition. It is closer in content to the politics of narcissism, to the childlike hope that we can in adult life without constraint be what we want to be, do what we want to do, 'love – and do what you like'. Trotsky thus historicises Shakespeare, only to universalise Goethe and Faust. Notwithstanding his rebuttal of Nietzsche, his brave new world is implicitly that in which 'everything is possible'. If citizens are arguing over the Sahara, then we have reason to doubt the extent of their civic development, and if this is so, then it is not clear either that everything is not also permitted. The only apparent balance to this system would be the by now well-worn back door of police-socialism, where the Party decides what is permitted (another policy canvassed here by Trotsky with reference to what constitutes revolutionary art).

Towards the conclusion of *Literature and Revolution* Trotsky turns, unexpectedly, to the advocacy of functionality in art. He criticises Tatlin's design for a circulating memorial tower for the Communist International from the perspective of a blunt utilitarianism: 'What is it for?' On this more pragmatic level, Trotsky now introduces an even more empirical test case for the work of art: the humble penknife. It suits Trotsky's case, because it combines art and technique (or at least design and technique). The shift in register is puzzling; to this point Trotsky has been discussing visual art, poetry, formalism and futurism. The shift of motif is significant, because Trotsky now by sleight of hand introduces science as the premise of art, and identifies production as the defining characteristic of culture – not just in pre-history, but in socialism, too. 'Does this mean that industry will absorb art, or that art will lift industry up to itself on Olympus?' The metaphors jar; art is now redefined in terms of the technique which we have earlier been assured is the logic only of the sphere of necessity; the image of classical antiquity is tacked on, but not blended in. Having posed the question, Trotsky advises readers that the answer can go either way, because both answers signify the massive expansion of the scope of humanity. The atmospheric ether of this expansion is the expansive power of industry itself.[55]

Trotsky proceeds to unveil his image of utopia beyond restraint. 'The wall will fall not only between art and industry, but simultaneously between art and nature also.' These may not be the falling walls of our own times, but the least implication for Trotsky is the collapse or the slicing up of Olympus. The scenario opens:

> The present distribution of mountains and rivers, of fields, of meadows, of steppes, of forests, and of seashores, cannot be considered final. Man has already made changes in the map of nature that are not few or insignificant. But they are mere pupils' practice in comparison with what is coming. Faith merely promises to move mountains; but technology, which takes nothing 'on faith', is actually able to cut down mountains and move them. Up to now this was done for industrial purposes (mines) or for railways (tunnels); in the future this will be done on an immeasurably larger scale, according to a general industrial and artistic plan. Man will occupy himself with re-registering mountains and rivers, and will earnestly and repeatedly make improvements in nature.

Man will rebuild the earth, if not in his own image, at least to his own taste – his own *good* taste, Trotsky the cosmopolitan hastens to add.[56] The optic opens yet further. The walls of the social laboratory collapse. The world is society's procrustean bed. Nothing can be left unturned.

> Through the machine, man in Socialist society will command nature in its entirety, with its grouse and sturgeons. He will point out places for mountains and for passes. He will change the course of the rivers, and he will lay down rules for the oceans. The idealist simpletons may say that this will be a bore, but that is why they are simpletons. Of course this

does not mean that the entire globe will be marked off into boxes, that the forests will be turned into parks and gardens. Most likely, thickets and forests and grouse and tigers will remain, but only where man commands them to remain. And man will do it so well that the tiger won't even notice the machine, or feel the change, but will live as he lived in primeval times [for]... The machine is the instrument of modern man in every field of life... The passion for mechanical improvements, as in America, will accompany the first stage of every new Socialist society.[57]

To read these passages and reread them is to be amazed anew, each time, as we enter the decade before the twenty-first century. For the capitalist Prometheus has achieved much of Trotsky's hopes, albeit in the image of capitalism, and not socialism. Socialism has had its moments, its five-year plans, in the construction of the socialist dams of the *Dneprostroi*, the impossibly massive hospitals, the mega jetplanes. Plainly this utopia in Trotsky is closest of all to Bellamy, or to Wells' caricature of the Webbs. Morris and Marx would have been carried out kicking, pleading like Weber 'who will live in this world?'

For Trotsky seems to have made a fetish of the backwardness of Russian history, and equally of its necessary replacement by his own conception of Soviet modernity. His own idea of rural idiocy was far more contemptuous than that of Marx, for he was the peasant's son who fell in love with Odessa, and then with Paris and Vienna. Rural life was a sort of intellectual suicide, even more than idiocy, for Leon Trotsky. But in the process of criticising the banality of ordinary everyday life he seems to have acquired nothing but contempt for the realm of necessity. Rationality he identified with consciousness and planfulness. Domestic life he described in terms of its present and worm-eaten texture, the care for family, food and education as a millstone on the present-day, presocialist family. Thus his hypermodernist scenario he envisaged, also, as a feminist utopia, for only with the arrival of the new society would woman at last be able to free herself from her semi-servile condition.[58] Writing in the context of a culture torn in strips, in all directions by war, civil war, famine and pestilence the young eagle's mind could respond only by soaring to Olympus, rising to a sense of utopia which makes Marx's automated society of the *Grundrisse* look like kindergarten. The obvious objection from any critical perspective, socialist or feminist, is that the food still must reach the table, and that the habits and practices of everyday life, however tedious, do still constitute part of being into the new century.

But Trotsky has not yet finished. There is more yet to his utopian vision in *Literature and Revolution*. Experimentalism, not tradition will become the norm under socialism.

Communist life will not be formed blindly like coral islands, but will be built consciously, will be tested by thought, will be directed and connected. Life will cease to be elemental, and for this reason stagnant. Man, who will learn how to move rivers and mountains, how to build peoples' palaces on the peaks of Mont Blanc and at the bottom of the Atlantic, will not only be able to add to his own life richness, brilliance and intensity, but also a dynamic quality of the highest degree. The shell of life will hardly have time to form before it will burst open again under the pressure of new technical and cultural inventions and achievements.[59]

Fourier in the laboratory, a veritable feeding frenzy, this is the content beneath the everchanging forms of Trotsky's utopia. For, as Trotsky assures us, 'Life in the future will not be monotonous.' Men will be as gods.

Man will at last begin to harmonize himself in earnest. He will make it his business to achieve beauty by giving the movement of his own limbs the utmost precision, purposefulness and economy in his work, his walk and his play. He will try to master first the semi-conscious and then the subconscious processes in his own organism, such as breathing, the circulation of the blood, digestion, reproduction, and, within necessary limits, he will try to subordinate them to the control of reason and will.

Artificial selection will open further possibilities. The unconscious will be sorted out, instincts raised to the heights of consciousness, made transparent, man will seek to 'extend the voices of his will into hidden recesses, and thereby to raise himself to a new plane, to create a higher social biologic type, or if you please, a superman'. Trotsky here manages the remarkable, for he synthesises the aristocratic radicalism and nihilism of Nietzsche with the worst kind of rationalism, a species hard to find among the central thinkers of the Enlightenment, into a new Frankenstein monster. Trotsky hates the past; its only redeeming moment is in the image of Sparta. He loves only the future, and he fetishises his own image of it, as relentlessly moving, shifting, rupturing, restless, impatient. So much is Trotsky persuaded by the gushing of his own rhetoric that he confesses he is unable to envisage where all this may end:

It is difficult to predict the extent of self-government [!] which the man of the future may reach or the heights to which he might carry his technique... Man will become immeasurably stronger, wiser and subtler; his body will become more harmonized, his movements more rhythmic, his voice more musical. The forms of life will become dynamically dramatic. The average human type will rise to the heights of an Aristotle, a Goethe, or a Marx. And above this ridge new peaks will rise.[60]

The 'lazy animal' of *Terrorism and Communism* dispatched, we now see the new socialist man in full vision. Aristotle here seems an anachronism, a classical throwback to times Trotsky feels that he should appreciate. Marx's character-type is not especially edifying in terms of the new socialist man; would-be revolutionary, he spent far too much time engaged in solitary scribbling. Goethe, the real aspirant to all that is human, this makes better sense as an ideal-type for the society of the future. Trotsky in full flight from the exigencies of everyday life has no capacity, as did Marx in *The German Ideology*, to view socialism as the utopia where those with the talents of Raphael are able to flourish as artists. A technocratic Leonardo in the spirit of Bogdanov, this would seem closer to his ideal citizen.

Yet there is more to Trotsky even than this. As Peter Murphy observes, Trotskyism as a tradition attracts those who are prepared to worship a special and singular category, that of the *sublime*.[61] The sublime, and not the beautiful is the zenith of human achievement for Trotsky; thus the Dionysian thrust of his utopia. For as Norman Hampson reminds us, in discussion of Burke in his study of the Enlightenment, the idea of the sublime is invariably counterpoised to that of stability, or harmony, so that the sublime necessarily contains within it an element of terror, related to an idea of pain and danger.[62] The developmental romanticism in Trotsky inspires the sense of 'delightful horror', delightful terror of nature now ascribed to man as God. Men will be gods, creating the intense, the oceanic, the immense, dealing in infinity, and in vertigo, leaving no silence, no stone or tiger unturned, installing creative frenzy everywhere, occupying the mind eternally, leaving no place for rest, or for tradition. In *Literature and Revolution* the sublime then departs from its own sphere of existence to become politics, nay, to become all of life itself. Beyond creation, beyond development, there is nothing.

On examination Trotsky thus emerges as a striking and peculiar example of the humanist utopian.[63] To change the world, this fundamental premise of Marxism and socialism becomes, however, for Trotsky not a means but an end in itself. The scenario sketched here does not seem to be atypical in the way that the utopia of *State and Revolution* is in Lenin's work. Trotsky's is a line which runs back to Bacon's *New Atlantis*. Happiness and freedom are bound to experiment, and evolution facilitated by revolution liberates the developmental dynamic which makes us what we are. Not freedom but perfection is the aim of social organisation. Stupidity, darkness and evil will go the same way as the idiocy of village life. Trotsky thus unwittingly presents himself as the whipping-boy for the critics of the Enlightenment, for even despite his numerous empty hopes, Marx does not answer to the caricature presented by postmodernists of Marxist rationalism. Trotsky does, and without flinching. At the same time, along-

side this heroic persona in Trotsky we find a more ordinary, social democratic humanism, which helps to explain the continuity of his utopian
images. Trotsky's ordinary hopes are that ordinary people might live better
lives, lives more fulfilling than those of the miserable poor peasants who
were Russia to Trotsky in his childhood and thereafter. Thus in his less
pyrotechnic moments Trotsky, like Marx, Mill and Fourier argued that the
progress of modernity would be determined by the place it gave to women,
could seriously discuss problems of domestic labour and its allocation,
would regale against the masculinism of comrade-communists and their
drunkenness, argue like Bebel in defence of collective provision of services, discuss civility and the cinema, and thus he could argue that abundance would open the way to the sublime, an apparently long but logically
short step from the problems of everyday life.[64] In Trotsky's thinking the
developmental fantasy of *Literature and Revolution* actually nestles, await-
ing, within the shell of his ordinary politics, for this was a mere step, from
the lazy animal to *homo faber*, to *homo activus*. Three or four hours of
necessity would then give way to spiritual reflection. And all of this could
be afforded by the Taylor system. To take too seriously the cultural
criticisms of Tolstoy or Ruskin would be to accept that we must descend
back to barbarity, for Trotsky.[65]

UTOPIA IN LENIN AND IN TROTSKY

With the exception of the outburst in *State and Revolution*, Lenin's utopia
was more modest than Trotsky's. Lenin's early utopia was closer to the
shrewdness of the *muzhik* or peasant than to the dreaming of the narodniks.
As he argued, for example in *The Agrarian Question in Russia Towards the
Close of the Nineteenth Century* (1908), the relations of the *mir* or feudal
commune were unable to prevent the proletarianisation of the peasants, for
the *mir* was ultimately a medieval barrier which was eroded by the development of capitalist relations themselves.[66] This argument reflected the earlier
view, developed in *To The Rural Poor* (1903), where Lenin had argued that
the *mir* was a rotten economic union between exploiters and exploited,
whereas what socialism called for was rather a voluntary political association of the people who would unite with the urban populace against the
rich.[67] Lenin's utopian hope was not for the nostalgic aura of the *mir*, but
rather for the populist union against the 'power of money'. The Bolsheviks
were not medievalists, but the extent to which they were avid westernisers
varied, say, from Lenin to Trotsky. Unlike Morris and Cole, the Russian
and German Social Democrats harboured mainly bad recollections of the
age of the guilds. Their eyes looked firmly forward, not hopefully back. The
difference between Lenin and Trotsky, subject to so much debate, was not

over the necessity of the revolutionary dictatorship of the proletariat and peasantry, for this view can be found for example in Lenin's *Two Tactics* and in Trotsky's *Results and Prospects* alike. Their dispute had rather to do with the more ruptural and futuristic conception of socialism advocated by Trotsky and the more gradualistic scenario envisaged by Lenin.

This proximate coincidence of views between Lenin and Trotsky would seem to cast some doubt on the substance of Marx's hope for a 'Russian road' incorporating larger elements of the past such as the *mir* or village commune. In terms of the scope of the present study, this would confirm the substantive claim stressed by Marx, Weber and Durkheim alike that socialism was irredeemably bound up with modernity and with industrialism, though it can equally well be objected that such a conclusion only inadequately addresses the question of the critical status of industrial civilisation itself. Marx, in his time, both accepted industrial civilisation as fate and yet pondered the possibility of alternative paths of development. The path of subsequent development itself suggests that the so-called Russian road was a mere idea, a mere possibility, lacking the strength, say, of later guild socialist argument for which the guild was an outer idea or housing within which qualitatively new social relations could be imagined.

Lenin and Trotsky agreed that capitalism was necessary to socialism, but only for Trotsky was this a hyperdevelopmental message. In this sense both the Bolshevik leaders were Americanists, but only Trotsky had a futuristic conception of Americanism. Lenin viewed the Taylor system as an example of capitalism's need to enslave men to the machine. At the same time it aided the process of the development of social production. Socialist Taylorism, that is to say... this was another thing.[68] Thus state capitalism combined with Soviet political forms or superstructure meant something very like socialism. For Trotsky the semantics of socialism could not so easily be undermined, though he too viewed Taylorism with relish.[69] Notwithstanding their differences, Trotsky here was closer to the later Marx – socialism was bound to be industrial, therefore the substantive image of utopia was definitionally developmentalist.

In strictly analytical terms, the vital question here concerns the status of the utopia in *Literature and Revolution*. In the past there were doubtless those enthusiasts who, before the horrors of the twentieth century, viewed Trotsky's scenario with dewy-eyed delight. Today probably some people would excuse it as a circumstantial flourish; after all, it can be argued, eugenics was in the air, and so on. Doubtless others again would argue that Trotsky's real utopia is to be found in the moderate political economy of the mid-late twenties. On balance, it seems that the utopia of *Literature and Revolution* represents the authentic high-point of Trotsky's socialism, and that the utopia therein is continued into the later classics such as *The*

Revolution Betrayed and *The Transitional Program*. Trotsky, in short, did not dedicate his life to the idea of a peasant–proletarian utopia, but to the actuality of the idea of Permanent Revolution, a revolution which would sweep the globe and install an industrialised socialist system in the place of the unevenness of capitalist civilisation. The scenario of Goethes, Aristotles and Marxs hanging about on street corners is entirely consistent with this predictive framework.

Certainly it ought to be acknowledged that the atmosphere of War Communism still pervades *Literature and Revolution*. But Trotsky's was always, after 1917, an heroic Marxism. Heroic Bolshevism had its heroic thinker: it was Trotsky, not Lenin. Hero-worship became a major motif, subsequently, especially in the work of Isaac Deutscher, who echoes back not to Nietzsche but to Carlyle.[70] Trotsky's utopia in *Literature and Revolution* was emphatically not that of Carlyle, where any work was good work and the air smelled of the twelfth century. But neither was Trotsky's union with Lenin ever more than partial and circumstantial, at least when it came to the image of socialism itself. For Trotsky the NEP was only ever a necessary strategic retreat or Faustian pact. The *smychka* between peasants and proletarians rested still on the power of the workers, this fundamental class. The alliance had as its purpose the development of industry of Department One, as Trotsky made clear in his economic writings of the early twenties.[71] Here he spoke of a new course, but it was still one directed to the same industrial end. As Richard Day has shown in his monograph *Leon Trotsky and the Politics of Economic Isolation*, Trotsky was in no way given to the absolute pursuit of the slogan of Permanent Revolution.[72] But nor was he ever able to make peace with the slogans which Bukharin drew from the NEP as an implicit extension of Lenin's views, that the peasants now ought legitimately to seek to 'enrich themselves', and that socialism was now to be achieved 'at a snail's pace'. For Trotsky this kind of concession would never do; the Soviet Union in the twenties had daily to confront the choice: toward capitalism or socialism?[73] Now, in 1925, he writes in somewhat less elevated register that 'Socialism means accounting'.[74] The mentality is close to Lenin, but it is reminiscent of the Lenin of *State and Revolution* rather than the minimalist pragmatism of 'On Cooperation'. For while Trotsky may momentarily have been a market socialist of necessity, the market was never to become a virtue in his theory: socialism was essentially about planning and control, whether under the sign of accounting or under that of the reign of the supermen.

In Lenin, the politics of socialism is in some ways that of the ordinary humanism latent in *The April Theses* – where there is milk, no child should be without milk. This motivation to revolution echoes throughout the work of the early Trotsky, the Trotsky of *1905*. In the work of Lenin and Trotsky alike it indicates a minimalist humanism, for which humans first of all must eat. In Lenin this residuum is too readily vulnerable to the charge that it is indeed 'socialism of the stomach'. Too late does Lenin discover that humans do not live by bread alone. Trotsky's humanism, by comparison, both works at this level and then soars to altogether empyrean heights.

In both cases these difficulties are accompanied by the political myopia of Bolshevism, which never understood the significance of the bourgeois revolution or of its revolution in civil rights. This remains a point of some contrast with Marx. For while Marx too scoffed at the all-too-human achievements of the bourgeoisie's political life, he did understand that the industrial revolution conferred incomplete, formal freedom upon citizens as wage-labourers. The Bolsheviks, along with the syndicalists and libertarians continued to view wage-labour as wage-slavery. It was only later, with a thinker such as Gramsci, that the realisation occurred: if the bourgeoisie offers us freedom, let us then hold them to their claim, and replace their social domination if this proves to be impossible.[75] Such a position remained beyond the instrumental grasp of the Bolsheviks, and necessarily, because it rests upon an ethics, a recognition which their 'science' obliged them to refuse. They were vocational revolutionaries, Marxists on a mission. Here, finally, Lenin is even less salvageable than Trotsky. Perhaps because Trotsky had ridiculed Lenin's Jacobinism in his 1904 *Our Political Tasks*, Trotsky was able to become a practical Robespierre but was hardly ever able to defend this shift other than as an alleged coming of age. Lenin in this regard remains the more politically dangerous, the practical embodiment of the pursuit of the sublime – restless, unable any longer to listen to Beethoven lest his vigilance slip, given to outbursts of sexual puritanism, given to the practical advocacy of the Republic of Virtue which Trotsky only imagined, but did not himself consistently strive towards. For the Bolsheviks did, after all, believe that October was their predestination; they did, in different ways, view themselves as the Elect.[76]

BUKHARIN AND PREOBRAZHENSKY

Bolshevism was, and remains, a distinct phenomenon, and for all its transient characteristics it remains a problem for both east and west. Certainly there is no justification for the desire of some to simply reverse the signs, to turn Lenin and Trotsky from heroes into anti-heroes. Yet the phenomenon might be better understood if we expand the analysis to take in the other leading Bolsheviks, Nikolai Bukharin and Evgenii Preobrazhensky. Both were leading figures in the high Bolshevik disputes of the twenties. Each provides a direct echo and extension of the themes raised in the discussion of Lenin and Trotsky. For Bukharin was to extend Lenin's strategy of compromise, while Preobrazhensky was to take to its logical conclusion the utopianism of War Communism itself.

Bukharin has long been recognised as a leading thinker within Bolshevism, not least of all because of his attempt to produce a Marxist sociology in his 1921 study, *Historical Materialism*. Bukharin's project was to argue for and to develop a proletarian social science, a proletarian sociology called historical materialism. The project was doomed, the breadth of Bukharin's scholarship notwithstanding.[77] Bukharin discussed Marx, Weber and Durkheim but nevertheless managed to work mainly in the shadow of Spencer. For Bukharin travels wide and far over nineteenth century sociological terrain – causation and teleology, determinism and free will, equilibrium and disturbance – before concluding his survey on the theme of the classless society of the future. Here Bukharin's enthusiasm extends only to allegedly disproving Michels' iron law of oligarchy. Bukharin's is the bad utopianism for which domination is dismissed with a gesture: if socialist administrators have power, it will be over machines, not over men. For communist citizens, after all, will be 'highly cultivated persons, conscious of themselves and others', who 'will become a single, harmoniously constructed human society'.[78]

The picture of socialism in the work of the early Bukharin becomes clearer in the text he co-authored with Preobrazhensky, the aptly-titled *ABC of Communism*. The lessons offered by the schoolmasters are clear. Under communist society there will be no classes, but rather a '*society of comrades, a communist society based on labour*'.[79] Thus Bukharin and Preobrazhensky think of their utopia in Marx's terms in *Capital* volume III. But they also see its features in terms anticipating the then still unknown *German Ideology*, for under communism 'there will not be persons who do one and the same kind of work throughout their lives.'

Under capitalism, if a man is a bootmaker he spends his whole life making boots (the cobbler sticks to his last); if he is a pastrycook, he spends all his life baking cakes; if he is the manager of a factory he spends his days in issuing orders and in administrative work; if he is a mere labourer, his whole life is spent in obeying orders. Nothing of this sort happens in communist society. Under communism people receive a many-sided culture, and find themselves at home in various branches of production; to-day I work in an administrative capacity, I reckon up how many felt boots, or how many French rolls must be produced during the following month; to-morrow I shall be working in a soap factory, next month perhaps in a steam laundry, and the month after in an electric power station.[80]

The utopia here is that of *The German Ideology* placed within strictly modern industrial confines; it joins Marx's Fourieresque tease to Lenin's axiom that Russian socialism was electrification plus soviets. And as in Saint-Simon, as in *State and Revolution*, Bukharin and Preobrazhensky also do away with the state. There will be no classes, therefore there will be no state.[81] Under capitalism there are capitalists, landlords, and labourers; under communism there are simply people, only 'comrades'.[82] It was only in the twenties that Bukharin was to become mortified about the fearful prospects of those 'comrades' who were 'commissars'.

Who then would 'run' society? Obviously, the comrades themselves would:

> ...all will work in accordance with the indications of... statistical bureaux. There will be no need for special ministers of State, for police and prisons, for laws and decrees... Just as in an orchestra all the performers watch the conductor's baton and act accordingly, so here will all consult the statistical reports and will direct their work accordingly.[83]

If the imagery of statistical bureaux conjures up the presence of Sidney Webb, the idea of the orchestra indicates just how thoroughly well read were the authors in the works of Marx, and how ill-prepared they were at this stage to think outside of them. This is utopia made easy – 'Within a few decades there will be quite a new world, with new people and new customs.'[84] Social parasitism and waste will simply disappear, along with gluttonous capitalists, drunkards, priests and prostitutes.[85] The working day will shrink and human culture will climb to heights never attained before.[86] For however astonishingly, Bukharin and Preobrazhensky were nevertheless able to assert in their communist ABC that the choice was stark; chaos or communism.[87] The period of War Communism was, however, the most bizarre kind of chaos itself, but this did not prevent Bukharin and Preobrazhensky from arguing for the end of money with the end of the state.[88]

At this point of the argument it becomes necessary to separate out again the ideas of Bukharin and of Preobrazhensky. While both were conspicuously left-wing communists in this period, Bukharin alone was to proclaim the obsolescence of his views, henceforth to develop a right-wing or pragmatic defence of Lenin's own legacy in 'On Co-operation', privileging now the NEP rather than civil war, and developing the two-class image of utopia, peasants alongside workers, organised in co-operative forms. More than this, from the early twenties he actually was to argue, like Durkheim, like the later Cole, for the necessity of intermediate groupings in civil society to stand between the state and the individual.[89] Alone among his peers, Bukharin had the courage to renounce his leftist utopia as exhausted and to turn to an internal, post-revolutionary defence of evolutionary socialism. Now, into the mid-twenties, he not only viewed the two-class utopia as a domestic scenario but also as a global framework. Henceforth, he believed, the *smychka* was not just a local goal and strategy, but also a global link between the world city or proletariat and the world countryside or peasant.[90] In this argument Bukharin harked back to his earlier, leftist analysis of *Imperialism and World Economy*. The difference was that now Bukharin was prepared to take the idea of uneven development even more seriously than Trotsky, whose own conception of uneven development rested still on the principle of the ever-expanding productive forces of capitalism. Like Marx, Trotsky was committed to a sense that the civilising mission of capitalism included its global extension as an industrial culture and system. Bukharin now revised this view. Socialists would inherit a less-developed earth than Marx had hoped: capitalism would not peacefully mature within its existing historical husk, only to throw it off at the moment of revolutionary ripeness, but rather would continue to represent a contradictory momentum.

As Elie Halévy argues in *The Era of Tyrannies*, what this forces on us is the realisation that Bolshevism and war were inseparable.[91] It is not 'merely' that the Soviet experiment was born in the crucible of War Communism and civil war. Even more, Bolshevism is deeply marked by the experience of the Great War, by that of imperialism, just as Stalinism is deeply marked by its own civil war against the Russian populace and by the devastating experience of the Great Patriotic War. The Bolsheviks were among those whose politics were formed in and against capitalist war, yet who came themselves to be perpetual warriors, pistols under pillows, dressed in military garb and using civil war as an image of the cathartic society. Bukharin, like his leftist colleagues, was prepared to defend compulsion left, right and centre. In *The Economics of the Transformation Period* (1920) he argued the position later taken on by Isaac Deutscher, that 'proletarian compulsion', from executions to compulsory labour, constituted the method of the formation of a 'new communist humanity' from the 'human material' of the capitalist epoch.[92] And from this, the classless, stateless communist society would emerge.[93]

Such was the view which Bukharin finally rejected, for he came to espouse a more minimal and populist image of socialism by the NEP. While Trotsky rejected the militarisation of labour in a strategic gesture, Bukharin renounced the entire idea of the militarised society. Like other Bolsheviks, Bukharin did not renounce the necessity of industrialisation, yet he was prepared to place it indefinitely in the back seat. Holding the worker-peasant union together became the consuming prerogative for Bukharin, and not just as a strategy but also as a goal. Preobrazhensky, meanwhile, came to represent exactly the position which Bukharin chose to renounce. Preobrazhensky was to stick fast to the industrial image of socialism, and consequently was to develop a persistent case for what had earlier been called 'primitive socialist accumulation'. Preobrazhensky was prepared to argue what even Trotsky could not countenance: that in order to achieve the utopia of an industrialised socialism, the peasants must pay, in order that Department One – heavy industry – be able to develop sufficiently for Marx's later hopes to be realised within the boundaries of the Soviet Union.

Preobrazhensky was unable to prise himself free of Marx's industrial-postindustrial utopia. As Richard Day indicates, Preobrazhensky's utopia – if not his historical location – is Marx's, replete with its images of necessary abundance, communal stocks and the end of money.[94] While Lenin's head in 1918 was somewhere in Germany, Preobrazhensky's was even further west, in the British Museum, in Marx's intellectual laboratory, light years away from the Soviet conjuncture in the period of heroic Bolshevism. It seems plain that it was Bolshevik heroism which was the red thread that connected Preobrazhensky to Marx's laboratory in this way. For Preobrazhensky's mind, like that of the younger Bukharin, was already in Marx's so-called higher phase of communist society, and the young leftists wanted to stamp on the accelerator rather than to linger too long in the land of the *muzhiks*. Bukharin was eventually to part ways with Stalin over this issue, upon which Preobrazhensky and Stalin then made their pact.

The central text in Preobrazhensky's work is his *The New Economics* (1926). Like Trotsky, but even more emphatically, Preobrazhensky viewed the twenties in the Soviet Union as a life-and-death struggle between capitalism and socialism, between the law of value and the law of primitive socialist accumulation.[95] Preobrazhensky's new differences with Bukharin are rehearsed across the thirty pages of the Foreword (and in forty pages of its appendix) to the second edition. Bukharin, for his part, now saw the theoretical and not just strategic basis of the NEP as the collaboration of 'capitalism' and 'socialism' within the boundaries of the Soviet Union.[96] In practical terms, this debate reduced itself to the issue of which economic sector was to support the other. Preobrazhensky's view was that the necessity of industrialisation meant that the agrarian sector – the peasants – had to be 'pumped' in order to fuel growth in industry. The direct comparison struck up here with the primitive accumulation of capital, the long and bloody process analysed by Marx in the first volume of *Capital* whereby peasants were driven from the land into cities by enclosure and forcibly made into a working class was too much for Bukharin, even for Trotsky to bear. But not for Preobrazhensky. If socialism's utopia was industrial, then this river of fire had first to be passed. There was no speculation about the

'Russian road' for Preobrazhensky, merely a rapid dismissal of narodnik apologies for the wooden plough, for economic and cultural backwardness.[97] But how could this be achieved, if not by force? Bukharin was not alone in approving compulsion in his *Economics of the Transformation Period*; the road to economic modernisation was widely viewed in Bolshevik circles as a process which could only be achieved by pistol and by whip.

The theoretical stage was now set for Stalin, for it was Preobrazhensky rather than Trotsky who viewed this economic situation as an imperative pointing towards autarky, and it was Stalin who finally elevated socialism to the august condition in which internal colonisation became not only an economic proposition but the essence of the communist dystopia, the realm not of freedom but of slavery.

But this was Stalin's utopia, not Preobrazhensky's. For Preobrazhensky actually specified his own utopia, in a 1922 pamphlet entitled *From NEP to Socialism*. While the atmosphere of *The New Economics* is both earnestly theoretical and polemically political, *From NEP to Socialism* takes the classical form of utopian writing, a future scenario which looks back. The pamphlet consists of a series of 'lectures', delivered in 1970 by one Minayev, a professor of Russian who is also a fitter in a railway workshop. Here Preobrazhensky presents *The German Ideology* in Soviet cameo: professor and fitter, both in one, looking back on the period 1917 and after. In the twenties, Minayev informs his audience, it became possible to maintain merely a reduced army and bureaucracy.[98] Whereas the policies of War Communism had achieved egalitarian distribution of goods, the NEP represented an Hegelian negation of this equality, introducing rather, 'to use a moral expression here, distribution [which] was then extremely unfair'. But this policy was nevertheless necessary at the time.[99] Only gradually, however, did state industry and planning become dominant. And this was a crucial development, for only state planning could inject reason into economic life.[100] The concrete embodiment of socialist reason was Gosplan, the state planning commission.[101] Unlike Stalin, Preobrazhensky even in 1922 views this as a peaceful transition: thus 'capitalist accumulation was made an instrument of socialist accumulation', for there is no police state at work here.[102] And yet everyday life seems something less than idyllic in this picture of the twenties, for Minayev must draw to the attention of his audience, in remarkably matter-of-fact manner, that alongside some historic decree in *Pravda* or *Isvestia* one might encounter a report of the shooting of a group of citizens for stealing a couple of matchboxes from a railway truck.[103] But this is understandable – forgivable? – given the 'human material' available when state industry was being restored.[104]

Like Lenin in his state capitalist, 'German' phase, like Trotsky in his Americanism, Preobrazhensky took the inner socialisation of capital as the essential foundation of capitalism in its transition to socialism. Capitalism was finally a mere coating on the new economic forms of socialism. As soon as the socialist content of the socialised part of the economy began to be constricted by the capitalist form of its clothing it burst out of it, seeking new forms.[105] Dynamic capitalism provided the content; socialism was the new form, the result of the capitalist egg (or chicken). Here we sense again the presence of a too-abstracted Marxian theory, of the view where the concept of capital as an essence could divest itself of obsolete outer forms and transmute into socialism with altogether too little pain or worldly complication. For Preobrazhensky 'this new period' of development 'could therefore be described as the painless and gradual casting off by socialist economy of the husk of capitalist forms'.[106] Like Lenin in 1918, Preobrazhensky in 1922 persists in viewing this imagined Soviet state of affairs as resting upon a presumed successful German transition to socialism.[107]

In this regard, and like his entire generation, Preobrazhensky took as gospel the theses of Hilferding's *Finance Capital* (1910) regarding the emergence of so-called 'organised capitalism', which offered itself as a model for socialists throughout Europe.[108] But was Preobrazhensky then just a dreamer? Not at all, in the view of recent radical economists who see Bukharin's *smychka* as avoiding the central problem of a 'goods famine' resulting from the failure sufficiently to industrialise under NEP.[109] This is difficult issue to deal with, for if this view has purchase then what makes Bukharin an interesting political thinker after NEP is also what makes him a disastrous economist, while what makes Preobrazhensky a hard-headed economist (because industrialising) from the economic perspectives of our own times is also what makes him both politically dangerous and helpless. Given the current debate about the social and ecological limits to growth, it is, however, less than clear that, viewed as a general principle, Bukharin's pragmatism is altogether redundant, unhelpful though it may have been in terms of indicators of industrial performance in the twenties.

Was a peaceful transition to industrialisation possible in the Soviet Union? This question remains open, and in some ways it remains the central question for the Soviet Union, where markets are now presumed to solve problems as readily as central planning was in the period of War Communism or Stalinism.[110] The path of historic events was to lead to the death not only of Lenin but also of the themes of 'On Co-operation'. What then of Stalin's 'utopia'? Even Stalin, this world-historic, conniving murderer had his views on the society of the future, though as we shall see the real image of socialism in Stalin is not in his 'theory' but in the monuments to his practice of High Stalinism itself.

What then of Stalin's own views? Stalin discusses his image of socialism in *Anarchism or Socialism?* (1906): no classes, no exploitation, only workers engaged in collective labour; no state, merely a central statistical bureau, universal satisfaction of human needs: in all, a stunningly accurate prediction of Soviet society in the thirties, for all that he fails to anticipate is 'no peasants'.[111] Stalin's professed strategic utopia was not obviously different to Lenin's after 1912, with the exception that the Soviet peasantry could now be counted on as a major actor and not viewed merely as a reluctant ally for the historic class.[112] For Stalin did still lionise the proletariat and like Trotsky, he scorned talk of the new Soviet society as state capitalism.[113] Stalin coupled the idea of Americanism to the strategy of autarky. The difference was that Soviet socialism was certainly to strive towards the earlier objective of classlessness, by eliminating the *kulaks* as a class.[114] By 1930 Stalin was veritably dizzy with the murderous success of his program for constructing new socialist man over the accumulating bodies of Soviet citizens.[115] Herein lies the authentic dystopia of J.V. Stalin, in the imagery of Stakhanovism and in the reality of the Moscow Show Trials, in the bettering of capitalism by outdoing its own historic attack on humanity in the enclosure of land and in the development of industrial capitalism in the west. After Stalin, the image of Soviet utopia – no parasites, no classes – still miraculously pervades communist and fellow-travelling thinking, until it is replaced by the image of the multi-class antifascist alliance of the 'people's democracies' after the Second World War. The beginning of that story, with Kadar in Hungary and Tito in Yugoslavia, is the beginning of the end of Stalinism, as recent events have shown. The Webbs, in the meantime, however, had become the leading apologists for Soviet communism, thereby turning an already tragic situation into outright farce, to modern eyes at least.

CONCLUSIONS

From Marx, to Lenin to Stalin is a long way to go historically. Conceptually, it is a voyage which runs from the craft and Renaissance utopias of Marx, via the syndicalist utopia of *State and Revolution* to that of the peasant-worker union in 'On Co-operation', finally into the descent of Stalin's social laboratory. Stalin's social laboratory is a long way from the intellectual laboratory of Marx. It has some uncanny resonances, all the same, in the sublime hopes of Leon Trotsky, for while Trotsky may only have dreamed of a social laboratory, in actuality Stalin turned the Soviet Union into a playground for would-be Master Builders. While the Stalinists deluded themselves, they also deluded others, such as the hopelessly gullible Beatrice Webb, who wrote by way of preface to Pat Sloan's *Russia Without Illusions* that the Soviets had vindicated her own utilitarian calculus, 'by which I mean the greatest good of the greatest number, a calculus which I believe controls the Soviet Gosplan, in its planned production for community consumption'.[116] These were, of course, no small illusions, and while they tell us something about the mentality of fellow-travelling, they also suggest something of the power of the Soviet experience. For once Marxism had become the authorised, scientific exemplar of socialism, the October Revolution provided the lightning conductor by which socialism became Bolshevism via the storming of the heavens. Socialism had arrived, had worked, utopia could now come to concrete fruition, as it ought – or so was the hope of these modernising utopians. As Weber then remarked to Lukács, the Hungarian communist in-the-making, it is only with the closing of this experience that the incubus of the past is removed from the shoulders of the living.

Ironically, this came to pass in a setting where the Bolsheviks, alone among our traditions, were possessed of an acute sensitivity towards imperialism. Where the Germans fumbled over the problem of imperialism and the Fabians closed their eyes to it for some good time, the Bolsheviks understood imperialism and Russia's place in the world system as a subordinate partner. Unfortunately they also believed, from the early Bukharin through to the late Trotsky, that the capitalist world-system was decadent, that the global system and not just the concept capital was pregnant with imminent socialism. The world-system, too, became teleological. They misread *The Communist Manifesto* as indicating the ripeness of the world system for socialism, when in fact it traced the expansion and sorcerer's-apprentice dynamic of the global system of capital. But for the Bolsheviks history was ripe, ripeness was on their side. They could argue from the position of strength called state power, they could scorn the pathetic social democrats and mock the laughable Fabians. Thus it was that the leading Bolshevik, Leon Trotsky, chose to ridicule the Fabians who, he charged, like English pigeon-fanciers had succeeded in shortening the bill of the proletarian bird by artificial selection, the latter a strategy which he himself hoped in *Literature and Revolution* to apply to humans. This meant that, unlike the embryonic chicken of revolution, the English working class was unable to break out of its calcareous prison, for the 'bill of the proletariat is its party'. The result for Trotsky was that the 'unhappy pigeon perishes, a victim of its compulsory abstention from the use of force, and the further progress of the variety of short-billed pigeons is thus terminated'.[117] Here, however, Trotsky confessed, the evolutionary metaphor which he too found tantalizing came to an end, for the social organism could present the bill to its Fabian misleadership, and go the revolutionary road. Notwithstanding the conjunctural attraction of syndicalism and communism in Britain, however, the appeal of Fabianism remained, spanning the period from 1918 to the 1945–51 Atlee Government and after. Communism replaced Fabianism for the Webbs and many others in the thirties, but the local species of socialism still maintained its own continuity. To Fabianism's utopias we now turn.

3 Fabianism

Fabianism, of all socialisms, is most consistently painted grey on grey. The Fabians, and especially the Webbs played up to this; they seemed almost happy to be ridiculed as they went about their business, doing committee work, scribbling endlessly, making acquaintances and influencing people. Ironically enough, this has helped to produce the situation where Fabianism has been incredibly influential, and yet rarely taken seriously; where Fabianism has been mocked, caricatured to death, syncretised and homogenised, Fabians turned into the boy-scouts of European socialism. All Fabian cats have become apparently grey; and Beatrice and Sidney Webb, as has been remarked, have become a kind of composite personality in the history of British socialism.[1] The Webbs could just as well be 'the Webb', for all the tendency to identify their thought. As is so often the case in the analysis of the history of ideas, however, the interest lies in differences as well as in similarities or identities. The Webbs were in some ways more alike than is often thought, in other ways more different. Their common views require analysis, but so do their differences. A similar challenge confronts us in attempting to locate and characterise the arguments of other Fabians; for just as Beatrice was not Sidney, so are there real and substantial differences between them and their rebellious nephews such as G.D.H. Cole and H.G. Wells, and avuncular Fabian figures like Bernard Shaw. Cole at different times took up the radically democratic persona of guild socialist, and then became more orthodox and party-minded with the passing of the twentieth century. Wells, for his part, became the most explicitly utopian of Fabians, whether rampaging over the achievements of the elders as a petulant young man or writing the baffling panoply of social science fiction that was his and his alone. And then, finally for our purposes, there are the similarly slippery and extraordinary influential views of Bernard Shaw.

associated with
Beatrice + sidney Webb.

SIDNEY WEBB: HARVESTING THE SOCIALIST IDEA

Like other socialists and especially Marxists, the Webbs too were inclined
to deny outright the utopian elements in their thought. They were, of course,
self-styled practical people, viewing socialism as an evolutionary trend and
Fabianism, effectively, as its formal culmination. Beatrice was more given
to reflection on the spiritual dimension of life and of society; arguably hers
is the more sophisticated attempt at social theory, and the more nuanced
sense of the future. This is, at first sight, a puzzle; for although it was young
Beatrice Potter who was tutored by the hard-headed Herbert Spencer, it was
apparently Sidney Webb for whom the logic of social evolution was all-
compelling, while Beatrice remained more romantic. Yet this distinction,
too, has been subject to caricature, so that Beatrice is often thought to
represent the female part of their division of labour and Sidney the male.
Some of the early papers of Sidney Webb show this to be a difficult
dichotomy to defend. These issues can be illuminated by treating the views
of Sidney and Beatrice in turn, proceeding then to the work of Cole, Wells
and Shaw, the better known but less significant here for our concern,
utopians fallen among Fabians.

Sidney Webb provides the first public hint of his image of socialism in
his 'Historic' *Fabian Essay* of 1889. What were the utopic elements of his
early thought? Webb rejects the earlier, romantic conception of the self-
developing individual as the ultimate goal of social organisation. Society is
the primary category, not the individual. Thus, for Webb, 'The perfect and
fitting development of each individual is not necessarily the utmost and
highest cultivation of his own personality, but the filling, in the best
possible way, of his humble function in the great social machine.'[2] History,
evolution... socialism: these were the paths surveyed by Sidney Webb in his
Fabian Essay. Webb was part of that new climate of opinion in later
Victorian England explained by Shirley Letwin in *The Pursuit of Certainty*.
He drew in the air of argument popularised by Spencer, where organisms
were seen to become more perfectly adapted and specialised and society
itself was the larger organism.[3] Like the views of Nietzsche, these views of
Spencer were widely influential, even among those who did not read at all.
In England, they were shared and propagated by figures as central and as
different from Spencer as G.H. Lewes (whose biography of Goethe the
Webbs both devoured), Leslie Stephen, who like Webb related morality to
social function, and D.G. Ritchie, another early co-thinker of Webb.

For Webb, then, the process of social evolution followed the track
viewed by Spencer, but it issued in the socialism which Spencer could not
abide. Evolution itself led towards socialism for the young Sidney Webb:
for him 'the Socialist philosophy of today is but the conscious and explicit

assertion of principles of social organisation which have been already in great part unconsciously adopted'.[4] The problem, for Webb, was that static images had been allowed to dominate socialist, and utopian thinking. Comte, Darwin and Spencer had turned the tide intellectually; legislation and public organisation facilitated the process practically. In this context, for Webb, notions of the perfect city are not abandoned, merely restructured. Spencer's individualism was discredited by the process of social evolution itself; 'the perfect city became recognised as something more than any number of good citizens'.[5] For Webb the social organism need now be recognised not merely as prior but as paramount. Society came first; individuality was the result, not the premise.

Sidney Webb's early thinking about society, socialism and the future was plainly moral in motivation. As he explained to a prospective Fabienne, property brought with it the duty of stewardship. For those without private property, labour was the social duty – all people should work, in paid or unpaid work, and therefore contribute to the state.[6] Webb thus recognised the existence of female unpaid labour, but viewed it, as it were, as a public duty within the private sphere. Certainly the idea of duty loomed large for Webb, and this helped explain his ambivalent attitude toward Goethe. Webb used his own portrayal of the figure of Goethe in order to express his moral sensibilities to Beatrice. In 1890 he wrote to Beatrice that he had reread Carlyle's *Sartor Resartus*. Using literature as the language of love, he described Carlyle's as 'a noble book, much like you' and he found himself saying, 'Close your Byron and open your Goethe'.[7] Within days he was writing again, having consumed *Dichtung und Wahrheit*, *Wilhelm Meister* and Lewes' *Life* (twice). Now Sidney made it clear that his reservations about Goethe were to do with the latter's libertarianism, his recklessness of consequence to others, especially women, his 'real selfish anarchism'. 'What, *eigentlich*, did Goethe ever *renounce*, all his life long?' Against this conception of Goethe, Webb privileged the idea of duty and social service. More than this, he saw Goethe as Beatrice saw Spencer, as the lopsided human being, the result of the too zealous pursuit of one facet of personality, the intellect. Goethe 'never did really discover what his line was', as Sidney Webb put it in his disarmingly direct prose, seeking, as he was, as much to describe his sense of self-purpose and worth as to distance himself from Goethe.

'We are not isolated units free to choose our work: but parts of a whole, the wellbeing of which *may* be inimical to our fullest development or greatest effectiveness', he wrote to Beatrice[8] – the words echo those in his 'Historic' essay. Webb unwittingly agreed with Max Weber that the age of the Goethean figure had passed, though he also remained sufficiently needful to threaten the cooling Beatrice that '*you* need not be in the least afraid of having any Werther tragedy on your mind'.[9] For Sidney would continue to serve, but lived in hope of serving in tandem: '*together we could move the world*', he pleaded with her.[10]

The individual ought to *serve* society; even the individual-in-love was a subcomponent, whose function was constructed by the broader social purpose. Evidently these were personal and sociological maxims for Sidney Webb. The implications of these maxims were extended in Webb's 1891 *The London Programme*. Here Webb argues again that society has the higher right, before sketching a kind of gas and water version of pastoral, or a suburban edition of Trotsky's Olympia in *Literature and Revolution*. His closing chapter is entitled 'London As It Might Be'. Webb's utopia contrasted somewhat with that offered by William Morris in *News from Nowhere*. Webb's was an ideal, in his word, of dense urban communities uplifted through the collective action of municipal organisation. The issue of municipalism is a significant one, for the Webbs were never the mono-maniacal bureaucratic centralists they have sometimes been cast as. Nor were they as alien to speculation as is sometimes thought.

The London Programme, like Morris' *News from Nowhere*, makes a great deal of the centrality of water to life . The Thames is equally central to both future vistas; Webb, indeed, quotes Thales, 'all things come from water'.[11] Water, for Webb, is for cleaning; drinking water ought to be as pure and as soft as from a Welsh lake. London ought to provide its citizens with free public baths, railway stations with drinking fountains and hand-basins, parks should offer bathing and skating ponds. More, water should be supplied to every floor, if not tenement, and gas and hot water laid on.[12] Webb's London might not be white, like that of William Morris, but it will be repainted – 'Bright is the future indeed for the painter.'[13] In this context Webb views Alfred Marshall himself as a visionary and romantic, with his image of London piped, heated, lit, cooled and detoxified.[14] Webb's own view is more comprehensive. Public libraries are effectively to replace public houses. The object is a system of urban planning in the manner of Chicago.[15]

In Webb's mind, this developmental trend toward socialism and municipal evolution was certain to impinge upon productive life as well as on consumption. The new London was to be a pacesetter of wages and conditions; it was to extinguish sweating, and to end the indecent spectacle of the scramble for work at the dock gates. 'With decent housing, short hours, regular work, and adequate wages the worker will at last have been placed in a position ready to take advantage of the opportunities for civilisation which life in the capital of the Empire should imply.'[16] Like Spencer, the Fabians viewed civilisation as something to be used sparingly; all citizens should participate, but differentially, according to their station in life,[17] perhaps, later, according to their talents and interests. The Webbs' utopia was not one of the mass society, proletarian or other. Their view remained structured by Spencer's, even if with the collectivist twist characteristic of later Victorian thought. For the Webbs there was no essential struggle between Man and the State; with each in their place, co-operation would rule.

Co-operation was a principle which Sidney and Beatrice shared prior to their partnership. Indeed, it is striking that they both, in solitude, wrote on Marx, on political economy and on co-operation prior to the formation of the firm of Webb. Co-operation was the natural value of English socialism from Robert Owen onwards. The Fabians and those who followed them – Laski, Tawney, Cole, MacDonald – viewed co-operation as an anthropological attribute. Radical social thought at the turn of the century became replete with the language of the social organism, of function and of co-operation. This came to be the basis of Fabianism's utopia: functional differentiation within a multi-class economic system. The development of Fabianism across the twentieth century then involves a shift, eventually, from municipality to state and from co-operation to central government.

Yet throughout its earliest years Fabianism's utopia is exactly the humble scenario of gas and water socialism. Clearly Sidney Webb was impressed by the humility of his claims and by the practicality of his utopia. His claims were thus both to political modesty and to sociological accuracy. In *Socialism in England* (1890) Webb rejects earlier utopias, from Plato to Comte, on the grounds of their static nature.[18] Significantly, his attitude towards the forerunners is sociological and not dismissive. Plato, Campanella, More, Fourier and Owen were not merely idle dreamers but aspirant planners. Their limit was that they presented the future in images of perfectly balanced equilibrium, without taking into account the need or possibility of future organic alteration.[19] Nowadays, according to Webb, now repeating the argument of his *Fabian Essay*, and

> owing mainly to the efforts of Comte, Darwin and Spencer, we can no longer think of the future society as an unchanging state. The social ideal from being statical has become dynamic. The necessity of constant growth and development of the social organism has become axiomatic.[20]

In this way, for Webb, utopianism in the conventional sense has simply become anachronistic. Today we have no 'utopia'; rather we pursue the functional evolutionary *Social Organism*.[21] Webb's argument here parallels Kautsky's, and Marx's, in that it declares blueprints to be obsolete; science henceforth explains the autogenetical emergence of socialism. Webb sensed the parallel later, when he dated 'practical' utopianism from *The Communist Manifesto* of 1848; the point now was not to dream, but to reorganise the existing order.[22] The difference between Social Democracy and what Webb sometimes called by the same name was that the Germans privileged the evolution of productive forces, where the Fabians gave pride of place to functional differentiation.

By the time Webb wrote *Socialism – True and False* (1894), his views on utopianism conventionally defined were less kind or fair; partly this is so because his motivation, in this context, seems to be bound up with his attempt to legitimise Fabianism now as a serious, businesslike form of socialism. Webb volunteers to discuss the romantic roots of the Fabians, born out of the Fellowship of the New Life, but here to smirk at its 'alternative', less than fully businesslike inclinations.[23] Writing long before him, Webb nevertheless evokes in the mind of the modern reader the images of sandal-bearing, carrot-juicing cranks later so painfully lampooned by George Orwell. The Fabian Society of course grew up and away from the fantasy world of communes and colonies; it let go, as Sidney puts it, of all faith in the recuperative qualities of spade husbandry, an apparent allusion to Robert Owen's fetish for the same.[24] The useful harvest, rather, was that of the socialist idea.[25] 'Three acres and a cow' gave way to *The London Programme* just as happily as Spencerian individualism passed into empirical collectivism.[26]

Public administration, for Webb, then replaced 'utopianism'. The idea of the 'new beginning' in Paraguay or Peru, Mexico or Matabeleland gave way, again, to the sensible monitoring and direction of the incipient forces of industrial civilisation.[27] Prophecy changed in form, if not in content: for the wise prophets ought henceforth to cease contemplating the project of founding utopia. The project now was not to initiate a small, local or partial community which adopted the whole faith, so much as to pursue the partial adoption of the new faith by the whole community.[28] And this was a new faith, a faith of a scientific kind, for Sidney Webb. While Beatrice Webb maintained a sense of faith closer to religion, even if hers was the 'religion of humanity', Sidney Webb's faith was in what he saw, or believed he saw in the evolution of English socialism. Sidney Webb's Perfect City was thus not postulated, but to him actual, a developing state of affairs characterised by municipal socialism, gas and water, pavements and town hall clocks expressing and embodying the gradual inevitability of the evolutionary process.

Yet there were also moral and philosophical well-springs for these views. Sidney's Perfect City may have seemed grey to his various critics, but its motive forces were brighter and more complex. For reasons we can only wonder about, Sidney Webb was happy to participate in the production of the image of Beatrice, the doubter, and Sidney, the wire-puller. Perhaps Sidney was more given to self-protection than Beatrice; but the result of the story is that those who read *My Apprenticeship*, or Beatrice's *Diaries* fall in love with her almost as much as Sidney himself had, while Sidney for all the world looks the clever philistine. Some early papers in the Passfield Collection cast an interesting light across this presumed emotional division of labour. What becomes clear in particular is that Sidney was also a religious thinker, and that the roots of his socialism also lay not in an ethic of efficiency – as is often thought – but in the idea of humanity. In an undated notebook young Sidney Webb wrote two essays, each running from one end of the notebook to the other. One was entitled 'The Existence of Evil'; the other, 'On Serving God'. 'The Existence of Evil' reveals a studiously rather than passionately religious Webb, discussing theodicy and the popular explanations of theodicy – Episcopalian Church of England, Calvinism. Notwithstanding all of the antinomies to be found here, Sidney concludes that '*Any* religion is better than *no* religion.'[29] Theodicy is interesting, for Webb, but somehow theology – even the life of the mind – is less attractive to him than to Beatrice. But for good reasons, to his mind: 'The first thing and the greatest connected with the sin and pain on earth is to do what we can to remedy it; to discover its cause is but an after amusement'.[30]

'On Serving God' is of a piece with 'The Existence of Evil'; here is Sidney Webb, spiritual but earnest, believing, but not lyrical. Webb here opens issues linking the service of God to the service of Humanity, a theme we have come to associate with Beatrice. This theme is further developed in 'The Ethics of Existence', a lecture given by Sidney to the Zetetical Society in October 1891. Here again we find themes more often associated with Beatrice's *Diaries* or her *Apprenticeship*: our lives are painful, but our daily occupations take us out of ourselves. Sidney Webb here shares this sense of anthropological pessimism, coupled with its release valve of vocational optimism. As he writes:

> The hopeful Utopian may look forward to a time when increased knowledge and increased intelligence may render injurious excesses less frequent, but within our practical ken there seems but little hope. It must be very many generations before such a change could set in the characteristics of our progress, as to prevent our urban population being universally afflicted to some slight degree with disease of the digestive organs, and with a deficient oxidation.[31]

Viewed in this context, the greying gas and water socialism of *The London Programme* becomes more suggestive. For while Webb here, as elsewhere, relies on the utilitarian language of pleasure and pain, the emphasis is on pain, the image of the future is at best despondent. So although Webb rejects the arguments of nihilism and of Schopenhauer in particular, he does puzzle over the significance of the question of suicide in this context of civilisational melancholy.[32] More generally, however, he also proposes that pessimism depends largely, if not chiefly, on health: so that the necessity of social reform becomes an anthropological and civilisational issue, and not merely an instrumental fancy of the administrators apparent.[33]

FROM CO-OPERATION TO COLLECTIVISM: THE VIEW OF THE PARTNERSHIP

Sidney Webb agreed with John Stuart Mill's *Autobiography* (which he does not, however, cite) that happiness comes not of its own pursuit, but of the pursuit of something other.[34] By 1892 the Webbs had made their own personal and historic pact to this end. By 1897 they were sharing different combinations of these and other views in *Industrial Democracy*. By 1897 the 'religion of humanity' looked somewhat less problematical a solution to the human condition than it had to Webb in his early writings. In place of the premodern, simple 'capitalist entrepreneur', socialists now, they claimed, faced an emergent hierarchy of specialised professionals – 'inventors, designers, chemists, engineers, buyers, managers, foremen, and what not, – organised in their own professional associations', standing midway between classes.[35] The Webbs' argument here displayed an uncanny similarity to that of Durkheim. The more developed the division of labour, the better, provided only that the professional groups themselves could bond individuals to each other and to the positively evolving order. For the moment, at least in the pages of *Industrial Democracy*, suicide had disappeared and modernity had emerged as possessing far more by way of hopes than fears, or gains than losses. Henceforth there could and ought to be not only the further development of the economic division of labour, but also its pursuit into the social order, as Durkheim had hoped in *The Division of Labour in Society*, so that there was an ever increasing differentiation between the functions of 'the three indispensable classes of Citizen-Electors, chosen Representatives and expert Civil Servants'.[36] The civil savant, the professional expert had arrived, for the Webbs, in order to resolve Carlyle's quandary, in *Past and Present*, of the contradiction between Democracy and Sovereignty.[37] The experts, the priests of Beatrice's 'religion of humanity' arrived like Hegel's civil service in *The Philosophy of Right*, to know and to represent the general will, or at least the best interest of society.

Here was a fundamental divide between Fabianism and Bolshevism. If the working class did not represent the general interest, then the image of the future could hardly be proletarian. It needed rather to be popular, and given the difficulties presented by the mass of 'ordinary sensual men', experts were both required and indeed necessary. But was this not, then, an image of socialism constructed as a middle-class utopia? Sidney Webb discussed some of the implications in a paper entitled 'The Economic Function of the Middle Class' (1885). Here there was no extolling of the virtues of the priests of humanity. Webb proceeded, rather, in a deliberately critical way, addressing the question, are the middle classes parasitic? His argument, predictably perhaps, was that the middle class seemed to do its best to look superfluous, whereas it was in fact functionally necessary. It was indispensable in terms of management, invention and profession. In addition, it saved, and it increased culture. Yet the middle classes were careless, presuming interest-income as their right, while the working class and their children expired young, and without pleasure. Sidney Webb could simply not accept this situation: interest, without adequate service rendered 'is simply – robbery'.[38] Yet Webb at the same time added his final pre-Fabian personal defence of private property, even though in the same breath he agreed explicitly with Marx's proposal, in *Capital*, that only labour, not capital, begot money.[39] Webb's final defence was an interesting case of sociological special pleading, revealing again the pervasive cultural influence of Herbert Spencer. Webb wrote that it was a rule of sociology, as of biology, that difference of function precedes difference of structure, therefore there must be a function for the middle class which it has so far refused to take up.[40] Clearly the middle class did have a vocation, if not as the priests of humanity then as something administratively approximate to that task.

The middle class had thus far failed to recognise, let alone live up to its Faustian task of renunciation. Duty had failed to moderate economic interest or philosophical self-interest. Its place in the social order was functionally circumscribed, but its own autonomous sense of duty had failed to germinate. Now Webb appealed to yet another key value for late Victorian radicals, that of service. Webb explains some of his views here in a lecture on Rome, given at Hampstead in 1888 as 'a sermon in sociology'.[41] Webb warms to the image of Rome because it offers senses of individual duty to community, city, state. Not for him the Athenian utopia of the supreme individual. For Webb, Rome with its 'supreme devotion has been a beacon light to all the successive ages, and is beyond all question our most important heritage from Rome'.[42] Rome, for Webb, is utilitarian, not indulgent, collectivist, not given to individualism. The argument then begins to parallel that in his 'Historic' *Fabian Essay*:

> One grand lesson in Sociology stands out conspicuously in Roman history and sums up the characteristics separately brought forward. If the progress of humanity is to be the ultimate end, and not merely our own

personal happiness, we must have regard not only to the development of the individual but also to that of the Social Organism.[43]

There follows the exact same phrase from the *Fabian Essay*, regarding 'the perfect and fitting development of the individual', and Sidney's final return to Goethe's inadequately practised maxim: renounce, renounce, renounce.[44]

For Beatrice and Sidney Webb alike, then, political theory led from society to individual, and this meant that the image of the future society must be constructed not in terms of interests, but in terms of notions of community, duty and service. Socialism need be based on that neighbourly feeling of which local life was made up, and of that willingness to subordinate oneself to the welfare of the whole without which national existence is impossible.[45] The individual did thus have a place in this utopia, even if he or she was often the last performer on the theoretical stage. Democracy, the Webbs explained, had as its purpose the lightening of the load of participation in productive life, setting free time and enthusiasm for culture, art and science, the pursuit of beauty, friendship, religion and wit. By 1921 they could write in *The Consumers' Co-operative Movement* that 'the final end to be served by social organisation can be nothing but the largest possible amount of the highest possible development of individual personality.'[46] Here they returned to some of the elements of Sidney's *London Programme*, reinforcing Ian Britain's case in his brilliant study *Fabianism and Culture* that even if the Webbs were not constantly cultural, culture was nevertheless a fundamental concern for Fabians. For the Webbs argued, in closing *The Consumer Co-operative Movement*, that culture and socialism would grow proportionately as did abundance. 'The beauty of the landscape may even come to be deemed as important as the wheatfield; the purity of the atmosphere and uninterrupted sunshine as valuable as a multiplication of factories.' More and more, they hoped, the life of the community 'will be organised, not mainly to produce goods, but to enjoy them'.[47]

FROM ENGLISH UTOPIA TO SOVIET SOCIALISM

Yet while the Webbs publicly and actively spurned syndicalism and proletarian socialism, the partnership also came to be infamously seduced by the image of the Soviet experience. How did their Fabianism, this most native of socialist forms, come ultimately to look firmly eastward? Much ink has been spilled over this turn, the bulk of it simplemindedly, presuming either that reformism and Stalinism are merely statist sides of the same coin, or else that the senility and depression drove the Webbs to lose their earlier, crystalline sense of vision. The explanatory challenge is in some ways more straightforward than either of these ideologically-motivated responses suggests. As Brian Lee Crowley argues, for his own axe-sharpening purposes in *The Self, the Individual and the Community*,[48] a crucial explanatory text falls between Sidney's 'Historic' essay or *The London Programme* and the mid-thirties volumes *Soviet Communism – A New Civilization*. Between the local, municipal pastoral and the hymns to Stalin falls another proximate blueprint, their 1920 *Constitution for the Socialist Commonwealth of Great Britain*. The Webbs' *Constitution* is arguably the most conspicuously utopian book in their life's work. Here again we find the proposal for a functional society, differentiated on the basis of the role accorded by the division of labour and bonded together by this interdependence and its professional corpuscles. For the Webbs the project of socialism is modernity without parasites, for parasites, those without function, are actually premodern. The rich, those who 'live by owning', are obsolete exactly because they possess no function.[49] Now the Webbs take function so seriously that they introduce a differentiation between the functions of democracy. Those without economic function pose one problem. But in the society of the future there ought also to be separated realms of producers' democracy, consumers' democracy, and political democracy, the last again divided into social and political parliamentary functions. Thanks to the detail of this case, it becomes possible to set the Webbs' British utopia even more clearly apart from that of Bolshevism. For the Webbs' utopia, as sketched in the *Constitution for the Socialist Commonwealth*, is a consumers' regime, not the regime of the associated producers, and in addition theirs has elaborate political institutions of a sort, where Bolshevism, exemplified in Lenin's *State and Revolution*, has none at all. The point of similarity, however, becomes evident, that like Bolshevism this dominant variant of Fabianism does manage to imagine modernity as a cluster of social forms without truly political forms, without politics in the classical sense, so that for all their differences Lenin and the Webbs can finally agree, in principle, that the substance of politics under socialism should be administration.

Political democracy, according to the Webbs, ought optimally to be functionally disaggregated into political functions – those concerning law and order, diplomacy, and defence, and social functions – those taking up issues of social welfare and rational 'housekeeping' in the manner shown by the powers of the London City Council.[50] The national parliament ought to be split into two departments within the House of Commons, one to follow police functions, the other housekeeping.[51] 'Housekeeping' seems more suggestive of Beatrice's biography than Sidney's; it also evokes the Victorian sense of differentiation between private and public spheres. As

Sidney had argued elsewhere, the existing democratic machinery was essentially sound, provided that the House of Lords was stripped of its veto power.[52] Thus modified, however, by functional disaggregation, parliament could more effectively achieve its national ends. For the Webbs, politics might then become the realm of measurement and publicity; the public agenda could henceforth be set by the *'searchlight of published knowledge'*.[53] This would be a process where, as evolutionary positivists could agree, the facts led consistently leftward, or at the very least upward, upward from above via the model of service which the Webbs proclaimed, again Durkheim-like, to be embodied in the learned professions and the civil service.[54] Consensus could thus be reached by the cogency of accurately ascertained and authoritatively reported facts, driven home by the silent persuasiveness of public opinion. Politics would consist of a 'stream of reports' from independent and disinterested experts retained expressly for this allegedly public purpose.[55] Beveridge was already summoned to the lobby of history.

Not only political, but also economic activity would be restructured in the world to be legislated into existence by the *Constitution for the Socialist Commonwealth*. The Webbs envisaged a complex reorganisation of industry, under which there would be three major sectors: nationalised leading sectors, municipal and local, and co-operatives.[56] As will be seen later with further reference to Beatrice Potter's work, the Webbs always favoured consumer co-operatives; their position was adamantly against so-called associations of producers, and for the native tradition which could be traced to Robert Owen and the Rochdale pioneers. Producer organisations such as trade unions were, however, to play a major role in economic and social life for the Webbs. Indeed, for them trade unions ought to become the basis of an extensive network of professional and vocational groupings. Like Durkheim, the Webbs viewed vocational groupings or corporations as autonomous, yet functional components of the social system. Such groups were not, however, to be viewed as specifically political or representative in electoral terms; for the conduct of politics, after all, the bicameral, internal or domestic and external or international parliamentary bodies already existed, exactly because functions such as those of political and economics were to be differentiated and not merged into each other. Vocational groups were thus by definition outside the state, and were explicitly not to be representative. Vocational groups would develop their own sense of purpose and civil service, developing the professional honour of the corporation, perfecting the science and art of the particular service that its members render to the community as a whole.[57]

In terms of the traditions of social and political theory, then, we witness here an affinity not only with Hegel's conception of corporations and of the civil service as a universal class, but also a striking echo of Durkheim's own case for corporatism in *The Division of Labour in Society*. As Durkheim exhorted, 'the categorical imperative of the modern consciousness is coming to assume the following form: *equip yourself to fulfil usefully a specific function*.'[58] In late nineteenth century Europe Kant's categorical imperative ceases to be an ethical maxim and becomes a systemic demand; and with this, any hope of the fully-developed personality recedes back through the pages of Goethe to the mists of the Renaissance. As Sidney had argued in his *Fabian Essay* and elsewhere, the perfect development of the individual was now no longer possible or desirable. Durkheim could well have been doing his puzzling on behalf of Sidney Webb when he asked himself the leading question, 'Is it our duty to seek to become a rounded, complete creature, a whole sufficient unto itself or, on the contrary, to be only a part of the whole, the organ of an organism?'[59] Plainly Durkheim, too, had breathed in the air of Spencer's theory. The good citizen, for Webb, for Secrétant and for Durkheim alike was the man who ploughed a single furrow. As Sheldon Wolin sensed in *Politics and Vision*, Durkheim lurks in this political realm, and with him, so too does Rousseau. For his own part, Wolin connects Sidney Webb to F.H. Bradley. Goethe's counsel, he reminds us, was 'strive to be a whole; and if you cannot, then join a whole'. Bradley amended this to read, 'you cannot be a whole *unless* you join a whole', for which Webb's sociological equivalent was simply that there were no individuals beyond social wholes.[60] But if Webb and Durkheim largely shared social diagnoses, Durkheim's political prognosis was arguably closer to that of Fabian *enfant terrible* G.D.H. Cole, who although deeply influenced early by Rousseau, retained his sense of romanticism well into the twenties. For unlike the Webbs, Cole envisaged corporations or guilds as the basis not only of economic but also of specifically political organisation, in the form of the National Guild Congress.[61]

While Cole was throughout this period largely hostile towards the state, the Webbs grew more and more friendly to it. Certainly the state, and the lexicon of collectivism was part of the new century in a similar manner to the way in which, say, co-operation was a watchword of the nineteenth century. But this is not to say that the Webbs were only ever just statists: what is remarkable into the postwar period is rather the way in which the state becomes a part of almost all discourse in political and social theory. In his leading 1916 essay, *Towards Social Democracy*, Sidney had presented the Webb position accurately when he identified the two leading characteristic trends in modernity as municipalisation and co-operation.[62] Fabianism seems rather to have slowly accommodated its pact with the state as the missing prime mover, the massive actor and legislator necessary to deal with apparently intractable social problems, and to have done this in part, and theoretically, via the Webbs' embrace of the Soviet experience, in part, and practically, via the experience of the 1945–51 Labour Government and the Beveridge Report.[63] Partly this was possible because, as H.G. Wells had earlier, and acutely observed, the idea of permeation led too easily to the sense that the world (and the state) was acting in the interests of Fabianism, even if the world or state did not know this;[64] in any case, Beveridge was certainly seen as a socialist and as the half-witting agent of Fabianism itself.[65]

Were the Webbs then ever great democrats? This is probably a more interesting question to pursue than that of their statism, yet it is likely no easier to answer. The Webbs were never Stalinists, at least not in the strict sense; at most they accepted the morally compromised relativism for which Soviet socialism was well and good for the Russians who could be expected to know no better. Certainly the Webbs were personally jaded by the early thirties, both by the failure of parliamentary Labour in Britain and by the cataclysmic experience of the Great Depression; by 1923 events were already sufficient to convince them that capitalist civilisation had reached senility.[66] The Great Depression confirmed the thesis of capitalist anarchy and collapse and at the same time reinforced the universal planomania characteristic of the times.

But what did the Webbs themselves mean by democracy? And had they not long been inclined to technocracy, whether that of Beatrice's service of humanity or Sidney's dedicated band of professional experts? Writing in *Towards Social Democracy*, Sidney defined liberty as 'the practical opportunity we have of exercising our faculties and fulfilling our desires' – and, he added, 'nothing else is worth the name of Freedom'. Co-operation, or socialism or social democracy facilitated liberty, wrote Webb.[67] The development of democracy meant that the typical figure of the Middle Ages, the Lord of the Manor, had given way to the characteristic personages of the nineteenth century, the improving landlord and the capitalist mill-owner, and in the twentieth had in turn given way to the elected councillor, the elementary schoolmaster, the school-doctor and the borough engineer.[68] Democracy was not, however, anything to do with the workplace; as Beatrice Potter had cleverly caricatured the case of her opponents in 1891, the message of socialism was surely not 'the sewers to the sewer-workers'.[69] Workplace democracy was neither desirable nor, when the argument came to it, was it practicable. Unlike social democracy, then, or at least some variants of it, and unlike Guild Socialism, democracy did most emphatically stop at the factory door for the Webbs.[70] Where social democracy then sought the extension of democracy from the political sphere to the social and finally the economic, Sidney Webb's conception of the matter was that the defence of democracy involved the 'extension of representative self-government from the political to the industrial sphere, and from political to industrial and social relations'.[71] Democracy, for Sidney Webb, apparently only ever meant representation, along with taxation. If the 'organic' conception of human society had replaced the 'atomic', then all the parts must need whir harmoniously.[72] Politics was not for the average sensual type, and autonomy could not be a core human value.

In the terms of political theory, the Webbs did indeed hope for human cultivation, but not on the lines of developmental participatory democracy.[73] Democracy seems ultimately for the Webbs to have been a mechanism or device, an instrument of mass approval or plebiscite; here they were already creatures of the twentieth century, for they were taking sides with, say, Schumpeter rather than with John Stuart Mill in viewing democracy more as means than as ends. Genuflecting before the specialists, ordinary citizens would nevertheless benefit, in the Webbs' worldview, and spiritually as well. Here Sidney Webb approvingly cited T.H. Green, along with his sense that the new atmosphere of personal obligation results, paradoxically, in an actual popular increase of individual faculties. Collectivism, for Webb, remained the mother of freedom.[74] Democracy, to put it in other words, was a systemic principle for the Webbs, neither a moral imperative nor a first principle but an administrative strategy which had its place and therefore its limits.

This secondary or systemic status of democracy for the Webbs may help to explain its further displacement from their worldview in the thirties. For Sidney, democracy was a problem because autonomy smelled too much of careless, do-as-you-like individualism in the manner of his Goethe. For Beatrice, in this connection more complex a case, Soviet communism also filled an emotional vacuum. Barbara Caine confirms here Margaret Cole's sense that without this new enthusiasm, Beatrice would likely have joined her sisters in sharing a miserable and lonely old age. The Great War had destroyed the civilisation she had known and, as she had said herself, now posed a set of problems with which she was unable to cope.[75] Her 1932 visit to the Soviet Union opened new vistas and hopes which were to become compatible with a worldview not itself based on values of participatory or developmental democracy. For Beatrice Webb the novelties of Soviet socialism were cosmetic, those of the planners and ideologues and not to be found in the practices of everyday life. By the thirties the formal organisational attributes of Soviet communism had solidified, leaving far behind the images of the proletarian utopia in Lenin's *State and Revolution* or even those of the peasant–worker *smychka* in the New Economic Policy and taking on rather a self-identity closer to that of the functional society, only now without guilds, unions, soviets or any other kind of effectively autonomous intermediary organisations.

The suggestion that there was in fact some kind of elective affinity between the Webbs' 1920 *Constitution* and Stalin's 1936 Constitution had earlier been advanced by the ever-insightful Leonard Woolf. Empirically the Webbs' *Soviet Communism* anticipated Stalin's Constitution by two years; what Woolf was onto was rather the idea that the Webbs' conversion in old age to Marxist socialism and their admiration of the Soviet system followed logically from their fundamental social philosophy, their belief in the overwhelming importance of social structure and function.[76] Woolf's clue, itself first laid by Beatrice herself, is worth pursuing. Beatrice had confessed in her 1932 *Diary* that what attracted them in advance to Soviet Russia was that, on the one hand, it bore out their own *Constitution* and that, on the other it supplied a 'soul' to that conception of government which their *Constitution* lacked. Their personal dislike of the communist 'soul' did not prevent it from doing the job. And there was no 'd—d nonsense' here about Guild Socialism! Finally, the Religion of Humanity here came into its own.[77] As they faced the Soviet Union's self-image in the thirties, the Webbs saw a society without the functionless – neither landlord nor capitalist was there to blight the Soviet silhouette, only the local parasites, Trotskyists and wreckers. Syndicalists and hooligans had not only bitten, but also turned into dust. The Soviet social landscape seemed to resemble the land of their hopes and dreams: for here was a society with a universal bureaucratic class, an extensive degree of municipal organisation, and a developed system of vocational groups (the by now completely integrated set up of trade unions). More, the Soviets made a functional distinction between man as citizen, man as producer, and man as consumer, and viewed leadership itself as a vocation. In the Webbs' view, this sense of functional differentiation confirmed their own: 'The USSR... is a highly integrated social organisation in which... each individual is expected to participate in three separate capacities: as a citizen, as a producer and as a consumer.'[78] The uncanny similarities extended further. The Soviets were also committed, on paper, to Measurement and Publicity.[79] The Soviet Union, for the Webbs, fitted almost exactly the requirements of their *Constitution for the Socialist Commonwealth of Great Britain*, without the benefits of the representative democratic apparatus, burdened only by what they called 'the disease of orthodoxy'.[80] Scanning approvingly the Central Aero Hydro-Dynamic Institute and the Campaign Against Rheumatism, they glowingly told their readers about how Research was Planned and Executed but not about the planners and researchers who were themselves executed.

Far from representing a mere lapse in judgement or the weakness or limits of the passing years, then, there is rather a striking logical consistency between the Webbs' earlier and later views on the political and social forms appropriate to the socialist future. That they misread the formal framework of Soviet social organisation as its reality was an extraordinary blunder on the Webbs' part, but it was not theirs alone. Fellow-travelling was by no means a peculiarly Webbian phenomenon.[81] Fascism was widely viewed as the greater threat to humanity, and the Soviets as an ally against it. What is perhaps a more potentially fruitful line of inquiry to pursue here, is how it was that the Webbs were able to depart from their own espoused empirical methodology in order to fall into the trap of formalism. For even their passing critical moments in *Soviet Communism* claim to rest on their own methodological stance, elaborated earlier in their research handbook *Methods of Social Study*. Social scientists, the Webbs argued in *Soviet Communism*, were bound by their training to investigate the contemporary facts for themselves, using the generalisations of previous writers, but only as hypotheses.[82] Sadly, when it came to the Soviet experience, the Webbs expected or claimed to expect that the physicians might heal themselves.[83] Certainly such a view was consistent with their own theory of the professions – professionals ought to behave like this. It seems that the Webbs themselves had become hopelessly entrapped, fly-like, within theoretical premises which were formalistic and based on faith and prescription rather than on empirical research. By the thirties, then, their research methodology had become diverted from the path of empirical research, and most notably from Beatrice's early path of social investigation.[84]

BEATRICE WEBB: FROM CO-OPERATION TO COMMUNISM

Faith was more generally the realm of Beatrice Webb. Sidney, happy to be seen as the stringpuller, reinforced this sense by claiming that he had no biography, because he had 'no inside'.[85] His exaggerated attack on individualism did represent something, for his interest like de Bonald's was not in *l'homme interieur* but in *l'homme exterieur*.[86] Beatrice, by comparison, poured her insides out in her diaries and in *My Apprenticeship*. As Royden Harrison has observed, Beatrice privately confessed that she viewed their study of the Soviet Union as their 'last and biggest baby', an act of 'supererogation', a theological service performed beyond the call of duty; something fit to be ignored or criticised, but not anything which might warrant blame.[87] In Harrison's equally paradoxical representation, Beatrice employed a Cartesian regard for the method of universal doubt together with a Rousseauesque intuition into the mysteries of the human psyche.[88]

Even the most cursory reading of Beatrice's work is powerfully suggestive of the depth and character of her mind. Beatrice Webb inspires, where Sidney Webb explains. Beatrice's romanticism endows her sociology with a sense of insight which Sidney's published work rarely reaches. Beatrice shares with Tönnies, for example, and against Durkheim, the profound sense that the experience of modernity involves loss of community, of tradition and meaning, as well as progress and gains, and with Weber she identifies the loss of religion as a major incipient social problem in the twentieth century. But this should not be taken as a mere confirmation of the view that Sidney ought to be viewed as some kind of stand in for the unfortunate Engels in the all too typical portrait, 'Marx clever, Engels dull'. As we have seen, Sidney had a spiritual side which, though fundamental as a motivating force, he preferred publicly not to discuss. And yet, despite this hitherto unacknowledged nuance, it remains difficult to resist the sense that in one regard at least the division of labour between Beatrice and Sidney Webb did indeed resemble that between Marx and Engels. The Webbs shared obvious attractions to Comte, to Spencer, Goethe and Carlyle. Sidney signalled the way forward to the still liberal Beatrice in his 'Historic' *Fabian Essay*. As Nord observes, this essay was designed exactly to win over the hearts and minds of well-disposed not-yet-socialists such as Beatrice herself.[89] Sidney eventually won Beatrice's mind, and heart, or part of it; and it was this persistent sense of the spiritual and romantic which Beatrice brought with her to the Fabian union, and which gave Beatrice's work the depth of character less conspicuous in Sidney's published work.

Beatrice Webb veritably had two souls. While Sidney claimed Goethe's professional ethic – 'renounce, renounce, renounce' – Beatrice's capacity to renounce was never free of some sense of longing. Troubled as she was by self-doubt, Beatrice has an immediate fascination for those who share this attribute. As she wrote in *My Apprenticeship* – itself a Goethean title – her own life was a struggle between 'the soul that affirms' and 'the soul that denies'.[90] One could just as well say that it was a struggle between science and religion, for faith had taken Beatrice to social science, only to leave her there, in need of a God. As she was to confess in later life, this need became transformed, finally, into the need for a Church.[91]

Like Sidney Webb, Beatrice Potter had a sense of duty instilled into her from early years. Herbert Spencer had taught Beatrice and her wayward sisters the significance of function even at a young age. Her sense of function was reinforced by her own class location; readers of her 'private' musings fairly readily come to meet that fundamental middle-class motivation, guilt. The young Beatrice came readily upon a greater quantity of social gadflies and parasites than was likely to infest the London home of young Sidney. Indeed, it was Beatrice's need to be useful which helped to propel her into the craft of social investigation.[92] Beatrice yearned to belong, to be useful, to contribute, to fulfil her duty. When she speaks of her relatives in the co-operative region of Bacup, there is an element of longing mixed in with her ordinary respect for these good people.[93] For the maturing Beatrice had acquired what she called the 'class consciousness of sin', or the 'consciousness of collective sin'[94] which would drive her into social service and lead her to esteem the vocation of public service. While Sidney Webb had climbed into and up the Public Service, Beatrice had worked out of the private sphere and into the social and sociological margins inhabited by Charles Booth, the 'social explorers' and the socially explored.

In Beatrice's work with Booth we encounter a different research universe from that of *Soviet Communism*: statistics and participant observation are given priority, not formal attributes and authoritative hearsay. Beatrice Webb and Charles Booth had set out to refute contemporary claims that one in four Londoners lived in dire poverty, only to find the actual situation to be worse, and of course to say so. But Beatrice was no mere factgrubber, and criticised the philanthropic investigators precisely on grounds of what they did not do, the questions and problems which they were content to leave covered by masses of data.[95] After Booth, Beatrice embraced socialism – the facts led leftward, as it were. Characteristically, she exclaimed in her half-public inner voice: 'At last I am a Socialist!'[96] Her own, pioneer work on co-operation, *The Co-operative Movement in Great Britain*, published in 1891, signalled some features of her personal transition to socialism. Shifting already towards socialism, Beatrice had begun to sketch in some attributes of her own utopia. Robert Owen was its guiding light. Like Sidney Webb, Beatrice Potter had read Carlyle, and inveighed with both against the callous cash nexus.[97] In this context, amidst the suffering and destitution of the nineteenth century, there emerged the figure of Robert Owen. Beatrice was more taken by Owen's practice than by his theory; like Sidney Webb, she was no advocate of spade-cultivation as the harbinger of the new society.[98] Again like Sidney, her conception of the socialist future was distinctly urban, or at least suburban. So it was the image of the mill at New Lanark which drew Beatrice Potter to Owen, not that of the enclosed rural utopia. Here was a comfortably British, not foreign doctrine, calm and legislative, neither anarchical nor murderous.[99] Owen's practical utopianism combined the 'socialistic legislation of the last fifty years' and the principle and practice of co-operation.

In Beatrice Potter's understanding, Robert Owen too insisted on the biological principle of functional adaptation, and applied it to the collective character of the race.[100] She accepted without apparent difficulty Owen's materialism, approving his sense that the good race was the product of the well-engineered environment.[101] Owen's paternalism presented no obvious problem for Beatrice; the social betters, after all, had it as their duty to form the character of their dependents by placing them in healthy moral, and enjoyable surroundings.[102] Politically and economically, Beatrice was convinced by Owen's insistence that the future of humanity depended on the elimination of profit. The profit-maker was to be replaced by an ideal civil servant.[103] Yet her position was by no means simply elitist or techno-cratic; she quoted at length from *The Dream of John Ball*, agreeing with Morris that 'fellowship is life, and lack of fellowship is death.'[104] The limit of Owen's hopes, for Potter, was less in his practical image of socialism than in his sense of the strategic means appropriate to the transition. Speaking in terms anticipating Sidney Webb's later use of T.H. Green, Beatrice argued that Owen was politically premodern, for he had failed to grasp the significance of Democracy as a form of association whereby the whole body of the people acquires a collective life, an internal Will. Cobbett, by comparison, had clearer political vision, for he had understood the mind of the English Democracy, and had recognised growth as an essential element of social reformation.[105]

At no stage in their apprenticeships or during their partnership did the Webbs have any time much for syndicalism. They had abhorred Lenin as a syndicalist, and had admired Stalin exactly for his allegedly advanced views on socialism as the utopia of the functional society.[106] As early as her 1891 book Beatrice Potter had chosen explicitly to distance herself from the utopia of the associated producers. Co-operation, in her lexicon, referred to consumers in league, not producers. Association did represent a general social trend, provided only that it maintained proper functional and insti-tutional distinctions. The 'unearned increment' of interest could and ought to be abolished, or redistributed, but only through separate organs which managed one and only one department of corporate life.[107] Workers' self-management was a ridiculous proposition; the mines ought no more to be run by the miners than the sewers by the sewer-cleaners.[108] Expressed in a less barbed way, her logic seems impeccable: all citizens, for example, are affected by the railways, so why should the rail system be run by the railway workers alone?[109] Political representation ought rather, she argued, follow the parliamentary model.

Workers not only could not run their enterprises, nor ought they. Reject-ing the labour theory of value and Marxism's consequent privileging of the proletariat, as good Fabians always did, Beatrice explained the principled difference using the authority of Alfred Marshall. Professor Marshall had explained that productive labour could not strictly be defined as the prero-gative of the proletariat; as he argued,

> It is sometimes said that traders do not produce; that while the cabinet-maker produces furniture, the furniture-dealer merely sells what is already produced... There is no scientific foundation for this distinction. They both produce utilities... The dealer in fish helps to move on fish

from where it was comparatively little use, and the fisherman does no more.[110]

People had rights as consumers, more than as producers; each part filled its function in the great social machine, no part less significant than the next, the higher no more vital than the lower. Socialism was thus characterised by the extensive evolution of good co-operatives, not bad ones, a process open-ended to the extent that there could be forged a veritable 'State within the State'.[111] Beatrice Potter thus argued, in parallel to Sidney Webb, that the evolution of democracy and socialism amounted to the emergence of Social Democracy. Associations of producers, meantime, were actually retrogressive, literally reactionary; and here Beatrice echoed Adam Smith's barb, that they were directly opposed in their interests to the interest of the community.[112] Trade unions had their place, but they should recognise it, like everyone else, and stay within it. The 'Child of Promise' begot of the partnership between co-operation and trade unionism meant the defence of separate spheres: the citizens organised as consumers, the workers organised as producers.[113]

As elsewhere, however, the views of the Webbs on syndicalism were not as absolute or resolute as is often imagined. A significant document which warrants mention here is the 1912 pamphlet penned by the Webbs: *What Syndicalism Means: An Examination of the Origin and Motives of the Movement with an Analysis of its Proposals for the Control of Industry.* Twenty years after the publication of Beatrice Potter's first book, syndicalism had a far better press, indeed, workers' control had become a major stream in the labour movements of Western Europe. In this paper, published by the National Committee for the Prevention of Destitution as a supplement to *The Crusade*, the Webbs showed a more subtle understanding of their enemy. Syndicalism, they argued, rested not only on the rejection of capitalism or the wage system, but also on the disillusionment with democracy – and not just parliament. A class doctrine, it managed in these times to hit a nerve; syndicalism as such was 'natural' and 'pardonable'.[114] Though the Webbs did not develop this case, they evidently viewed syndicalism as the product of uneven development. The gears of capitalist economy moved at a great rate; when meshed with artisanal labour traditions, teeth flew off. Who, in this context, could deny that syndicalism was a pardonable excess? Yet it was at the same time an obstacle, its eyes turned backwards or so far forward as to be impracticable and unconvincing. Indeed, the Webbs proposed, it was 'ethically objectionable'.[115] It discouraged citizenship or participation in the political system, conventionally defined; and it brought about deterioration in moral character, via sabotage.[116] In practical terms, economic activity would still remain to be organised; there would still, under syndicalism, be individuals who gave orders or who took them. And there would still need to be some kind of parliament, or General Council – so how would they differ? For even in a parliament of producers, there would still be conflicts of interest to resolve. Like Weber in his theory of bureaucracy and critique of socialism, then, the Webbs here claimed that the imagined syndicalist community would be more complicated than capitalism, not less. More, syndicalism offered a concrete step backwards in its premise that the trade union could act as an employing authority, thus destroying its utility as a trade union (an insight later forgotten when it came to the Soviet experience).[117] Further, syndicalism worked with an over-proletarianised conception of the individual: who was to represent the non-unionised?[118] And surely the way out was not to succumb to the ridiculous, by introducing compulsory unions and bogus unions, poets' unions and so on?[119]

What is striking here is the philosophical underpinning of the Webbs' case. For they proceed to attack the privileging of work, as such. Syndicalism offends because it identifies life and work, and this is too much even for the dedicated priests of humanity themselves;

> important as may be material production it is not the only interest, and not even the highest or most vitally important interest of the community. We do not live to work; we work merely in order to live.[120]

The implication is clear: all individuals have a social duty, but it is as though the obsession with duty is a personal anthropology, not a moral imperative. As they explain:

> A constitution based exclusively on wealth production seems as lopsided as a constitution based exclusively on wealth possession. Surely we shall not fight for any ideal smaller than Humanity itself; and that not only as it exists at present, but also as it may arise in the future.[121]

We all need to work, for the Webbs, and to serve, but we also need to be free beyond work – here the argument is far closer to Kautsky than to Lenin – in leisure, and in civilisation.[122] More:

> Over and above the tribute of work that we have to pay to the world – a tribute that may be lightened by a more equitable sharing of the burden and sweetened by the sense that it is no longer aggravated by the toll levied by the idlers and parasites – there will be, in the Socialist State of the future, to which we personally look forward, all the rest of life to be lived; and lived for the first time, as far as it lies in us so to live, in the utmost liberty possible to a civilized society.[123]

Duty, not work, emerges as the central moral view of the Webb utopia; and here, in 1912, duty is the precondition of culture.

But if there are anthropological reasons for this desire to locate and limit production and productive life to its own sphere, then there are also social factors explaining the Webb view. Beatrice had made it clear in her early study of co-operation that hers was not simply a personal or political preference for the rights of consumers over those of producers: consumers were in some ways structurally more significant than workers, in that consumption determined the conditions of production. By buying cheap or dear, consumers sent market signals which bred sweating, or decent working conditions; 'cheap is nasty' held true not only for consumers, but reached in its effects into the realm of production as well.[124] This is a significant thread in the Webb case, for it helps to explain the distance of the Webbs from anything like the notion that 'small is beautiful'. Small, for both Sidney and Beatrice, was sweatshop. Granted the development of industrialism, scale was a positive virtue. Size, however, was proportionate to complexity, so the Webbs had no time to entertain Lenin's fantasies about cooks governing, or each taking their turn at the administrative tasks of the day. Size was proportionate not only to complexity, but also to responsibility. In the cities, in comparison to Bacup and other small communities, 'the mill-owner, coal-owner or large iron-master is forced to assume, to some slight extent, the guardianship of his workers' – compelled by state regulation and trade unions to curtail the worst excesses of formative, decentralised industrialism.[125] The Webbs' utopia was thus not only urban or suburban rather than rural, but also urban in a modernist cast, industrial rather than artisan. Only on this basis could Beatrice hold up her hopes for the 'future religion of humanity'.[126] As optimistically as Sidney, she viewed this as no mere vision of a 'Moral Utopia', but rather the 'Child of Promise', itself begot via the evolving principle and practice of co-operation.

By 1921 the partnership had effectively finalised its views on co-operation and the co-operative society. The tenor of *The Consumers' Co-operative Movement* was more sober than that of Beatrice Potter's own independent study, at least so far as its conclusions were concerned. By 1921 the Webbs were keen to confirm that Democracy meant Representative Democracy.[127] Co-operatives had developed strongly into the new century, confirming their shared worldview. This trend served to reinforce their sense that co-operation was one sphere of social life, best functionally differentiated from other spheres, where trade unions and professional associations (and perhaps even the self-governing guilds which might grow out of them) would reign supreme.[128] This theme of differentiation, division of mental and manual and separation of proper spheres of authority and capacity indicates again the perpetual motif of corporatism anticipated by Sidney Webb as early as his 1889 'Historic' *Fabian Essay*. Further along this path, Sidney had also provided Clause Four of the British Labour Party, where workers by hand or by head were offered the fruits of the socialist harvest.

By 1918 the Labour Party had become for the Webbs the active and realising agent of the Fabian utopia; and by the 1945–51 Labour Government, Fabians and radicals of all stripes, from Tawney to Cole and the Webbs, had embraced the Labour Party as the historic receptacle of their differing socialist projects. For the Webbs the party-form successfully edged out mass political forms such as syndicalism. Their capacity to embrace the party evidently aided their predisposition to the principle and practice of state power, as it encouraged their later embrace of the Soviet experience. The Webbs' apparent and passing sympathy for guild social-ism, like their momentary sympathy for syndicalism, again gave way in Clause Four to the sturdier image of social differentiation. Clause Four after all spoke of the wealth of all the different producers, not of the economic rights of the industrial workers. The Webbs never finally rejected their sense of plural organisation; as they wrote in *The Consumers Co-operative Movement*, 'what is desirable in the Co-operative Commonwealth of Tomorrow is that there should be, not any one rigid structure, but all sorts and kinds of democratic organisation, central and local, compulsory and voluntary.' Co-operatives offered the principle of decentralisation, while Political Democracy had necessarily to insist on a larger measure of the centralisation of authority and of subordination of the parts to the whole.[129]

With specific reference to life in the socialist countryside, however, the Webbs doubted the efficacy of agricultural co-operation.[130] Smaller scale activities such as dairies and creameries were plainly compatible with the co-operative form, but afforestation and farming would be better lent to state ownership. For if the Webbs did not agree that small was beautiful, they also chose not to prefer scale for its own sake: unlike Kautsky, they did not have a conception of an agrarian utopia that was massively indus-trialised and organised practically along the lines of the factory. For the Webbs the model of socialist agriculture was, like industry, to be varied and diverse. There seemed to be no reason obvious to the Webbs why peasant agriculture should not, like the individual practitioners of the professions and the arts, coexist with all possible expansion of associations of con-sumers in agriculture and manufacture alike.[131] It is obvious that the Webbs envisaged no parallel British program to that of Stalin's dystopic assaults of forced industrialisation or collectivisation of agriculture. Yet despite this, the Soviet experience in agriculture as elsewhere was for them exemplary by the thirties.[132] Somehow the images of vocational austerity and the impressions of efficiency were simply too much to resist.

The caricature of Sidney Webb's administrative hand can be detected in all this; so too can the image of the romantic aura around Beatrice's head. As has been suggested here, there was more to both of them than this. Sidney was not without his romantic motivations; his sociology, and his utopia, rested on fundamentally philosophical and ethical foundations. Beatrice also had occasion to be something less than romantic; she had a politically hard head, whether shown in her no-nonsense attitude to the idle poor in Britain or in her stance against the 1926 General Strike, or later against the wreckers and troublemakers who wilfully clogged up the works in the Soviet economic and political machine. Yet if Beatrice was hard of head, she was also needful of spirit. It was she who developed the spirited case for co-operation, and who argued for the co-operative dimension of the Webb utopia. And it was likely she, as well, who initiated the Soviet enthusiasm, with its consequent identification of the Webbs' 1920 British *Constitution* and the Stalin regime. Beatrice had responded positively to Bernard Shaw's news, on his return from the Soviet Union in 1931, that the Soviet Union had somehow taken on their own utopia. For Beatrice was deeply vulnerable to Shaw's axiom, that the Bolsheviks were people like us but who actually did what they spoke about.[133] Ironically, then, Beatrice was evidently responsible for both the romantic, co-operative dimension of the Webb utopia, and for its final, fatal ensnaring in the Soviet dystopia of the mid-thirties. She seems to have contributed to Fabianism both one of its best components, in the sense of co-operation and difference, and one of its most malignant vulnerabilities, in its sense of functionalised difference, its cult of things proto-Soviet and then pro-Soviet.

COLE AND WELLS: UTOPIAS GUILD AND TECHNOCRATIC

Certainly there is enough variation in the Webbs' views to allow contemporary responses varying from political rescue operations to outright critical rejection. The crucial point of division, here, is whether the Webbs were in fact authentic in their own identification of Fabianism with Soviet communism. The symmetry between their own hopes and the claims of Stalin is conspicuous, yet it does not immediately follow that there is an identity between these views or their utopias, nor does it follow that the historic association between the Webbs and Stalinism is sufficient to discredit their own worldview. In understanding the principle of differentiation the Webbs were in the vanguard of socialist sociology. Ultimately the adequacy of their views becomes merged with a debate still going on, whether corporatism can possibly be a strongly democratic option into the new century.[134]

G.D.H. Cole did not use the language of corporatism, and his guild socialist utopia was vitally concerned with the issue of democracy.[135] For Cole democracy was the primary value, not duty, and the primary thinker was not Goethe, however construed or criticised, but Rousseau. A major difference between Cole and the Webbs here was that Cole was generally cynical about categories like the state and consequently was dubious about practices such as representation. Whether implicitly or explicitly, Cole's attraction was to the idea that small was desirable if not beautiful, that simplicity and proximity were preferable to complexity and scale. In short, Cole was spiritually attuned to medievalism, for while he rejected ideas of social reversion and the blissful peasant utopia, he saw the guild as a type of organisation which had still not exhausted its modern potentiality. Throughout the earlier decades of his life and writing Cole was concerned with the producers' case. Against the Webbs, he privileged work and production, and consequently put the case for local producers' democracy, not national consumers' democracy. His earlier views – essentially those of the period prior to the Second World War – were thus closer to Bolshevism, if we speak of Lenin's utopia in *State and Revolution*, for Cole's early utopia was basically that of syndicalism. More significantly than Lenin, however, Cole's concern with work aligned him directly to local tradition in the figure of William Morris. While the Webbs, like most other British radicals, had claimed some affinity with the firm of Morris, Cole followed a more direct line. Cole drew actively on the romantic current from Ruskin to Morris. Like Morris he saw a necessary relationship between work and aesthetics. Where the Webbs, like Kautsky, viewed work as central yet drew strong distinctions between a future of necessity and a future of freedom, locating freedom outside work, Cole wanted the future to be about freedom in work.

Like other *fin de siécle* radicals, Cole also used the language of function, but with reference to the division of social powers. In his *Self Government in Industry*, for example, Cole had argued that it was necessary to divide the functions of the state from those of trade unions.[136] The state's realm was consumer representation; unions were to represent the producers. But what were Cole's hopes in all this? As Jack Vowles has argued in his lamentably unpublished thesis, 'From Corporatism to Workers' Control: The Formation of British Guild Socialism', the guild movement was neither always nor necessarily socialist. The Guildsmen were not only socialists, but sometimes outright medievalists, sometimes capitalists. Indeed, as Vowles observes, Ruskin could be counted as a preindustrial, agrarian syndicalist.[137] More generally, the guilds themselves had been something less than democratic, a fact which some Guildsmen such as A. J. Penty heartily endorsed.[138] So democracy was not necessarily a core value for the guild movement.

The guild movement was then turned, in part, into the guild socialist movement by the likes of Cole, who came by the Great War to advocate a functional democracy, neither a political nor a mass democracy, but a Rousseau-like utopia, adding in the corporations which Rousseau himself had rejected.[139] Plainly syndicalism was beyond, and well after Rousseau's vision; yet Cole's attachment to syndicalism was no less limpet-like than his intellectual attachment to Rousseau. Guild socialism effectively became a kind of formal nomenclature which legitimised this half-holy marriage. What Cole could not bear, especially in the period around the First World War, was the kind of boring collectivism he associated with the Webbs. Still politically petulant, he chose to argue that the option between syndicalism and collectivism put right-thinking radicals in no bind at all. Forced to choose,

> It would be the duty and the impulse of every good man to choose Syndicalism, despite the dangers it involves. For Syndicalism at least aims high... Syndicalism is the infirmity of noble minds: Collectivism is at best only the sordid dream of a business man with a conscience. Fortunately, we have not to choose between these two: for in the Guild idea Socialism and Syndicalism are reconciled.[140]

But was Cole's utopia a new synthesis, a new principle, or something else? Guild socialism seems in Cole's theory to work as an emblem for something new which is actually old – medieval; and to cover the commitment to something newer, but also backward-looking – syndicalism. Like Sidney Webb, Marx, and most other modern socialists, Cole argued that guild socialism was not an imagining of utopia in the clouds, but a giving of form and direction to definite tendencies already at work in society.[141] Thus while evolution was a moving force, the process of evolution itself reached back to the guilds, and to notions of commutative justice such as the 'Just Price'.[142] Taking on the spirit rather than letter of the guilds meant arguing for a National Guild, an association of all workers by hand and brain concerned in the carrying out of a particular industry or service which would then facilitate the running of that industry or service on behalf of the whole community.[143] Only in this way could self-government and freedom be achieved in *work*.[144] Yet this case referred not only to Rousseau, or silently to the Marx who shadows Cole's utopia. As Reckitt had wittily put it, Cole was the Bolshevik Soul with the Fabian Muzzle, but he was also more than that: he was also an English pluralist, taking up a positive stance with reference to the work of J.N. Figgis.[145] So the argument developed, in

Cole's hands, that there should be all manner of guilds, for producers, for consumers, for civic service, for citizen groups, that there should be no single or central source of power, that power ought and need be pluralised. This was why the state had no special or general claims, for Cole. Like the Webbs, and their principle of differentiation, Cole thus thought it a good organisational principle that power be dispersed, but unlike them he saw no special, sometimes even no legitimate role for the state in society. Having thus modified the work of his hero, Rousseau, by adding corporations, he also refused the very idea of a general will. It was not simply his line of objection that representation was difficult, if not impossible, that made Cole argue for democracy while the Webbs argued for Democracy. For Cole there could be no elect, no Hegelian or Webbian civil service; socialism was to be conceived as functional democracy, but with the decentred parts working in happy autonomy and not to the governing hum or clatter of the planners' office. Here, Cole's authority was not Figgis or Rousseau, but Lenin's *State and Revolution*:[146] writing in 1920, Cole does not blink an eyelid at this peculiarly diverse bunch of witnesses, united, like his varying guilds, only by their differences.

Yet above these varying guilds would still remain a National Commune or Association of Guilds, differing from the old state in that each part was functionally representative, making no claim to general representation at all.[147] Where the Webbs had their functionally differentiated principle of formal representation, Cole envisaged nothing more than a council of councils, to deliberate over the competing claims of functional groups and to perform ancillary tasks such as external relations and coercive functions.[148] In the countryside, Cole consistently argued, collectivism was also inappropriate, and here he argued against Kautsky's views that agriculture must follow similar patterns of concentration to industry.[149] But he agreed with classical Social Democracy and Bolshevism that economic power precedes political power, that labour representation of itself would change nothing.[150] Attracted simultaneously to co-operation and to syndicalism, to evolution and revolution, Cole did indeed represent something of a puzzle, a quandary which is resolved at least momentarily by Anthony Wright's shrewd suggestion that Cole's was a bifocal vision, coupling a longer view, more rigid, with pragmatism about immediate concerns.[151] In the longer view, Cole could afford to be romantic, looking back to the Middle Ages, forward through the hopes of the new working class struggles after the First World War, thinking pluralistically and optimistically; in the shorter term, more and more dominant into his later years, Labour, locally and the Soviet Union internationally would loom larger. Cole thus shifted, however gradually, from a position closer to Marxism to one more akin to liberalism, with which his pluralism already showed affinities, just as his practical concerns shifted gently from social theory to social policy and his identity from that of prickly critic to practical adviser. In the lower bifocal, Cole was eventually to come far closer practically to his earlier irritants, those Webbs – and to argue, thus, that work was more like necessity, leisure more akin to freedom and so on.[152] Guild socialism finally became, for Cole, a utopian project in the bad sense: the upper, pinkish lens eventually fell out of his vision.

Probably Wright is correct in his assessment that where the Webbs became Sovietists, Cole became a circumstantial statist. In response to continuing economic crises, the state took on a new practical legitimacy for Cole.[153] And yet, analytically, the remnants of the superior vision also remained evident, for Cole was prepared to argue in his monumental *History of Socialist Thought* that both labourism and communism were in fact forms of evolving state capitalism.[154] Perhaps because of his historical sense, Cole did not seem morbidly bitter about this outcome. Doubtless he had pondered Morris' epigrammatic wisdom in *A Dream of John Ball*, how it is that 'men fight and lose the battle, and the thing that they fought for comes about in spite of their defeat, and when it comes turns out not to be what they meant, and other men have to fight for what they meant under another name'[155] – for he had argued, as early as 1922, that the exhaustion of guild socialism was to do with the fact that it had done its work, not least of all in influencing the Webbs' *Constitution for the Socialist Commonwealth*.[156] A similar case, as Cole later understood, could be made in defence of the terminal tradition called syndicalism.[157] But was the bifocal not smashed, then, by the rifle butt of Stalinism? Cole had himself earlier anticipated the problem of the relationship between the Webbs' *Constitution* and the Soviet experience, the logic of his argument suggesting that guild socialism had not been integrated into Fabianism but rather had disappeared into it without trace.[158] Dispositionally like Morris, a libertarian and an optimist, Cole was no more able than Morris to ignore that John Ball's dream would be lost in the long night of Stalinism and the dissolution of modern socialism into communism and statism as such.

Alongside the sober yet hopeful Cole, there stepped onto the Fabian stage two more debonair types – Bernard Shaw and H.G. Wells. Before Cole had much impact at all, Shaw and Wells were breaking into public notice as futurists, Shaw with *Man and Superman*, Wells with *Anticipations*. Shaw we will return to, for despite their dispositional differences, Michael Holroyd is right to indicate his special relationship with Sidney Webb.[159] Wells, like Cole, was a bad boy in Fabianism's earlier history, and Wells was even badder. For while Cole clung to Rousseau, inoffensively, Wells took on the role of the modern Goethe – in the eyes of the Webbs, at least.

Wells has the reputation, unique among Fabians, of being the wilful utopian, the professional writer of utopias. As Krishan Kumar has shown, this recognition is richly deserved, for Wells was also the author of an idiosyncratic personal sociology. Sociology he viewed as the realm of utopia – and here, as Kumar suggests, the precedents are not Comte, Marx or Webb but Plato, Bacon and More.[150] Like Shaw, Wells was to cultivate an open contempt for democracy (and Democracy) in tandem with a cult of the intellect (and intellectuals, a new class of 'Efficients'). And alongside function, and evolution, Wells forcefully draws to our attention another leading theme of the epoch – eugenics. For in Wells' vision science loomed large, and though Wells was critical of science as well it nevertheless governs his utopianism.

Symptomatically, Wells' leading statement is to be found in his *A Modern Utopia* (1905) – for it is a modernist utopia, a new utopia, Bacon advanced and extended as were guilds in Cole's utopia. Notwithstanding his fictional and sociological enthusiasm for utopia, Wells offers a similar stance to Sidney Webb's, that other people have utopias, what we have is science. Other people's utopias, for Wells, are absurd because they are based on perfect and static states.[161] In these premodern utopias 'change and development were dammed back by invincible dams for ever'. The Modern Utopia, by comparison, is not static but kinetic – 'We build now not citadels, but ships of state.'[162] The new world, significantly, is global – this is not a utopia based in London; and this world is consequently migratory. All fixed points of identity have dissolved.[163] Already we sense the restless figure of Faust in the margins.

Organisationally, this is a world of varied property forms, encouraged by separate associations of citizens.[164] Eugenics emerges because it is necessary, in this world, to resort to 'a kind of social surgery'.[165] Duty and service are values for Wells; thus motherhood is defended as a vocation, a service to the state, supported by a kind of guaranteed minimum income system.[166] The social system is regulated by the Samurai, a deliberate invention, a meritocratic elite. The class structure – for there are indeed classes, defined not by function but by personality – is four-fold: Poetic, Kinetic, Dull and Base, and here as elsewhere Nietzsche's Zarathustra is in the air.[167] All the same, the atmosphere is relentlessly modernist; so that Wells comments in passing that there 'are no more pathetic documents in the archives of art than Leonardo's memoranda'.[168] Like Spencer, Wells was a Scientist, and proud of it. In his eyes, Leonardo should have been one too.

Wells conspicuously enjoys the literature of utopianism, speckling his story with references to Morris, Bellamy, Bacon, and Plato. Bellamy's own pervasive influence is especially evident in Wells' 1899 novel, *When the Sleeper Wakes*. Where *A Modern Utopia* steps boldly, if offensively into the twentieth century, influenced peculiarly by the outcome of the Russo–Japanese war, *When the Sleeper Wakes* comes out of the nineteenth century cast, where the somnambulant awake in horror into a dystopic world, at least in the direct sense that the future is worse than the present or at best, it is still evil.[169] Surpassed by the technocratic optimism of *A Modern Utopia*, the *Sleeper* is somewhat less central for our concerns than the 1911 work *The New Machiavelli*. In this work Wells vigorously attacks the Webbs, appearing here as Oscar and Altiora Bailey, ascribing to them various fiendishly technocratic views which actually bear uncanny resemblance to his own. The novel is a kind of thinly veiled if one-sided public shadowboxing match between Wells and the Webbs over both the politics of the Fabian Society and the issue of Wells' philandering with Amber Reeves. It was through his behaviour in incidents such as these that Wells came in the eyes of the Webbs to act the role of the libertine Goethe – impulsive, unanswerable, self-indulgent, Byron-like, a cad, individualistic to the point of explosion.

In *The New Machiavelli* Wells presents images of his own utopia as well as those which he ascribes to the Webbs. Order and devotion, he says, are the very essence of his socialism, and a splendid collective vigour and happiness its end. 'We projected an ideal state, an organised state as confident and powerful as modern science, as balanced and beautiful as a body, as beneficent as sunshine, the organised state that should end muddle for ever.'[170] Wells' utopia, transmitted here through his main character, is not without its nobility: he aspires to an England uplifted, transcendant, with neither wretched poor nor wretched rich, a nation armed and ordered, trained and purposeful amidst its vales and rivers.[171] Faust-like, he lives through a motivating symbol which represents the challenge of improvement, 'the image of an engineer building a lock in a swelling torrent – with water-pressure as his only source of power.'[172] Wells, portly and short, somehow manages nevertheless to stride through these pages as the taut, lean, white-coated savant, something of a contrast to the black-leathered figure of Trotsky. It is as though Wells somehow imagined himself Prometheus, in comparison to Trotsky, who dreamed of those who would transcend Aristotle, Goethe and Marx. Beatrice Webb meantime dreamed of a leader who might 'unite the intellect of an Aristotle, a Goethe or an Einstein with the moral genius of a Buddha, a Christ or a St. Francis'.[173] Readers of *The New Machiavelli*, however, would hardly be given this impression of Beatrice Webb. For Oscar and Altiora Bailey were firm-lipped megaphones of socialists, completing each other's sentences like the nephews of Donald Duck, advocating their own hegemony as would-be Samurai.[174] 'If they had the universe in hand, I know they would take down all the trees and put up stamped tin green shades and sunlight accumulators. Altiora thought trees hopelessly irregular and sea cliffs a great mistake'[175] – so scoffed Wells, powerfully influencing the public image of the Webbs as two typewriters clicking as one, apparatchiks governed by three-by-five filing cards, worshippers of ascetics rather than aesthetics.

Somehow the Webbs managed to deflect all these slings and arrows, never replying in kind – for that would show them to be as humourless as Wells claimed; and after all, Wells' outrage was largely to do not with their refined but austere collectivism, so much as with their criticisms of his own personal strategies for race-breeding. While it is today less than fashionable to separate the personal and the political, Wells' personal morality is of less concern to us here than his politics. The Webbs were right to identify the libertine, libertarian philosophical underpinning of Wells' socialism – he was, for them, a kind of Goethean stalking horse. Given that the Edwardian distinction between public and private was somewhat more emphatically drawn than it is today, however, it is also fruitful in this connection to discuss Wells' private, though clearly political polemic against the Webbs. For *The New Machiavelli* was in some ways a stylised caricature of a more specifically political, but private polemic published in the dark by the Fabian Society in 1906. For the Fabian Society, too, had its internal struggles – long forgotten, or Wells-disguised – and they were not only those of fathers and sons; the Society had its own, discreetly quiet attempts at revisionism, not only from young firebrands such as Cole, but also at the hairy hand of Wells. Wells' For Members Only publication was entitled *Faults of the Fabian*. The document itself was a premature post mortem, a savage critique disguised in parts as a friendly jostling of the Old Gang. Wells' premise and conclusion was straightforward – the Fabian Society was too small, too lethargic, too poor, too much formed by its humble origins, insufficiently given to the revolutionary task which actually stood before it. The point was to change the economic basis of society, not just to alter the way people thought about it. The Fabians were too silly – too much given to the politics of the sect, to mockery and giggling, too much marked still by their bohemian roots. And they were conceited – for they believed society to be advancing whether people recognised this or not. Here Wells' critique anticipated Gramsci's comment on Trotsky, that certainty is a kind of advance guarantee against defeat, as it reminds us of Bernstein's characterisation of Marxism as a Calvinism without God. The Fabians, like spritely schoolchildren, win mock victories too easily, failing to realise that these are pyrrhic:

But you are socialists! We chalked it on your backs when you weren't looking!" ... [nothing institutional will change, PB] yet socialism will be soaking through it all, changing without a sign of change. It is quite a fantastic idea, this dream of an undisturbed surface, of an ostensibly stagnant order in the world, while really we are burrowing underground, burrowing feverishly underground – quite a novel way of getting there – to the New Jerusalem.[176]

The Society – the Old Gang – had miraculously managed to convince themselves of the impossible, that evolution, like Marx's old burrowing mole in *The Eighteenth Brumaire*, was written into the order of things.

Wells was characteristically scathing as well as witty in his broadside. In half-humour he tells the story of the mouse who 'permeated' the cat – strangely, the cat is still alive and well, or seems so, and the mouse cannot be found.[177] With equal ease, Wells demands readers to take up their Plutarch: the problem with this man Fabius, was that he never struck at all.[178] And strike, they should, and must: for otherwise the Society was simply kidding itself, catnapping while congratulating itself. True to form, the Fabian Society established a Committee of Inquiry to look into the matters raised by Wells' charges. The Committee, which included Shaw, Sydney Olivier, Maud Pember Reeves and both Wells and Mrs Wells, in turn produced its own document calling for the tightening of the Fabian Basis, replacing the language of political economy with that of a fuller-blooded socialism.[179] So Wells, like Cole, took his stand against the Bureaucrats in the party. For Cole, after the First World War, this was a fully authentic stance. For Wells it was more ambivalent: for he ranted and raved yet, as Kumar says, always managed finally to defend a middle-class socialist utopia, whether that of the scientist or that of the shopkeeper.[180] Shaw, for his part, would likely have agreed with the desire for fuller blood, without sharing these images of utopia. An idiosyncratic man, he needed his own.

UTOPIA ON ANOTHER SHAW

Bernard Shaw's views on the future were partly compatible with those of his old friend, Sidney Webb, but they were also different. In some ways Shaw does not deserve a place in this analysis, for even within a deliberately open definition it can be argued that he was no social theorist. Extraordinarily influential, however, he was, and a fascinating condensation of certain themes of the age. Most strikingly, Shaw was the early advocate of Social Democracy who came to despise democracy itself, and not just Democracy but the entire field of meanings of the concept. The critique or dismissal of democracy was not his monopoly, nor Nietzsche's. Cole, for example, had argued in a public lecture in 1920 that the Soviet system was preferable to the parliamentary system; likely his error of judgement here was to do with the images emitted by those systems rather than with their formal properties or content, and he was, after all, still then something of a syndicalist.[181] Wells, too, was a technocrat who differed from the Webbs only in believing the Soviet system to be inadequately Comtean.[182] Shaw was instead attracted not only to Stalin but also earlier to Mussolini, to action and to the decisive, to the sense that democracy had exhausted itself, perhaps not before time.

Readers of Shaw's *Fabian Essays* would not, however, have been struck by advance warning of these later idiosyncracies. The early Shaw stuck to his brief; his literary projects had so far been thwarted, and the tenor of his essays was not noticeably different from that of, say, Webb's own contribution to the volume. Shaw's connection to the nihilistic stream in modern culture itself emerged gradually; its exact nature remains difficult to determine, though Shaw seems to have been consistent in one thing at least – a hostility to liberal myths of democracy and progress.

In 1889 Shaw was happy to view Social Democracy as a state of affairs achieved through Democracy, whereby the whole people was gathered into the state, so that the state could be entrusted with the rent of the country, and finally the land, the capital and the organisation of national industry.[183] By the turn of the century his politics were more florid. He had always been, and remained an incorrigible individualist – yet, at the same time, was a collectivist in sociology. Into the new century, the intellectual salon of his mind was populated not by Marx or Morris, but by Ibsen, Nietzsche, Schopenhauer and their local anticipations. His sense of utopia is correspondingly different from that of the Webbs, Cole and even Wells.

Shaw's commitment to Nietzschean politics was suggestive rather than substantive. The central text here, *Man and Superman* (1903) is aptly subtitled *A Comedy and a Philosophy*, and true to form Shaw spends most of our time keeping us guessing. Shaw is both wit and comic, critic and eccentric. The way in which he uses 'superman', it could just as well be the 'new man' who populates the entire genre of reforming literature. The figure of Nietzsche, like that of Superman, is thus symbolic, for as Shaw argues, Nietzsche only says what Bunyan had earlier.[184] Plainly Shaw, the iconoclast, is only ever able to feel at home in the company of other iconoclasts. As he has his revolutionist, Tanner, say: 'I no longer break cucumber frames and burn gorse bushes: I shatter creeds and demolish idols.'[185] So Nietzsche belongs here, but Shaw views him as one of the gang. Thus he later has the Devil remind the audience that Superman is as old as Prometheus, adding that the worship of the Life Force is 'the newest of old crazes'.[186]

Bergson does not seem to be one of Shaw's gang; perhaps this is because Shaw's 'Comedy and Philosophy' precedes Bergson's *Creative Evolution*, which was first published in 1907 (Bergson was only later to lecture in London, in 1911). Yet Shaw is very clearly in the grip of vitalistic thinking. Shaw has Tanner confess to his would-be beloved, who asks why he seeks her hand, 'The Life Force. I am in the grip of the Life Force', and then turns this, too, into a joke; she replies 'I dont understand in the least: it sounds like the Life Guards.'[187] Plainly those who engage in this kind of parody cannot resist the temptation to self-parody either, so that it becomes even more than usually difficult to determine the relationship between the views of author and characters. For Shaw evidently enjoys placing some personal words into the mouth of his revolutionary, especially when it comes to concerns about the Life Force, Creative Evolution and the New Superman in his appendix to the play, 'The Revolutionists' Handbook'. Here Tanner–Shaw's utopia is more clearly revealed to be analytical in its premises, but disturbing in its conclusions. The premises involve arguments that civilisation is corrupt, and that in this context it is hopeless to expect much of democracy – the downtrodden will never be able to change the world. The conclusions are that only some process of sexual selection will place the human race in a situation where it can rise to this hitherto empty challenge.[188] Tanner–Shaw here praises the 'perfectionist experiment at Oneida Creek'. The logic here in some ways resembles Trotsky: race-breeding alone can achieve a utopia where, in England, there ought to be not one but various Cromwells, a Cromwell-everyman, in France a Napoleon-everyman, in Rome a Caesar-everyman, a Germany where all are Luther–Goethes (and the women apparently are perpetually pregnant if not barefoot with these heroes).[189]

If the Tanner–Shaw utopia is reminiscent of Carlyle's hero-worship refracted through Darwin and collectivism, it thus offers a kind of jarring sense of the clash between themes of progress and disillusion characteristic of the turn of the century. Half of Shaw's soul is with his old friend Webb; the other half with H.G. Wells, triumphantly optimistic yet cynical about the raw human materials to hand. The latter trend seems to be predominant when Tanner–Shaw anticipates the possibility that unless we are all to become supermen, the world will remain a den of dangerous animals for the accidental supermen – Shakespeares, Goethes, Shelleys... Wellses, Shaw? (there could only ever be one of him) who will be fated to labour stoically on.[190] Unlike Sidney Webb, then, Shaw refuses the unqualified ideal of progress and the idea of natural evolution to socialism. Those who simply propagandise, for Shaw, are as pathetic as St Francis or St Anthony sermonising the birds and fishes. Even will is not enough: we need, rather, the will of Superman. This returns the argument again to eugenics, for the 'only fundamental and possible Socialism is the socialization of the selective breeding of Man: in other terms, of human evolution. We must eliminate the Yahoo, or his vote will wreck the commonwealth.'[191] Yet within moments Shaw is again pulling the reader's leg, joking about a joint stock human stud farm, which might be piously disguised 'as a reformed Found-ling Hospital or something of that sort'[192] and like the Webbs cast as the Baileys, we can only laugh or remain silent. For like Wells, Shaw argues that King Demos must be bred like all other Kings.[193]

Shaw is probably closer to the Faustian personality than the other Fabian characters surveyed here, for while each was frenetic in his or her own way, Shaw was prepared to turn this into a maxim: 'Activity is the only road to knowledge.'[194] Tearing about, Toad-like, in motor or on bicycle was only the outer manifestation of this hostility to the contemplative life; writing about absolutely everything on the face of the earth was another. Shaw always had views on absolutely everything, but he turned his wit and insight to the writing of popular encyclopedias only in the interwar period. In between times he wrote his 'metabiological pentateuch', *Back to Methu-selah* (1921). Shaw here repeats the argument that his inspiration is as indigenous as it is Germanic; Bunyan pre-empts Nietzsche, Cromwell anti-cipates Schopenhauer.[195] But it is Darwin who attracted his real interest, if not enthusiasm. Shaw proposes, in effect, that Darwin has been massively oversold, so that every idiot is now a Darwinist. Darwinism ignores the Mind, in Shaw's eyes; Creative Evolution offers a better view of humanity, inasmuch as it argues that as the weight lifter can develop or 'put up a muscle', so can the convinced and earnest philosopher 'put up a brain'.[196] Neo-Lamarckianism presents a superior alternative to Darwinism: as giraffes grow long necks by use, so can humans extend themselves, up-wards and onwards if not to celestial heights.[197] Shaw embraces this theory as Functional Adaptation or Creative Evolution,[198] a view at once as English and organicist as it is continental and Nietzschean. Nietzsche's place is appraised in what he himself describes as Lamarcko-Shavian Invective: 'Nietzsche, ... thinking out the great central truth of the Will to Power... had no difficulty in concluding that the final objective of this Will was power over self, and that the seekers after power over others and material possessions were on a false scent.'[199] Again, the argument is likely Nietzschean by coincidence, rather than in substance. What Shaw rebelled against was the Darwinians' indifference to imagination. So called natural selection explained the easy part; it said nothing of morality, purpose, intelligence, accident.[200] Darwinism was too materialistic: it pleased Owen, and other would-be reformers of character, leaving socialists with the mistaken conclusion that in improved environment lay the road to utopia. Shaw, for his part, took sides here with Lewes, in his *Life of Goethe*. Lewes had poured scorn on the idea: how could the world be thus true to Darwin, if there were pampered idiots born into the ruling class?[201]

Yet Shaw's theoretical populism prevents him from following such ideas through. The combination of sociological simplification and iconoclasm leaves the reader unhappily puzzled. Shaw's work presents itself as a kind of moving vignette, showing signs of very many dominant and popular ideas without explaining them or their significance, let alone placing them in any broader theoretical framework. Thus, again, for example, he offers in *Back to Methuselah* a great insight – that the Edwardian reception of Marx was influenced by the reading of works such as Buckle's *History of Civilization*, thus opening the entire issue of reception of ideas, and then lapses into a bad joke about Marx's *Capital* being widely read.[202] Consequently, it is only to the very end of the long Preface to *Methuselah* that Shaw comes cleaner regarding His Own Part in the Matter. Now he explains that his earlier attempt in *Man and Superman* to use the Don Juan theme was too baroque; *Back to Methuselah* was to make up, by bearing the legend of Creative Evolution more plainly and forcefully, shifted this time to the Garden of Eden and its futuristic variations.[203] But is this then Shaw's utopia? Is Shaw's image of the future only a more romantic turn on Wells', socialism with lolling, idyllic supermen instead of enterprising Samurai? The answer to these questions is no. For while Shaw's wilfully utopian tracts inform and amuse us, we must look further yet for glimpses of his future. Nihilist Shaw was not; but he was, in all likelihood, something of an anarchist loosely disguised as a Fabian.

We have seen that the citizen of Shaw's abstract utopia, as evident in the plays, is the figure of the superman. All citizens, implicitly, are super people: there is no herd, no separate population of inferiors or outsiders as there is in Wells' world. What then of the future as portrayed in Shaw's political encyclopedias, such as *The Intelligent Woman's Guide to Socialism and Capitalism* (first edn, 1928) or *Everybody's Political What's What?* (1944)? No pretence can be made here to anything like a comprehensive analysis of Shaw's public-political-pedagogical works. As ever, Shaw's views on everything are everywhere. The synoptic view offered by his analytical summary to *The Intelligent Woman's Guide* is, however, instructive; imaginably many more readers of both sex read this than the dizzy excursions into nether realms that follow. Shaw states some of his views on the future here with admirable clarity: they represent a kind of synthesis between his own wild spirit and his Fabian sobriety. Distribution of social and economic goods, he proposes, is the perpetual issue confronting human beings. Though all must eat, not everybody must work: civilisation produces surplus. If everyone worked, everyone would have a good deal of leisure. But humans were especially talented in the art of contriving more highly elaborate and unequal social arrangements. The theme of leisure is significant, because although Shaw shared the period distaste for idleness or parasitism, he evidently placed great store on leisure as the realm of freedom.[204] Socialism represented equality of shares of goods, and leisure. Eugenics could be countenanced, in this scheme, but the human stud farm was now rejected as too dangerous; consequently humans were thrown back on natural sexual attraction as the basis for breeding. For Shaw also respected Nature. Only equalising income could have a tangible effect on breeding.[205]

Idleness was a problem not just because the rich could be idiots, but also because they were unproductive. There were obvious exceptions – Shaw uses the cases of John Ruskin and Florence Nightingale to illustrate his claim, because Webb-like (Shaw-like?) they combined unearned incomes with lives of great public service. Anthropologically Shaw is claiming not that idleness is a vice – given his commitment to the *vita activa*, the logic of his case is that it is in fact impossible to be idle, even for rich idiots who will, given the chance, eagerly go flapper-dancing or pursue a frenzied panoply of sporting activities.[206] Hence the need that all should work, under socialism. For work is not itself a curse, any more than what we experience as 'leisure' is a release. We ought not to work at pleasure: what we need is work with some pleasure and interest in it to occupy our time and exercise muscle and mind. We ought not live to work; rather, we need to separate out work from leisure, and rest.[207] Shaw is thus anything but the advocate of a 'leisure society'. His sense of legitimate, Faustian frenzy is that it ought to occur in work, not leisure; and yet work itself cannot be fetishised for its own sake, a view entirely consistent with his romantic view of man as imagination.

In work, however, we are made into cretins, divided, as Marx put it, by the division of labour itself, so that we are doomed to be less than fully human: we are all, now, idiots, incapable of wholeness in life or work.[208] Leisure does seem to take on a greater significance for Shaw than, say, Cole, however, in that 'disablement' is firmly located within the realm of production; it does not reach into the realm of leisure, so that it is important that workers should have plenty of leisure.[209] The place of women in all of this is something less than clear, perhaps because Shaw's addressee is the educationally enthusiastic middle-class woman, she who ought always to be thinking of England. Thus he discusses women in the labour market, but says little of domestic labour, past, present or future.[210] Yet in all this, labour and liberty nevertheless remain counterpoised, and here Shaw reintroduces the theme that civilisation is to do with surplus, and with the saving of labour: feudalism gives you the sweeping brush, capitalism the vacuum cleaner, Socialism ...? Socialism gives you liberty; liberty is leisure, and leisure liberty. The logical implication is evident: labour is the realm of necessity, leisure that of freedom, so that Shaw does here seem to be taking a step in the direction of Kautsky, and towards the utopia of leisure. 'Genuine leisure is freedom to do as we please', so quoth Shaw.[211]

It remains uncertain whether such views are the conclusions to or premises of Shaw's now middle-class, now aristocratic socialism, for he keenly argues in defence of the 'rent of ability'. What matters here is that brains are put to good use, that is, applied to the social interest, and plainly Shaw shares the sense of the Webbs that their own labours are such[212] – perhaps not under socialism, but at least under capitalism (fascism, and sovietism). Civilisation obviously rests on its ideas people, its blueprinters witting or other, and Shaw in this connection endorses the Webbs' proposals for parliamentary modification in their *Constitution for the Socialist Commonwealth*. His enthusiasm for these political changes is muted; the problem is simply that the older Westminster system is obsolete, more akin to the sweeping brush than to the vacuum cleaner.[213] Government, and implicitly strong government, is necessary to the future in any case: for without its compulsion, too many might shirk the responsibilities of social service. Compulsion, however, may lead to chaos, as it will likely elicit a potentially sinister alliance of the 'useless classes' and the trade unionists.[214] The transition to socialism, however, ought to itself be parliamentary, though we are left wondering whether parliament will be changed before, during or after the transition, for Shaw takes his distance from any too gentle interpretation of Webb's proposed 'inevitability of gradualness'.[215] Yet amidst such forceful resolution Shaw nevertheless recoils from regulation or overregulation, for his love of liberty is not restricted to the realm of leisure.[216] Certainly Shaw makes it abundantly clear that he has no time for proletarian socialism or Direct Actionism, for it is actually only Poor Man's Capitalism, like Poor Man's Gout.[217] A middle-class utopia this is, but with the ambivalence remaining between compulsion and liberty. Characteristically, this ambivalence runs also through Shaw's views on fascism – better than liberalism, but too slavish before private property, a potential utopia beyond capitalism which refuses yet to take that bull by the horns.[218] For such remains Shaw's hope, or at least half of it; as he concludes his Appendix, 'Instead of a Bibliography',

Socialism means equality of income or nothing [!], ... under Socialism you would not be allowed to be poor. You would be forcibly fed, clothed, lodged, taught and employed whether you liked it or not. If it were discovered that you had not character and industry enough to be worth all this trouble, you might possibly be executed in a kindly manner; but whilst you were permitted to live you would have to live well.[219]

Shaw was nothing if not playful, as well as frenzied; and he played, too, with revolution. 'All very serious revolutionary propositions begin as huge jokes', he wrote elsewhere, in his essay on Ibsen.[220] As readers we remain in an interpretative limbo, puzzling still over whether Shaw still means to pull our legs or plans rather to remove other strategic parts of the torso. Under the Fabian disguise, even that of the anarchist pales into erratic individualism. So it was that Shaw read even Ibsen as a way to communism via the most resolute and uncompromising Individualism.[221] This returns us again to the theme of democracy. As we have seen, Shaw's *Fabian Essays* viewed Social Democracy as coextensive with socialism. The Superman, however, left democracy in his shadows and Democracy a formal commitment of a more or less mechanistic kind, as encountered in *The Intelligent Woman's Guide*.

There is little further enlightenment in Shaw's *Everybody's Political What's What*? Now Shaw sides with Cromwell, Dickens, Ruskin, Carlyle, Hitler, Pilsudski, Mussolini and Stalin against parliamentary forms.[222] The stance was continuous with his earlier sympathy with Morris, also an opponent of parliament. He rejects what he calls the 'Hitler plan', but anticipates greater things to come in 'ultra-democratic Russia'.[223] The muddle thickens as Shaw recommends that a change from 'our system' to the Russian system would be no change at all as far as the multiplicity of governing bodies is concerned; a bit of liquidation of slackers will help, for 'What the Russians can do we can do.'[224] Shaw evidently favours the image of corporate life, and locates the existing malaise in the party-system,[225] as well as in adult suffrage.[226] He again endorses the Webbs' dual parliament strategy in their *Constitution*, but goes on to suggest now that it is the Soviet system which is to socialism as perhaps the Webb *Constitution* is to capitalism.[227] A weaker than hitherto proposed variation on the breeding argument suggests that democracy equals equality, which can best be pursued by 'sufficiency of means, equality of opportunity, and rational intermarriageability for everybody, with production kept in its natural order from necessities to luxuries'.[228] The remainder of the book tells us a great deal more of Shaw's eccentricities than of his politics, unless we are to take the one for the other. Shaw concludes by discussing Great Men, himself included – 'I happen to be classed by the sect of Shavians as a Great Man myself',[229] reminding us of his earlier throwaway, that there was little won in having someone else praise one's work when one could do the job oneself.

CONCLUSIONS

The utopia of Bernard Shaw may be interpreted in two distinct ways (at least). Shaw's wilfully, playfully utopian writing in the plays is suggestive of a radical future, part English, with a weak Germanic wash. His more specifically political writing varies from social democratic to resolutely undemocratic. Beneath both variants lies an amateur sociology, part governed by his sense of Buckle and Marx, Lamarck and whoever else he read or heard, for which democracy was a period or phrase rather than a norm (and as we have seen, Shaw all too readily took the socialist escape clause on defining democracy, viewing it as equality or liberty or something like that). Perhaps more revealing of this than his published views is the attitude he took in correspondence to Friedrich Adler. Shaw wrote:

> We must get the Socialist movement out of its old democratic grooves... The movement had its chance; and it proved just as incapable of seizing it as the Paris Commune of 1871.[230]

Socialism had lost its moment, Shaw argued, as had the Frankfurt School; but they did not celebrate this. Shaw, for his part, wrote days later in 1927, again to Adler:

> Now we as Socialists, have nothing to do with liberty. Our message, like Mussolini's is one of discipline, of service, of ruthless refusal to acknowledge any natural right or competence. We admit no liberty whatever until the daily debt to society is paid by the day's work. Liberty belongs, not to the day's work which it is a business of a Socialist government to organise, but the day's leisure, as to which there is plenty of room for Liberal activity.[231]

Shaw viewed democracy as part of the loss, a price to be paid for moving on; the argument is essentially syndicalist, revealing again the historic and theoretical connection between syndicalism and fascism. Cole, by comparison, viewed democracy as everything, but preferred direct democratic forms. The Webbs formalised Democracy into functionalised channels. Wells hoped for the replacement of Democracy by Science.

Cole was the closest thing to a Marxist ever to populate the lineage of Fabian celebrities. Wells was arguably unable to transcend his utopia of the angry young engineer who would be scientist. Shaw would have liked to be remembered as William Morris, the libertarian who faced by Bellamy's frightening utopia would lie on his back and kick; but he was too much given to authoritarianism. For their part, the Webbs spanned different streams across the two centuries, emerging, as Beatrice put it, from a milieu which was 'conservative by temperament and anti-democratic through social environment'.[232]

As we approach the new century, Cole's utopia fades into its own past. Shaw and Wells arguably offer nothing positive at all to the socialist project today. Surprisingly, the Webbs still have the most to say to us from the

Fabian tradition. For they understood, on balance, that modernity was a mixed blessing, and they were able to recognise the social necessity of differentiation in our time. The limit of their utopia is that they could not see the negative effects of this trend, but rather came to idolise the finely detailed but humanly dismembering fixed social division of labour characteristic of modernity. Perhaps it could be said that if the spirit of Cole's utopia still inspires, it is the letter of the Webbs' case which remains instructive. Fabianism as a tradition will not lead to the storming of heaven any more in the future than it has in the past. There is, nevertheless, much that we can learn from the detail of its arguments and internal tensions, from the combined strengths and weaknesses of its differentiation principle and the unfulfilled hopes of its pluralist norms.

4 Social Democracy

While the image of Bolshevism has been more or less shattered by the collapse of communism in Eastern Europe, and while Fabianism looks vague – promising, or hopeless, depending on one's position – as ever, the status of German Social Democracy is at first sight difficult to determine. On the one hand, and practically, German Social Democracy has been multiply ruptured – by the Great War, through Weimar, then to be delivered into the hands of Hitler, resurrected and transformed into Social Administration by Brandt and Schmidt. On the other hand, the theoretical legacy of Social Democracy remains potent. Social democracy as a project has never yet been fulfilled, but of the traditions analysed here its legacy is the most potentially positive.

As with Bolshevism and Fabianism, there are predictably stylised views of the nature of Social Democracy. The easiest, from left or right, is simply to declare it moribund because of the visible impasse of parliamentary socialism in Western Europe today. It is equally easy, subsequently, to view the leading thinkers of the movement – Eduard Bernstein and Karl Kautsky – as neo-Victorian idiots, relics, fossils or fools. Only more recently has there been an attempt to reassess both Bernstein and Kautsky, to actually read their works, and to discover the nuances and insights contained in them. For the experience of the Social Democratic movement, and the theoretical labours of its leaders were in fact monumental cultural institutions, which provide all kinds of insights into the tradition called socialism. The experience of the SPD, indeed, could be said to contain its own practical utopia – the 'state within the state', more accurately viewed as a society within a society which provided relations of identity, support, and sustenance for very many middle- and working-class German citizens up to and after the turn of the century. Theirs was, in fact, as Vernon Lidtke has shown, an alternative culture, and not just an island of socialist utopia drowning in a dominant sea of Junker capitalism.[1] In this sense, then, the practical utopia of Social Democracy can be seen in its voluntary associations, singing and bicycling clubs, clubs for smokers and for anti-smokers, just as the practical utopia of Bolshevism might be seen in the workings of the early Soviets and that of Fabianism in its municipal enthusiasms and summer schools.

Marx, of course, had viewed his socialism as other than utopian – in the fundamentally expressive catchphrase of Engels, there was an essential divide between socialisms utopian and scientific. Science arrived together with Marxism, in the account of the founders. Yet, as we have seen, Marx's own work was resplendent in its utopic dimensions, from the *Economic and Philosophical Manuscripts* through to the last writings. Kautsky and Bernstein, Marx's leading legatees, took on Marx's disdain for public blueprinting. As often as not, their public stance was to ridicule utopianism while presenting their own utopias as emergent states of affairs. This is true even though Kautsky was to adhere more closely to the utopia of the associated producers, with lives governed by the cleft between freedom and necessity, while Bernstein developed an image of the future more akin to that of civilised capitalism in its social liberal form.

DIETZGEN AND BEBEL

But before Kautsky and Bernstein there were other figures. One vital early figure who has long since slipped into the mire of obscurity is Joseph Dietzgen. Dietzgen was literally a home-grown utopian, a tanner by trade, without formal education. Marx actually liked his work, which is enough to warrant curiosity itself.[2] Dietzgen's work was enormously influential in Britain, where there was indeed a Dietzgen cult. It was published alongside that of Labriola by Charles H. Kerr of Chicago.[3] The significance of Dietzgen here is that his popularity arguably had a great deal to do with something which would likely have upset Marx. For Dietzgen developed a Religion of Social Democracy, and delivered it in sermons between 1870 and 1875. Dietzgen believed that socialism was a new form of knowledge, a new epistemology, but this new dialectics begot a religion, which was a science in its premises yet acted as the new philosophy or cosmos of belief. *Work* was the name of this new Redeemer. Socialism truly concerned itself with the salvation of mankind.[4] Redemption could now be sought through socialism, through the conscious, systematic organisation of social labour.[5] The logic of Dietzgen's position was that religion was a kind of human need – in order actually to dethrone a fantastic and religious system of life, it was necessary to put a new, rational system in its place.[6]

Throughout Europe socialism had developed as a kind of secular religion, as Stephen Yeo has demonstrated in his essay on 'The Religion of Socialism'.[7] Socialist churches and Sunday schools were merely the practical manifestation of this need. While Dietzgen was adjusting the horizon upwards, August Bebel was at the same time addressing more systematically the material dimension of the future. His 1879 tract, *Woman Under Socialism*, was according to Steinberg the most influential single SPD publication (Social Democratic readers in Germany as elsewhere disappointed their superiors by otherwise reading in natural science or romance).[8]

Bebel's is a work of major significance, not least of all in that it registers the arrival of the other sex in the socialist utopia, indeed, even privileges it. Bebel's utopia, like that of Bernstein two decades later, was not a proletarian society but a *new* society. It is a society to be based on large-scale production, but also on decentralisation.[9] In accordance with the Gotha Program of 1875, Bebel decrees that all will be obliged to work, but on condition that they will be free to choose their work. Following the images of freedom and necessity in Marx, Bebel's utopia is one where work, necessity, can be reduced to two-and-a-half hours a day.[10] Bebel's future rests on the integration of mental and manual labour and the combination of industrial and agricultural activity.[11]

Bebel thus recognises differentiation, but does not tie individuals to their ascribed functions. As I have observed, his is no masculinist utopia – at the very least, and unlike Lenin's compulsory post office model of socialism, women do indeed inhabit this world, and unlike Wells', they are not portrayed as either madonnas or breeding machines. Bebel proposes, in fact, that women might spread their day's energies across trade, education, art and administration – almost an urban equivalent of Marx's rural idyll in *The German Ideology*.[12] He addresses the question of domestic labour, but argues, like Morris, as though it must remain the prerogative of women alone. Men do not participate in reproductive labour, here; and mechanisation is advanced as the solution to domestic labour, by means of central laundries, socialist kitchens and communal provision. Bebel waxes lyrical over the virtues of shoeshiners and vacuum cleaners; clearly he shared the overly optimistic hopes for technology which were part of the milieu of early modernism and essential to arguments such as those of Wells and to local Marxists like Lily Braun.[13]

Likely Bebel saw his task in *Woman Under Socialism* as being to explain and to popularise Marx's views for a significant section of the membership of Social Democracy, actual and potential. Thus he follows Marx in ascribing a centrality to work, and yet moderates the early Marx's anthropology by arguing that while there can be no enjoyment without work, there ought to be no work without enjoyment. Bebel also confirms Marx's sense that the object of socialism is not to universalise the role of proletarian, but to abolish the proletarian way of life,[14] and this latter theme spans an interesting debate, characteristic of all the traditions surveyed here, whether socialist culture is bourgeois culture or proletarian culture universalised, or whether it is something altogether new. Yet all this seems simultaneously to sound like a program of modernisation, which undoubtedly it was, appealing to a better life for all in all possible ways, and legitimating the SPD rather than seeking to develop Marx's fragmentary utopic elements into a systematic theoretical view. At the same time, the achievements of Bebel's book are considerable: without flights of fancy, without abolishing marriage and women, *Woman Under Socialism* presents a sweetly reasonable image of socialism, moderate and modernist, balanced and differentiated. A significant shift emerges when we turn to the work of the Red Pope, Karl Kautsky. The general orientation of his utopia is proletarian, based on universal labour for men and women alike, yet its impulse is also ultimately democratic.

KARK KAUTSKY: THE RED HOPE

At least since the leading work of Massimo Salvadori it has been acknowledged that Kautsky was more than the 'Red Pope'.[15] As Salvadori argues, Kautsky has a history which both precedes and postdates his office in the papacy of the Second International. For our purposes, it needs to be recognised that Kautsky not only developed a systematic and nuanced version of Marxism but also that he returned again and again to the image of socialism as a future. And yet by the time of Kautsky, and notwithstanding the obvious jokes about Marxism as a religion, Marxism had also become more secular. Where Dietzgen, like the early Marx, following Feuerbach saw socialism as spirituality recovered, and while other traditions like the Fabians viewed theirs as the religion of humanity, Kautsky's hopes were optimistic without being eschatological. With Kautsky and Bernstein, in fact, social democracy enters an epoch of sobriety which justifies its description as Weberian Marxism.

Kautsky discussed utopianism as early as 1896, when he wrote on William Morris for the SPD's humorous periodical, *Der Wahre Jacob*.[16] While he rightly viewed Morris as a romantic, he also took his distance from Edward Bellamy, whose *Looking Backward* he reviewed in *Die Neue Zeit* for 1889. Here his stance on utopianism resembled his position on religion – science stood supreme in the realm of knowledge, but this did not mean that religion or utopianism did not have their place. Utopianism as Kautsky understood it belonged not to the sphere of science, but to that of art. He wrote:

It is no surprise that one finds today a widespread craving to see what the future will be like, and this superficial optimism is harmless and by no means to be undermined, as long as it doesn't presume to have an effect on reality, on the political and economic struggles of the working class, as long as it asks nothing more than to be a branch of Socialist poetry. We even believe that utopianism could give rise to a significant work of art if there existed an artist who, full of enthusiasm and imagination, and possessing a profound knowledge of the human soul, as well as knowledge of the current development of society would envision the future. *Poeta vates* – The poet has a right to want to be a prophet.[17]

Kautsky knew the literature of utopia, and was prepared to take it seriously – to a point. In the same period, he wrote his major work on Thomas More. Kautsky possessed a strong sense that socialism could be legitimated by establishing its precedents or forerunners, even if at the same time stressing their differences from contemporary socialism after Marx. According to Kautsky two great figures stood on the threshold of socialism: Munzer and More.[18] Kautsky thus acknowledges from the outset that More is a premodern thinker, yet one with astonishing insight. In particular, for Kautsky, the idea that each individual ought to be attached to a particular handicraft is simply reactionary. The factory system had placed socialism on a different basis. Mechanisation meant that, once the proletariat directed society, the individual worker could shift from job to job, bringing into play a number of muscles and nerves whose harmonious activity would impart vitality just as unproductive gymnastics did in Kautsky's Germany.[19] Evidently Kautsky preferred dialectics to gymnastics.

Further, More seeks to restrict the needs of the citizens of the future: but here technology steps in to save the day, for it is in increased production, rather than restricted consumption, that the path to free time lies.[20] In all this Kautsky is prepared to view More with a degree of charity which he bestows on no other 'forerunner'. Indeed, he proposes that 'More's communism is modern in most of its tendencies, and unmodern in most of its expedients.'[21] So while Morris and others are good critics, More is the only utopian who for Kautsky offers an extendable legacy. It is difficult not to draw the conclusion that this preference was a personal one, however, for on balance Kautsky agreed with Durkheim that modern socialism rested upon a qualitatively different sociology to the premodern.

Alongside Kautsky's specific discussion of the utopian genre we find a series of utopic images in his substantive works: *The Class Struggle* (1892), *The Agrarian Question* (1899), *The Day After the Revolution* (1902), *The Road to Power* (1906), *Ethics and the Materialist Conception of History* (1906), *The Labour Revolution* (1925) and *The Materialist Conception of*

History (1927). It is here, rather than in Kautsky's response to the field which he constructs as utopian, that we discover the architectonic of his own socialist future.

In *The Class Struggle* Kautsky offers the rudimentary contours of his own picture of socialism. What is striking about this image is its unrepentant modernism. For Kautsky the future was bound to that of the city. It was free of ancient relics such as handicraft – small production was simply doomed to disappear. Factory labour would be universalised – 'woman will cease to be a worker in the individual household, and will take her place as a worker in the large industries.'[22] The proletariat in control would thus, for Kautsky, make its pact with machinery – and this does indeed suggest a difference of opinion between him and Morris. For in Kautsky's view, socialism would be characterised by freedom in leisure, beyond work. The hope was not the freedom of labour, but *freedom from* labour, which itself would allow freedom of life, freedom for artistic and intellectual activity, freedom for the noblest enjoyment.[23]

Kautsky wrote *The Agrarian Question*[24] in order to test, or prove, Marx's essential proposition that along with the centralisation of capital, capitalism produced the concentration of the mass into the proletariat. Socialism, as the process which would crown this prehistory, would necessarily extend its forms – if capitalism was characterised by massive scale and an intensive division of labour, so then socialism would be – and this would be a process which would mark not only industry, but also agriculture. Two features of the book warrant its inclusion here. First, Kautsky finds himself unable to argue, finally, that the process of capitalist concentration is in fact characteristic of agriculture: he is a better sociologist than Marxist, so to speak, and this aligns his work with that of the early Fabians rather than the Bolsheviks. Second, Kautsky provides here more hints by way of his image of the future.

In discussing agriculture under feudalism, to begin, Kautsky shows that his interest in history is not just contextual. Indeed, he quotes Heinrich Müller, the Swabian writer who in 1550 painted a picture of medieval abundance, tables groaning with food, wine drunk like water, 'and you could eat, and take away, anything you wanted – there was growth and plenty'. While Kautsky does not take this opportunity to launch into medieval sylvans, his discussion is suggestive of a modernism less than complete in its hopes. More predictable is Kautsky's general proposition, that small farming is simply wasteful – fifty peasant plots require fifty ploughs, fifty harrows, fifty carts, whereas a larger holding might work with a tenth of this number.[25] As in industry, the larger enterprise can develop the division of labour and thus facilitate the development of skill. Kautsky does not here seem to regard the mobility of individuals in agriculture as a virtue in the way he does in industry.[26] In economic terms, scale confers advantage in terms of credit, commerce, and transportation.[27] The argument is not unlike that which we find in Marx, or in Webb – rural idiocy prevents access to culture, which is a right for all.[28] But co-operatives have their limits; they are best given to medium-size enterprise.[29] The small enterprise is doomed, but less impendingly so than the classical premises of the Erfurt Program would have led the Social Democrats to believe. The general developmental process can in fact encourage an increase in small enterprises, according to Kautsky.[30] Thus, as Alavi and Shanin comment, while Kautsky sets out to prove the theses of Marx's *Capital* for agriculture, he ends up explaining the opposite, i.e. the permanence of the peasantry.[31] Next 'the possibility that the peasants might survive is conceded, explained and then politically and economically disregarded insofar as the dynamics of change are concerned.'[32]

Partly Kautsky's predicament resulted from his philosophical commitment to a general theory of societal evolution. Alavi and Shanin go so far as to suggest that Kautsky here privileges social development or progress over proletariat, party, even socialism.[33] Certainly Kautsky argued explicitly within the pages of this text that

> Human society is an organism, not animal or vegetable in character but of its own specific type although no less an organism. It is not merely an aggregation of individuals. And as an organism, it must be organised in a uniform manner. It would be absurd to imagine that one part of society can develop in one direction, and another part, of equal importance, in the opposite direction. Development can only go in one direction.[34]

Kautsky's bind is evident: he confronts uneven development, he needs to acknowledge empirical deviations from the capitalist/socialist telos, yet he also needs to restate 'the axiom that the development of modern industry necessarily leads to socialism'.[35] Yet social development, evolution, progress, take precedence over the interests of the proletariat.[36] At the same time, however, Kautsky fumbles with this concept of evolution, qualifying his earlier statement of unilinear evolution with the proviso that society is not an organism whose parts all develop at the same speed.[37]

Yet the overall logic of *The Agrarian Question*, and of Kautsky's work as such, is that big is beautiful. Co-operation undoes itself as it develops in size, now resembling other large capitalist enterprises, and the idea of 'village communism', Marx's so-called 'Russian road', is simply rejected.[38] The city is the site of utopia. Kautsky thus reenters the worlds of his chosen utopians – here, Bellers, Fourier, Owen – in order to discuss (and defend) child labour, not in its capitalist form but in its anthropological underpinning.[39] To exclude youth from productive labour is hardly better than licensing their exploitation by capitalism – for humans do need to engage in work. Schooling must also remain a vital part of the process of formation, though Kautsky also places considerable weight on experience and on the significance of popular culture.⁴⁰ In this context he briefly discusses the role of the state under socialism. He inveighs against the libertarian proposition that the state or public administration ought be abolished. Kautsky's proletarian state is not Lenin's:

> Such matters are currently far too complex, diverse and extensive to be carried out as a secondary occupation, as a dilettante after-hours activity. They require trained specialists, paid officials, for whom such matters are their sole concern. The idea of government of the people by the people, meaning that public affairs should be attended to by representatives of the people, unpaid, in their free time instead of by paid officials is a utopia, and a reactionary, undemocratic utopia at that.⁴¹

The hand may be that of classical social democracy, but the voice is the voice of Weber. For, somewhat like the Webbs, Karl Kautsky shared the characteristic ambivalence of Victorian and Wilhelmine sociology – an overemphatic enthusiasm about the principle of social organism and social evolution coupled with a clear vision of the necessity of differentiation and social division of labour. And this, again, is what drives a wedge between his views and those, say, of Morris. For while Kautsky in closing refers more positively to a possible (limited) revival of handicraft, as the demand for cheap articles will fall under socialism, his general scenario of the future remains as generally modernist as is that of the Webbs.⁴² Certainly Kautsky succeeds, however, in imparting to his reader the sense that central, large-scale industrial forms will dominate the socialist horizon, regardless of local peculiarities in its silhouette.

Kautsky becomes less coy about such details in his 1902 essay, *The Day After the Revolution*, where he turns directly to problems of the future. In the pretext to *The Day After the Revolution* Kautsky offers one of his characteristic moderations of view. Having already decided for the freedom/necessity, leisure/labour couplet he nevertheless offers the coda that even factory work can be improved, all the same: the factory can be turned from 'a place of monotony, repulsive forced labour into an attractive spot for the joyful activity of happy human beings'.⁴³ Once again, we see that Kautsky was not entirely dismissive of the romantic current. Yet the general picture remains hypermodernist. In *The Day After the Revolution* Kautsky sketches a utopia not unlike that of the Webbs' *Constitution*, with the difference that it is staffed entirely by proletarians. Kautsky explains, Webb-like that socialism will be characterised by a plurality of different property forms – nationalised, municipal, co-operative and private.⁴⁴ Now he openly rejects Morris' utopia: the 'machine will remain the ruler of the production process'.[45] Against Bebel, he also rejects the Renaissance conception of the individual, offering in its place an industrialised caricature where a seamstress, for example, can work in a nationalised factory, at another time make dresses for private customers at home, or establish a co-operative with her comrades.[46] Leonardo here is modernised, turned not into a scientist (Wells) but into a flexible labourer for whom diversity exists merely across a single industrial sector. The suggestion is less diverse than that of the Webbs, because there is missing here any sense, say, of social service, even though the latter theme can be said to exist in Kautsky's commitment to ongoing public administration. Again Kautsky's conceptual orthodoxy gets the better of his analysis. Following Marx's argument about the centralisation of capital and its accompanying tendency to proletarianisation, Kautsky fails to differentiate between proletarian and citizen. The only human identity we see here is the function of the proletarian. Kautsky's ethics are circumscribed by Marxist sociology – his commitment to the two-class theory with its axiomatic bipolarisation means that class subsumes to itself function and, more generally, action. Where in Bebel we get a diversity of practices, in Kautsky we are offered a diversity of property forms as some kind of insurance that there will be diversity in the conduct of everyday life. Only this sleight of hand allows Kautsky to assure the reader that his utopia will facilitate the greatest diversity and possibility of change, and then to close with some grandiose gestures towards the fraternal, pre-Trotskyist collective superman of socialism.[47]

To turn to *The Road to Power* is to return to the triumphalism of Kautsky's *Class Struggle*. Here, in 1906, Kautsky continues to defend what others stigmatise as 'prophecy', now as the materialist reading of the direction of social evolution. Again Kautsky denies that his view is teleological, yet assures readers of the inevitability of socialism, and offers his classic expression of automatism: that Social Democracy is a revolutionary party, but not a revolution-making party.[48] The truisms of orthodoxy are equally characteristic of his *Ethics and the Materialist Conception of History*, which was probably one of Kautsky's most widely distributed works in English, published like Dietzgen and Lafargue by Kerr of Chicago. This text helps better to explain the circumscription of Kautsky's ethics by the Marxism in his sociology. Kautsky, unlike Bernstein, rejects Kantian ethics as though it were glue for the bourgeois morality of reconciliation. Darwin's stress on struggle makes him, and not Kant, an ally of socialism. The end of evolution, or its proper beginning, is socialism. Social freedom has to do with the greatest possible shortening of the period of necessary labour.[49] Socialism's freedom is different from that espoused by the French Revolution, primarily because of the difference between attitudes to property.[50] But finally, Kautsky claims, the ethics of socialism differ because Marxism alone has a scientific basis. Moral indignation might come in handy in the struggle for socialism, but socialism is freestanding, as its proper concern is with the scientific examination of the laws of the development and movement of the social organism, for the purpose of knowing the necessary tendencies and aims of proletarian class struggle.[51] Science precedes ethics – here we find a similar flaw to that in the work of the Webbs, where sociology practically precedes ethics, where the question of how efficiently to organise the social organism typically precedes the questions, what ought I do?, how ought I live?

Kautsky penned *The Labour Revolution* after the Bolsheviks came to power. It was only now that Kautsky was to become an open and vital defender of parliamentary forms, to more publicly view socialism as the fulfilment of bourgeois civilisation and not just as the crowning of capitalist economy, and, in the process, to link up arms again with his old friend Eduard Bernstein, who had defended these views all along (and suffered for it, especially at the combined hand of Bolshevism). Unlike Bernstein, Kautsky still at this stage remained ambivalent about democracy, viewing it as the precondition of socialism and as a barometer of working class strength, and yet also seeing it as a positive institution in itself. Democracy in *The Labour Revolution* is never merely a means, but not yet fully quite an end either.[52] But now Kautsky enters more fully the kind of debate conducted between the Webbs and Cole over guilds and other organisational forms proper or improper to socialism, the rights of consumers versus those of producers, and so on. Such debates had been brought to a head by practical matters of socialisation following the German revolutions. As we would expect, Kautsky's case is closer to the Webbs. The Webbs had, indeed, sent Kautsky a copy of their *Constitution*, though it appears from their correspondence that it never arrived.[53] Certainly Kautsky shared the Webbs' reservations about guilds – he was unimpressed by the proposition that parliamentary forms should be welded to economic or functional interests.[54] At the same time, Kautsky simply rejects the suggestion that consumption leads production; to accept this, as did the Webbs, would be to deny the priority of class struggle.[55] Others, like Lenin, who also claim to march under the banner of the class struggle are still, however, befogged by syndicalist fantasy. Kautsky specifically reprimands Lenin here for his naivety in *State and Revolution*. What Lenin hopes for – the whole of society organised as one office and one factory – 'that is a prison, not a factory', says Kautsky. The only virtue of the fabulous ignorance of the Bolsheviks, according to Kautsky, is that it made them bold. 'For Russia and for Communism the luck was not so obvious.'[56] Unlike the Webbs, Kautsky was always to maintain his wits about him regarding the Russian experiment – his 1918 *Dictatorship of the Proletariat* was merely one instalment in a long and principled critique of the Soviet path.

The Labour Revolution rests on the now familiar argument about utopia and evolution – 'thanks to Marx', in the German tradition at least, 'we are now familiar with the idea of social evolution. We no longer seek the perfect society, which would render any further development impossible, but only a solution of the specific problems which capitalism presents to us.'[57] Kautsky's was thus a limited utopia, dependent on variable property forms, with the necessary bureaucracy subordinated to the practice of politics. Against Lenin, it need be acknowledged that a 'democracy which tried to dispense with bureaucratic assistance would only be capable of solving simple problems' – whereas complex social forms would likely continue to produce complex problems.[58] Kautsky also rejects the distributive principle 'to each according to their needs': productivity ought to determine remuneration, not the formal principle of equality.[59] At this stage Kautsky returns to the critique of guild socialism.

Even a critic as distant from English experience as Kautsky understood that the English labour movement had undergone a sea change in terms of its attitude to the state. For the mid-nineteenth century movement the state had been bureaucratic anathema. By the twentieth century, under the influence among other things of Fabianism itself, the state had come to be seen as the legitimate instrument of legislation. Guild socialism, Kautsky argued, represented the synthesis of these theoretical strategies: it unified state and syndicalism, allowing the latter to remain the dominant motif.[60] Like the Webbs, he rejected syndicalism as too complicit in the utopia of *State and Revolution*, and argued that it was simply too backward-looking, linked as it was in Germany and England alike to the building trade, with handicraft rather than with mechanical production.[61] Against Cole, and specifically in criticism of *Self Government in Industry*, Kautsky now advanced the case against guilds in detail. The essential problem about guild socialism, as with syndicalism, was that workers' democracy was too particularistic.[62] Yet as we have seen, Kautsky's utopia is for all this constructed in the image of a generic *homo faber*. Evidently Kautsky is, however, empirically sensitive to the existence of *homo consumer*, so that he offers the sound observation that rather than arbitrate later, social mechanisms involving consumers in decision making concerning production may dissolve potential problems in advance. Here Kautsky enters again the Austro-German socialisation debate, defending Bauer's *Der Weg zum Sozialismus* and endorsing the principle of joint control between production, consumption and science (which would seem to mean the state).[63] He remains unconvinced of the need to destroy either money or the state.[64]

For Kautsky the so-called 'second phase' of socialism is infinitely removed from the present; it may in fact be similar to 'the Millennial Kingdom'. Socialism, in any case, very clearly stands on the shoulders of capitalism – it develops its forms of life in order that it may bring to the 'whole of humanity not merely bread and security of existence, but also civilisation and freedom'.[65]

On the one hand... on the other – this seems to be the way in which Kautsky's Marxism proceeds, and it is this ambivalence which drove Trotsky and Lenin to view Kautsky as a renegade. Kautsky had rejected Bolshevism, and yet argued for a proletarian utopia, proletarian class struggle, proletarian democracy, only to baulk at the outcome when Lenin presented him with the baby of the Soviet utopia for his approval. When pressed, or thus distressed, however, Kautsky spoke against 'proletarian aristocracy'.[66] Kautsky sought after a class conscious and intellectually developed proletariat, even if he secretly hoped that its consciousness would resemble his own. Yet he was absolutely no Bolshevik in Lenin's sense of the professional revolutionary, the Jacobin who made a pact with Social Democracy, and he made this clear enough in his argument in *The Materialist Conception of History*, that belief was no precondition of socialism, that one did not need to be a Marxist in order to be a social democrat.[67] As I have suggested, however, the tension in Kautsky's thought was not merely that between philosophical generality and historical specificity, though this was indeed a central feature of his thinking. There is also a tension here between a liberal, or universalistic political current and a proletarian sociological current. Class analysis too often got the better of Kautsky, so just as he tended to be dismissive of the peasantry he also tended to blot out the middle class or the intellectuals, acknowledging them – just as he did the peasants – only to deny them, and to return to the general postulates of Marxism concerning the almost universal and burgeoning working class standing against the ever-diminishing ranks of capitalist magnates.[68] Lenin, as we have seen, was a different puzzle – theoretically dogmatic to the point of despair, he also became progressively more empirically pragmatic, taking seriously third classes to the extent of finally ditching the syndicalist scenario of *State and Revolution* in favour of a multi-class utopia.

One substantial issue on which Lenin and Kautsky actually disagreed – historiographical commonsense notwithstanding – was exactly this issue of class analysis. Kautsky took the intelligentsia seriously – he did not deny his own existence – but he was also given to a general sociology in which intellectuals were *Kopfarbeiter*, those who worked with their heads while others toiled with their hands. Yet, as we have seen, Kautsky fetishised science and consequently was obliged to argue that real Marxists were those who were possessed of such Science. This view he defended publicly in *Die Neue Zeit* in 1901–2.[69] Lenin then seized upon these arguments for his own purposes in his 1902 tract *What Is To Be Done?* Lenin's view was that the professional revolutionaries alone could provide the leaven of correct theory for the well-intentioned but ultimately aimless spontaneous activity of the working masses. Kautsky had argued that the vehicle of science was not the proletariat but the bourgeois intelligentsia; this historically accurate observation was turned by Lenin into the theoretical guarantee for his own claims to power.[70] Kautsky's theory, once again, was contradictory. On the one hand he praised proletarian culture and self-education, as we have seen, for example, in *The Agrarian Question*, where formal education is appreciated but not idolised; on the other hand, he viewed Marxism as a qualitatively superior form of knowledge which did not originate in experience. The tension is one that is evident in Marx's own work: on the one hand, the logic of experience (or the logic of history) drives the masses into action, on the other hand they really must read *Capital* in order to understand themselves and their world. Kautsky viewed intellectuals as both necessary, for theoretical development, and at the same time superfluous, because history itself was looking after these things. Lenin, by comparison, viewed theory as openly and plainly as any political operator – as a means and will to power. The status of theory is different, for Kautsky, and partly because of his primordial Darwinism. For Kautsky not only espoused the utopianism of progress, but also on every other day enthused for the utopia of absolute knowledge. This hope for a unified science sets Kautsky's project well apart from the pragmatic approach to knowledge characteristic of Lenin's practice, if not always his theory.

Kautsky returned again to these kinds of issues in his magnum opus, *The Materialist Conception of History*, though he had also examined them earlier in an essay which Lenin avoided, 'The Intelligentsia and Social Democracy'. Here Kautsky had defended the idea of an alliance between science and labour, and he imagined a reciprocal alliance at that.[71] He did not use the language, but he seems to have been thinking of something like Gramsci's organic intellectuals, not Lenin's professional revolutionaries. The point of comparison with Gramsci is one which recurs in *The Materialist Conception*, but there are many other resonances here as well. Kautsky viewed the book as his most important, but it was allowed to disappear, under communist polemic (Korsch) as much as behind the proverbial veil of silence. The general message which the book imparts is not unlike that suggested by the analysis of the Webbs' work, above: caricatured as philistines, these were actually sensitive and fascinating thinkers, whose legacy remains far more potentially productive than that of Bolshevism once the pyrotechnics have died down.

Partly this is so because of the milieu within which these *fin-de-siécle* socialists laboured. Kautsky, for his part, formed this milieu as much as he was formed by it – its real monument remains the journal he founded and edited through the period, *Die Neue Zeit*, which itself remains the best measure of German socialist culture in the period. Everything was to be discussed; everything was problematical, everything was interesting. Little wonder that Lenin turned Kautsky into a renegade. Kautsky opened his study with the proviso that subscription to the materialist conception of history was no prerequisite for adherence to the SPD. The reason for this pluralism becomes more clear as Kautsky proceeds to introduce the materialist conception itself. For as Kautsky confesses, what he has in mind is not a one-sided explanation of history to counter Weber, but a 'developmental history of mankind'.[72] This puzzle rests on another tension, that between Kautsky's commitment to encyclopedic knowledge and his sense of the tentative and fragile nature of knowing and being. Thus, for example, Kautsky here (as elsewhere) discusses everything under the sun, has apparently read everything, has views on everything (yet without the manic sense of overload characteristic of Shaw) and at the same time wants to establish limits to knowledge and to politics. Against Trotsky's open-ended scenario in *Literature and Revolution*, then, Kautsky posits a limited goal:

> Even after the general realization of Socialism, human freedom will of course remain limited, just like our knowledge of the world on which this freedom is founded. We shall never completely fathom all problems posed by nature, and we will hardly be able ever to foresee all consequences even of our own social activity... instead of speaking of a leap from the realm of necessity into the realm of freedom, one would probably do better to speak only of an extension of the province of freedom within the realm of causal necessity, the boundaries of which are unassailable.[73]

The argument is stated more succinctly later on:

> The final goal of the proletariat is not a final goal for the development of humanity... like the process of acquiring knowledge, that of social development is also unending... An enduringly perfect society is as little possible as an absolute truth. And both the one and the other would mean nothing other than social stagnation and death.[74]

Kautsky in this sense, and like the Webbs, was more thoroughly evolutionist a thinker even than Marx – no millennium could put an end to this process of change, no last instance could ever come – not even theoretically.

In stark contrast to the Prometheanism of Trotsky, Kautsky instead volunteered the proposition that human beings were naturally conservative. The mind itself was conservative, governed by habit and tradition rather than by the Faustian passion for change upon change.[75] Like Durkheim, he argued that morality, state and society transcend the individual sociologically.[76] Evolution was a complicated story, not simply the onward, upward arc toward socialism but a fragmented and halting process. Again like Durkheim he argued that morality rested less on class bases than on what societies *considered* to be good or evil. Morality is not freely chosen, but is autonomous.[77] Now Kautsky rejects the suggestion that society be viewed as an organism – Spencer and Schäffle are mistaken to do so, because unlike the animal organism the organisation of society is composed of individuals, each of whom possesses individual consciousness.[78] A new culture can only arise under socialism out of the abolition of the proletariat, not its universalisation; and yet the process must perforce remain indeterminate, for 'Nothing is more erroneous than to believe that the search for what is new... is inborn in the human spirit.'[79]

Anticipating Trotsky, Kautsky argues in his analysis of early civilisation that the small family farm is a necessarily barbarous institution, for it is all necessity and no freedom. If the proletarian movement takes hold of the whole mass of the people, the resultant process of mental diversification may actually enable the whole of civilisation further to be uplifted, and this not for single individuals but for the whole of humanity. 'The result could seem to be a race of supermen. But they would be supermen only in comparison with humanity as it has been hitherto.'[80] For in the meantime there would still remain a division of labour and co-operation within it. Here Kautsky argues against the growing interdependence theory of division of labour associated with Spencer and Durkheim and influential on the Webbs. Formal altruism, for Kautsky, cannot be overpowered by actual antagonism.[81] Yet property relations reflect the conservative character and the mind – when a certain technology and its associated system of property have existed for some duration of time, the *power of tradition* also comes into play.[82]

Kautsky's sense of continuity, of the weight of history and the place of tradition lead him to confirm a utopic vision that of all in Marx's work is closest to that in the third volume of *Capital*. This is already clear from the works discussed hitherto, but is further clarified in *The Materialist Conception*. Writing just after the publication of Marx's *German Ideology*, Kautsky takes time to argue against its utopia, huntsman–fisherman–shepherd–critical critic, at least inasmuch as he interprets this utopia as indicating a non-industrial future. But actually, for Kautsky, the Marxian message is different: it concerns not the flight from the division of labour, but its transformation. The rural examples which Marx draws on are redundant, but the idea of spreading activities over the day lives on. The socialist goal for Kautsky must involve both the reduction of the extent of the working day and the pursuit of different activities within its extent – four hours, say, of eight in the mine or factory, the remaining four in agriculture, or building, or driving, or in art or science.[83] For Kautsky this new, flexible socialist division of labour would have different results from those hoped for by Durkheim: rather than producing professional or vocational solidarity, this less fixed identity will serve to minimise the role hitherto played by interest in politics.[84]

Kautsky thus rejects not only Trotsky's Prometheanism, but also Marx's. At the same time, however, he refuses Durkheim's – and the Webbs' – sense, that identity can be given and social solidarity best achieved by a fixed and limited place in the social machine. This, and other dimensions of his thought arguably place him closer to Weber. Indeed, Kautsky repeatedly and systematically returns to Weber in *The Materialist Conception*, both methodologically, with reference to the place of mind or ideas in history, and later, politically. Kautsky discusses, and praises *The Protestant Ethic*.[85] None of this is surprising, except for the fact that Marxists hardly ever take Weber seriously, except as a stalking horse. Certainly it ought to be unsurprising given the sobriety and balance of Kautsky's own views, on mind, say, and given the somewhat arbitrary nature of his self-description as materialist. This then issues in specific discussion of 'Politics as a Vocation'. Kautsky agrees with Weber, as we have seen earlier, regarding the necessity of differentiation, organisation and bureaucracy: the two thinkers stand shoulder to shoulder against Lenin. And here it is difficult not to conclude that Kautsky simply rejected, to all intents and purposes, his own earlier claims to Marxist science, and drew rather upon the different major streams which made up *fin-de-siécle* German social theory.[86] Unlike Weber, Kautsky never, however, felt the calling to politics; he was happy to be an intellectual. The sociology of intellectuals was another theme to which he now returned. Here he proposed, as Mannheim did later in *Ideology and Utopia*, that intellectuals were not a class but could take up the cause of another class.[87] Now, into the new century, a new kind of intellectual was brought closer to the proletariat by new working conditions. This process of development made it necessary, further, to renounce the old definition of intellectuals. Intellectuals today included not only the academically trained, but all those who in a democracy found themselves placed in democratic vocations, as writers, as party or union officials, as parliamentary representatives.[88] The intelligentsia thus took on a new historic significance, though (on the other hand...) the major class divide, bourgeois versus proletarian, was still the fundamental class cleavage.[89]

Back, then, to the proletariat, Kautsky's fundamental class. The proletarian, for Kautsky, is a more universal figure than the bourgeois. And more, miraculously, the theses of *The Class Struggle*, – of *The Communist Manifesto* – still hold true. But now, Kautsky argues, economistic struggle expands into struggle for the transformation of state and of society. The key to this process is democracy. The democratisation of the state is one task; other, new and special organisational forms will still yet have to be created.[90] Not crisis, but only the strength of the proletariat can see the instauration of socialism; this involves the growing political power of the working class over the shrinking economic claims of the bourgeoisie.[91] Within this framework nestle both a minimum and a maximum program for the proletariat. At the least, the proletariat will grow in health and in strength.[92] On a broader horizon, individuals will outpace Rousseau and even Bentham, for they will encounter qualitatively new kinds of happiness.[93] Kautsky agrees with Marx, that all those would-be Raphaels shall be so under socialism. 'The general availability of education will facilitate the full development by everyone of all his [sic] potentialities, the promotion of which is in the interest of society.' The increase in free time will allow the individual further to develop potentialities should the nature of work limit these – leisure time will allow productive labour, work in science or art, or play or sport. 'In this regard, socialism will offer a hitherto unheard of possibility of the free development of the individual personality', but for Kautsky this could at most be a modernised and socialised Faust with collective sensibility overriding the will to be all.[94]

What emerges from any reading of Kautsky's work, as opposed to its Bolshevik resumé, is a sense of difference, distinction, and ambivalence. Kautsky is nowhere near as consistently given to the defence of democracy as Bernstein, indeed his primary values seem rather to be progress and proletariat. In this regard Kautsky does bear some responsibility for Lenin's views, as we have seen. Kautsky's early utopic visions generally lack any detailed sense of political forms, and it is of course the earlier Kautsky who is the vital figure in Bolshevism's intellectual formation. By *The Labour Revolution* and *The Materialist Conception* Kautsky makes his democratic credentials far more plain; they are there in the earlier work, but the citizen is still shrouded as the proletarian. Peter Murphy's critique of social democracy as a belated convert to democracy itself is thus well-aimed – at Kautsky, but not at Bernstein.[95]

BERNSTEIN: A GOOD MAN FALLEN AMONG LIBERALS

Eduard Bernstein has been even more extensively caricatured than Kautsky, for his period of Marxist orthodoxy was relatively short-lived, though he persisted long in viewing himself a Marxist. The stock response to his alleged 'decline' has, once again, been to blame the Fabians. Thus just as *Soviet Communism* has been uncharitably viewed as the declining view of two octogenarians, so Bernstein's refusal of orthodoxy has been viewed as a disease acquired while off the Continent, in England. Bernstein was obliged to leave Germany by the threat of imprisonment under Bismarck's anti-socialist laws. He was, indeed, something of an Anglophile, following as he did Marx's sense that England was further down the road of capitalist development and, especially, of the process of development towards democracy. Over a century an entire literature has been generated about the question whether in fact Bernstein was a Fabian.[96] The short answer to the question is no, but this has not served to prevent much ink being spilled over the issue. (Karl Korsch did in fact join the Fabians while on his own English sojourn; hopefully a fresh century of debate will be avoided in this case.)

Did Bernstein then have any substantive affinities with Fabianism? The answer to this question is also in the negative, but this time with qualification. Cosmetic similarities are apparent – Bernstein shared with the Fabians a generally evolutionary conception of socialism, but then, as we have seen, this was a general motif present in all labour movements in the nineteenth century. Certainly the company of the Fabians was conducive to heresy – and Bernstein actually came to realise that he was living a lie while addressing the Fabians on 'What Marx Really Taught' in 1897. He had set out to defend Marx, and came to realise that he could not persuade his audience because he could no longer persuade himself.[97] Subsequently Bernstein became not only the great (or miserable) reformist, but also the leading revisionist.

Bernstein was always something of a conservative among Marxists: he took tradition seriously, and viewed history as a process somewhat less than given to rupture. Unlike some others, such as Belfort Bax, he also shared with Marx and with Weber the sense that modernity was a mixed blessing. Bax, in debate with Bernstein, had identified modernity with capitalism and offered a completely negative appraisal of both. In this regard at least Bax was a less nuanced thinker than his co-author William Morris, for despite Morris' own medieval aura, he did not want simply to turn back. Bax attacked Bernstein as a rotten Fabian, an apologist for the culture which produced 'shoddy'.[98] Bax's own utopia, more or less explicit, seems suggestive of primitivism, Rousseau and the noble savage – for the savages, at least; this was a logic later to produce the moral approval of Bolshevism for the Russians but not for the British. 'Unlike Bernstein', said Bax, 'we regard modern civilization as, *per se*, a curse and an evil. (This, I suppose, is what Bernstein calls Romanticism).'[99] Capitalism, or modern civilisation, and socialism were absolutely antithetical for Bax – Bernstein had 'unconsciously ceased to be a Social Democrat' in order to deny this.[100]

Like all revolutionaries, Bax simply refuses to accept that to ask for everything is to demand nothing, to which the powers that be will only too happily oblige. Bernstein, by comparison, actually wanted the world to change but, like Kautsky and others, suspected that there were substantial obstacles – like tradition, habit and memory – to the scope of this change. Bernstein was not a postmodernist, or for that matter an antimodernist. He believed that progress was a value worth defending, that slavery was worse than wage-slavery, and so on.[101] Characteristically, he uses *Capital* to make his point. He then proceeds, in a series of articles in *Die Neue Zeit*, to discuss utopia more formally. He agrees with Marx and with Webb that utopianism in the old sense, 'the recipe for the cook-shops of the future', is obsolete. But there is a new kind of bad utopianism for which capitalism and socialism are worlds apart, for which socialism is a negative and apocalyptic view rather than one which affirms the world and then sets to work on it.[102] The Weberian resonances are unmistakable: in order to change the world, we must be of the world. But this does not, for Bernstein, add up to a disaggregated Fabianism, a patchwork of administrative policies for the reform of the respective compartments of social and administrative life. In individual investigations and as pragmatic socialists, the Fabians have achieved much that is excellent, according to Bernstein – but they have deprived the socialist movement of the compass which keeps it from just fumbling about in the dark.[103]

Like all other socialists, then, Bernstein makes rhetorical attacks upon utopianism while still, necessarily, working with an image of the future. And like Kautsky, he knows the literature of utopia and praises it as both inspirational and pragmatic. He praises Owen and Fourier for the detail of their thinking – for they were practical dreamers, so to speak, who viewed their proposals as feasible, discussed scale and architecture, needs and passions – they were reformers, offering defensible precedents for Social Democracy.[104] Bernstein appraises the desirability of local organisation, yet admits the impulse of modernity toward scale and differentiation. This raises practical, but also moral difficulties, and here Bernstein argues, like Weber, that the effects of welfarism upon the personality must be taken into consideration. Citizens must take on duties as well as rights in order to aspire to active citizenship.[105] Individuals, consequently, ought still to be responsible for their own welfare under socialism – responsibility is the reverse but coupled value of autonomy. The alternatives are tyranny or chaos.[106] Socialism thus involves the pursuit of social self-help, and like the Webbs, Cole and Kautsky, Bernstein here advocates intermediate institutions in order to facilitate the process. Most of the functions at present carried out by the state must be taken over by self-governing democratic bodies.[107]

Regarding work, Bernstein like Kautsky views it as a responsibility for socialist citizens: this is already implicit in his conception of individual responsibility. Again he turns here to Owen and Fourier, both of whom argued in defence of child labour on the basis of the anthropology *homo faber*. The point seems arcane, given the reconstruction of the image of the western child into the twentieth century, but the claim is consistent with the sense that humans need both to work and to play (Bellers).[108] It is also consistent with the claim that capitalism is the historical prerequisite of modern civilisation, but that this civilisation is by no means limited to the capitalist economy – child labour, like adult labour in its capitalist form is to be transformed but not abolished.[109] But now Bernstein was to let the cat out of the bag, and set it amongst the pigeons. For in 1898 he began to question the so-called 'final goal' of socialism. The 'final goal' of socialism Bernstein viewed as the utopia of windbags. The movement, the process of socialism was more important. The message of Bernstein's now clichéd phrase – the movement everything, the goal nothing – is in fact both sensible and defensible, only it produced so much purple outrage that his sundry enemies, Parvus, Luxemburg and the rest, were unable to concede the point (Parvus was sufficiently wild, and stubborn, to write no less than seventeen articles against Bernstein; Luxemburg wisely saved her energy and wrote instead one brilliant polemic, *Reform or Revolution?*).

The controversy preceded the publication of Bernstein's central work, *Voraussetzungen des Sozialismus*, characteristically mistitled in English on Ramsay MacDonald's mischievous advice as *Evolutionary Socialism*. The German title was significant, for Bernstein viewed socialism as a premise from which we depart, not a goal at which we arrive. Thus the *goal* is nothing, because socialism is not a goal but a principle. In response to criticism, Bernstein summons up the language which he used in the criticism of Fabianism: 'A movement without a goal would drift chaotically, for it would be a movement without direction. No goal, no direction! The movement needs a compass, but this goal is not the realisation of a social plan so much as the implementation of a social *principle*.'[110] Thus the so-called goal, or *principle* of socialism was intact; and the *movement* Bernstein defended as a gesture both theoretical and strategic. Bernstein defended the labour movement both as an institution and as a process, a moving towards socialism. And as Weber had pointed out, there was in any case nothing self-evidently reformist about this stand – the idea that the movement was 'everything' could just as well be the view of syndicalism.[111] Bernstein, for his part, argued (against Parvus) that not syndicalism, but state enterprise, municipal enterprise, co-operative enterprise led the way forward.[112] But more than this, Bernstein actually feared revolution, as he feared chaos. Certainly he was more hard-headed about state power than Parvus – for he simply argued that socialists could not spurn capitalism the day after the revolution unless they wanted economic life to come to a complete standstill, and thus set the stage for reaction. The theory of collapse was hopeless – like Gramsci, like Kautsky, Bernstein viewed socialism as a new order itself the product of order, not chaos.

Indeed, Bernstein proposed, if revolutions call forth all the slumbering potentials of humanity they also call out the idiots, and the world is still such a place that the idiots have a good chance. More generally, he suggested, socialists would do well to remember the power of memory and tradition – the world was not such a simple place, not even when old régimes crumbled.[113] In sad anticipation of later years he now wrote that when 'all trade has come to a standstill and all commerce has ceased, people do not ask whether something is socialist but whether it will help them get work and food'.[114] Bernstein was thus prepossessed both with ordinary human questions about suffering, and with postulates of social theory concerning the power of the imaginary. Like Weber, he argued against the dichotomy materialism and idealism, rather in defence of the category *interest*.[115] Like Durkheim, he proposes that moral concepts are more durable than economic developments, and that precisely because they are more conservative, they are to some extent independent of such developments. And thus he criticises Marxism's deafening silence on matters of ethics.[116]

Bernstein's own proposals become more clear when we turn to the book entitled *Evolutionary Socialism*. Reformism was not really the centre of controversy here; Vollmar and others had been counselling that for years.[117] But reformists and radicals had for too long been content to live with the combination of reformist practice and revolutionary rhetoric, since it had even been enshrined in the Erfurt Program of 1892.[118] Bernstein simply hoped to bring theory into line with practice; Rosa Luxemburg, by contrast hoped to bring practice into line with theory, while Kautsky, meantime, was happy to live with the contradiction. What generated the most hostility to Bernstein's case was, in retrospect, the least controversial of his claims. Bernstein had the tenacity to question the holy grail of classical Marxism – the proposition that capital would become more concentrated just as the proletariat would expand. Bernstein rejected the theory of capitalist collapse and the theory of class bipolarisation. According to his biographer,

Peter Gay, Bernstein sketched all this out not in a treatise but on an envelope:

> Peasants do not sink; middle class does not disappear; crises do not grow even larger; misery and serfdom do not increase. There is increase in insecurity, dependence, social distance, social character of production, functional superfluity of property owners.[119]

Bernstein argued that society was positively not becoming simplified but rather graduated and differentiated in its structure. The middle classes were a normal feature of this story and not an aberration.[120]

Crisis was not the motor of socialism; capitalist collapse was not inevitable. Socialism was better understood as the movement towards an order based on the principle of association. Consumer association was to be preferred to producer co-operation; co-operation itself could facilitate the process of the formation of social capital.[121] Unions were the democratic element in industry, but they were one actor alongside others, and were not representative of the proletarian state *in nuce*.[122] Politics was not primarily a matter of classes but of citizens. 'The idea of democracy includes, in the conception of the present day, a notion of justice – an equality of rights for all members of the community' – democracy actually meant the suppression of class government, not its extension into the proletarian state.[123] Thus social democracy 'does not wish to break up this society and make all its members proletarians together; it labours rather incessantly at raising the worker from the social position of a proletarian to that of a citizen, and thus to make citizenship universal'. The aim of social democracy, for Bernstein, was not to set up a proletarian society, but rather a socialist one.[124] Socialism was best viewed as the heir of liberalism; the security of civil freedom was always a higher goal for social democracy than the fulfilment of some economic program.[125]

Bernstein thus realises that the weight of both the Marxist and the German political traditions predispose social democracy to take both politics and democracy insufficiently seriously. While social democracy has been captivated by the figure of the proletarian, German political discourse has been constrained by the fact that even its language offers no special word for 'citizen' – there is only *Bürger*. Bernstein however is ultimately unfussed by this awkwardness – he already argued, against Lassalle, that 'we are *all* citizens (*Bürger*)', and against Luxemburg, he interpreted *bürgerliche Gesellschaft* not as bourgeois society but as civil society.[126] His opponents here suggested, as had Bax in a different setting, that bourgeois civilisation was entirely rotten: the challenge for Bernstein was rather to sort out what was defensible in bourgeois civilisation and what was not, for as he wrote elsewhere, socialism by definition cannot be completely new – history does not work this way, and never has since there were states, for no social principle alone is ever completely pervasive.[127] Luxemburg, by contrast, adhered to the theory of capitalist collapse,[128] while Kautsky at this stage sat on his hands, the two of them avoiding like the plague the ethical question why people ought to struggle for socialism at all.

Bernstein had let the cat out of the bag by claiming that socialism and liberalism were actually somehow related, and not just historically. Of course, this meant that socialism could never be a cultural, ruptural event; it also suggested, however, that socialists ought to follow liberals in turning their eyes to action, to behaviour, to conduct, to ethics and to politics. Like Marx, then, but also like John Stuart Mill, Bernstein proposed that the 'aim of all social measures... is the development and the securing of a free personality'. Autonomy is the precondition of social emancipation; democratic organisation from below leads the way to the realisation of socialism. The conquest of democracy, the formation of political and social organs of democracy is the indispensable precondition to the construction of the new order. More explicitly, Bernstein simply asserts that it is democracy which is the prerequisite of socialism (and not the other way around).[129] Democracy is not an instrument, but rather is the substance of socialism.[130]

Much of this argument represents a clear advance over classical Marxism's disinclination to take politics seriously. In some ways it is hard to believe that Lenin could have written *State and Revolution* almost two decades after Bernstein penned these principled yet pragmatic guidelines for socialism. Likely the outbreak of war explains this refusal of Bernstein's strategy: for Bernstein's case was indeed naively gradualist, resembling here the worst of new liberalism and not only its best. Thus advanced Rosa Luxemburg, polemical scalpel at the ready. Bernstein was certainly guilty of the central charge levelled by Luxemburg – he did indeed believe in the gradual accumulation of reforms, thus indicating altogether too teleological a concept of history as progress resting at the basis of his work. While Luxemburg's work and image still exert a great deal of influence within socialism, her own arguments here remain less than convincing; in a certain sense Luxemburg won the debate because the left was too readily inclined to kill the bearer of gradualist tidings, Bernstein himself.

Luxemburg's own utopia is difficult to glimpse. Plainly her axiom was the self-activity of the working class. This meant, however, that the question of reform or revolution reduced, in her eyes, to the class question whether the movement was to be petty-bourgeois or proletarian in character.[131] This qualm had been expressed earlier by Hans Müller, in his missile against the party elders, *Der Klassenkampf in der deutschen Sozialdemokratie* (1892). Müller had advanced the thesis that Bismarck's anti-socialist laws had effectively changed the class composition of the SPD, as its proletarian leaders, black-banned by old employers, were obliged literally to become petty-bourgeois in order to make a living. The consequence was that the identity of the party had been transformed.[132] While the account may be historically accurate, the implication – common to the views of Müller and Luxemburg alike – is puzzling, for socialism after all has never been a purely proletarian theory or practice, and indeed the idea that socialism should be proletarian has in fact been a major obstacle to its realisation. As Marx had suggested, socialism could be intellectual or experiential in its derivation; there is in principle no necessary (or historical) incompatibility between the middle class and socialism at all. Socialism has never been a movement composed solely of Dietzgens, real or imaginary. Socialism can be the sigh of the oppressed creature or the political choice of an intellectual; biography is plainly significant in the history of socialism, but it ought not to be viewed as a kind of magical explanatory 'last instance'. Rosa Luxemburg, for example, was hardly ever proletarian in her existence, which in some ways was reminiscent of Beatrice Webb's; only she was unable adequately to address the question, while Bernstein could simply respond that in the society of the future the individual would appear not as proletarian but as citizen.

For Luxemburg, the proletarian hammer blow alone would introduce the new régime amidst the context of crises and collapse.[133] The physiognomy of the new régime itself, however, remains unclear, for while Luxemburg lambasts Bernstein together with 'Mrs. Potter-Webb' they did, at least, give some sense of their imagined future, whereas Luxemburg keeps us guessing.[134] Like other revolutionaries, Rosa Luxemburg interpreted the historical exhaustion of German liberalism as indicating its intellectual end, into the bargain. The result is that while, like Trotsky, Luxemburg looks like the hero for today (or at least for the sixties), Bernstein, (like T. H. Marshall in the fifties or Agnes Heller in the nineties), actually explores questions to do with citizenship, democracy, and action because he transcends the economistic or systemic definition and reduction of civic life. Bernstein's utopia is like that of the Webbs (or Marshall... or Heller) in that it can be caricatured as a capitalist, or middle-class utopia. But virtually all save the most sublunar utopias can be thus criticised. The problem in the context of this discussion, however, is not only what constitutes a sufficiently radical utopia, but also what seems to be suggestive of a way forward. In this light Bernstein's socialism is interesting because, like Kautsky's, it bears some distinctly Weberian sensibilities, but also, and significantly, it posits socialism as one of the warring gods between whom we must choose. Bernstein was world-affirming where Luxemburg was world-denying. But more than Weber, Bernstein also saw a line which could run between these two sharp extremes, to affirm democracy and citizenship while denying the features of bourgeois civilisation which worked against them.

SOCIAL DEMOCRACY ON THE CUSP OF MODERNITY

The fate of the Social Democrats in Germany was closer to that of Weber's blackest fear, the iron cage, than that of seizing a future and acting on it. Certainly the SPD was never cured of its teleological habit, and while Bernstein's strategy was briefly enshrined in the Görlitz Program of 1921, it was only again to be replaced by the triumphant Kautskyism of the 1925 Heidelberg Program. Bolshevism meantime had become the source of inspiration, as Shaw and later the Webbs were to show. Bernstein, like Kautsky – like Weber – understood how badly the Bolshevik victory would set back their cause. As Bernstein wrote in a fragment:

> The socialistic theory of the bolchewists [sic] is, as much as it does not offhandishly recede behind Karl Marx, a marxism made coarse, its political doctrine is an overvaluation of the creative power of brute violence and its political ethics are not a criticism but a coarse mis-understanding of the liberal ideas that in the great French revolution of the eighteenth century have found their classical expression. But just as by the unbending language of facts they have already seen themselves compelled to subject their economic policy to a thorough revision the time will not stay away when in the face of the rebellion/revolt of the ineradicable striving of the peoples to freedom and right they will also have to fundamentally revise their policy and their ethics.[135]

While it is unlikely that there will be a Bernstein revival in Eastern Europe, the legacy of Social Democracy will in all likelihood be drawn on there as frequently as in Western Europe, by radicals arguing in defence of citizen-ship and the principle of civil society. This has a great deal to do with the fact that Bernstein and Kautsky effectively modernised Marxism's utopia, yet they did so in a way in which, unlike the Webbs, did not risk turning it into an administered society. They did not view administration as a sub-stitute for politics.

This is one factor which sets Social Democracy apart from Fabianism, though as I have suggested, Fabianism's faults were not necessarily those poked at by its jocular critics, nor is Fabianism without its instructive features. Yet Social Democracy arguably comes much closer to the so-called citizenship school, or to the tradition of ethical socialism, than Fabianism ever did. The problem with English ethical socialism is that, somewhat like the guild socialist tradition with which it has some affinities, the temptation is to gaze too solidly backward rather than forward, the implication being that if medieval ethics are superior to those of utilitarianism (which they undoubtedly are) then somehow medieval social theory will also be adequate to the tasks set us by modernity.[136] The same central issue thus arises again: how can socialism 'transcend' bourgeois civilisation while retaining its defensible practices and beliefs?

As has been suggested throughout this study, one binding feature common to socialist utopias since Marx is the claim that socialism is no longer a state to be postulated and realised, but rather an incipient and emerging state of affairs of one kind or another. Whether revolutionary or reformist, whether given to proletarian or multi-class organisation, however given to recognising or succumbing to social differentiation, labour's utopias view themselves as immanent rather than millennarian in character. Labour's utopias, at least those surveyed here, thus largely break with the image of Cokaigne, the idyll of earlier utopias, rivers of wine, garlicked fowls begging to be eaten and so on. Social Democracy takes this process of rupture the furthest, and consequently is the most modern or potentially 'postmodern' of labour's utopias. In this regard it is absolutely no accident that Kautsky takes on from the industrial pact, freedom beyond work, work as necessity, which Marx sketches in the third volume of *Capital*. Nor is it any accident that Kautsky and Bernstein have little patience for the Fourieresque idyll of *The German Ideology*. For in modernity the problem is not that I am free to be hunter, critic, shepherd, and so on, but that my necessary identity is that of parent, teacher, writer, administrator, editor, domestic labourer, son, lover and so on. After Weber we all of us bear many identities pertinent to our respective spheres of activity: the problem is less in trying to expand them, than in striving to live up to each of them and to the respective expectations which participants in each of these spheres of existence then place upon us. Doubtless in this setting Cokaigne still looms attractive, but likely the closest any of us get to this passed past is in leisure, in company or communing with nature as we know it.

What is striking about Bernstein and Kautsky's utopias in this regard is exactly the extent of the advance. We can see this by returning to two other leading works in German thought and in that of its labour movement – Ferdinand Tönnies' *Community and Association* and Paul Lafargue's *The Right to be Lazy*. Tönnies is usually read as a leading sociologist, as though he were not also an influential social democrat. Lafargue, on the other hand, is usually viewed as a socialist demagogue and not also as an interesting, if profoundly misleading sociologist.

Tönnies published *Community and Association* in 1887. The book was a vital prompt for Durkheim's *Division of Labour in Society*, for it viewed modernity largely as loss rather than as gain – it was a deeply romantic work, notwithstanding Tönnies' claims not to be taking sides. For as the title suggests, modernity for Tönnies introduces a rupture, a great divide between *Gemeinschaft* and *Gesellschaft*.[137] This was his essential proposal, wickedly reversed by Durkheim – that organic social bonds were dissolved, to be replaced by mechanical systemic relations. Though it was much more, the study also emerged in its reception as a positive reappraisal of medievalism – something which Bebel, Kautsky and Bernstein rejected, because they saw Wilhelmine Germany as still too much governed by a living feudal legacy.[138] The logic of Tönnies' argument, however, was directly to the contrary – the acid of modernity stood to dissolve the edifice of tradition. Household and economy would be further formally separated, town subordinated to city, obligation would decline, individualism become rampant, and all this would serve to produce a new and dismal cosmos and imagination. Plainly Tönnies' argument was influenced by Marx, for certainly it was his view that all that was solid would thus melt into air. It is equally plain that Tönnies' affinity with Marx was with the early Marx, with romantic hope of redemption rather than the modernist pact with the present.

Tönnies' view was also inward-looking, in a certain sense. The community could be self-sufficient; the individual in modernity cannot. Men may be obliged to suffer the market, but women can make peace in the home.[139] This is not Kant's world, the world of the cosmopolitan, nor Montesquieu's, nor Marx's – though it may be reminiscent of Rousseau. Tönnies too felt this impulse, for like Cole he came by 1922 to argue for something like guild socialism as a means to salvage part of the past.[140] The claim need not be made here that Tönnies was extraordinarily influential in terms of labour's utopia – it could just as well be the case that the theses of *Community and Association* reflected these views as formed them. It is certainly true that men and women in the German labour movement shared, for example, the noble, or simply practical but patriarchal view that women ought to be protected from modernity, or at least from its pernicious effects on the factory floor.[141] Yet what a contrast this is to the utopia of Bebel, or of Kautsky. For these moderns there was no necessity at all that the public sphere be a masculine realm, certainly not so far as paid work was concerned. Following Marx's positive anthropology, their premise was that human beings need to work, creatively to labour, regardless of their sex.

This is an appropriate note upon which to introduce Lafargue, for he too looked back for socialism, and rejected Marx's positive anthropology in the process. Lafargue drew broad respect in the Second International, not least of all as a philosopher. Lenin called him 'one of the most gifted and profound disseminators of the ideas of Marxism',[142] which says as much about Lenin as it does about Lafargue. Lafargue's work is a veritable mélange, combining true mediocrity with real insight.[143] In general his insights occur only occasionally in his ethnological considerations where there can be found some interesting anticipations of recent French structuralism.[144] Such insights are buried under an avid eclecticism and an unsuccessful mimicry of the grand heroic style of writing. Some central characteristics of Lafargue's thought can nevertheless be indicated. Lafargue combines a romantic critique of capitalist technology with an unbridled enthusiasm for the noble savage.[145] This combination produces what might be called an inverse Hegelian philosophy of history, where Europe represents the terminal senility of civilisation as we know it.[146] The anthropology at work in Lafargue is familiar: there is a strong emphasis on the healthy natural instincts of the savage, which are beaten out of him by so-called civilisation.[147] Lafargue admires Hobbes as the father of modern materialism, and presents arguments resembling those in Rousseau's *Émile*.[148] Religion and the work ethic are seen as the major fetters on essentially revolutionary forces.[149]

These arguments are stated more clearly in Lafargue's most famous work, *The Right to be Lazy*. Lafargue's treatise, a refutation of the earlier socialist maxim, 'the right to work', characterises that position as base and slavish.[150] He takes as his motif Lessing: 'Let us be lazy in everything, except in loving and drinking, except in being lazy.'[151] In an argument with distinct Nietzschean resonances as well as echoes in Wilde, Carpenter and Morris, Lafargue explains work as the product of a herd mentality which has permeated the labour movement: 'In capitalist society work is the cause of all intellectual degeneracy, of all organic deformity.'[152] The proletariat is *manly* but corrupted by Christian enthusiasm for labour; the noble savage is far superior to the mechanical slave of bourgeois society. The image of Athens haunts the background.[153] An extensive and absurd argument follows as proof of the corruption of work: the witless proletariat causes crises of overproduction by working too hard, while they should only take what they need from stock; their insistence on work and more work forces the bourgeoisie into a condition of unhappy laziness.[154] Here Lafargue reveals a class ambivalence towards hedonism, which is taken to be enervating for the bourgeoisie and yet at the same time a basic component of the socialist future.[155] Laziness, facilitated by automation, is understood as an instinctual return to a state of nature;[156] Lafargue shows no understanding of the need for work, so that his argument accords with the view of Adam Smith rather than with those of his unfortunate father-in-law.[157]

The glimpses of utopia in Lafargue's work recall Trotsky's *Literature and Revolution*. Parallels exist in the Olympian imagery, in the Nietzschean undercurrent, in the presumption of abundance with its actual concomitant – that some, the 'speaking tools', must continue to labour so that others might create or contemplate. The image of paradise portrayed in the essays presented together with *The Right to be Lazy*, 'Socialism and Intellectuals' and 'The Bankruptcy of Capitalism', confirms this utopian scenario. Like Trotsky's utopia it is dependent on mechanised production, Lafargue's radical criticism of technology notwithstanding.[158] Yet it is also, and essentially, the presocialist utopia of Cokaigne.

Looking back on Lafargue's work, the most surprising thing is that he was not laughed out of town (or city). Lafargue was indeed a respected figure, but it is difficult, on this intellectual basis rather than on that of his family affiliations, to see why this should be so. Like Wells, he seems basically to offer a personal program as a utopia. Doubtless the proletarian response to the process of capitalist industrialisation involved nostalgia for a past, real and imagined, as well as futurism or modernist desire to break with the past and embrace the future. Yet the proposition that the future will consist of inactivity rather than activity of a measured sort, and in hedonism rather than in contemplation sounds like little more than a preferred wish-desire, a fantasy in the bad sense rather than a utopia in the good sense.

While romanticism and nostalgia were certainly in the air for the German labour movement, so too was the sense of relative sobriety which we have come to associate with Max Weber. Indeed, it can be argued that Bernstein and Kautsky came to profess something like a Weberian Marxism, with the emphasis spread equally across these constitutive terms. Weber, like Tönnies, was also part of a certain liberal, social democratic milieu in Germany, and of course here as with Tönnies it can be argued that the milieu was as significant as the thinker. Weber was in correspondence with Bernstein, and the paths of such figures crossed in other ways as well.[159] As Harry Liebersohn has shown, the entire German intellectual scene between 1870 and 1923 was fruitful and fecund, to the extent that authorship of particular ideas is even more difficult than usual to explain. Kautsky, as we have seen, was thoroughly well read in Weber, but more so, these were people who each read what the others read as well as wrote and responded to what the others also encountered in German politics and culture. This meant that Nietzsche was in the air even for socialists, as Hinton Thomas has shown, and that the travails and ecstasies presented by modernity were encountered as shared concerns by several generations of German thinkers.[160]

CONCLUSIONS

Bolshevism, as we have seen, consisted especially in the figures of Lenin and Trotsky of an amalgam of eighteenth century views, often seizing on the mechanistic rather than the emancipatory moments of the Enlightenment. Fabianism was deeply scored by its origin in nineteenth century

British culture. The primary distinction between Fabianism and Social Democracy is the centrality to Fabianism of utilitarianism, however rendered or refined. Where Bolshevism was uniformly hostile to liberalism of all stripes, Fabianism was always deeply implicated in utilitarianism in particular. Social Democracy, by comparison, rejected utilitarianism but affirmed liberalism, especially in the case of Bernstein. Social Democracy took on from Marx the vital element of romanticism which Cole later suppressed and about which Beatrice Webb remained ambivalent. Social Democracy thus remains a more clearly ethical tradition, for it is more easily able to address the Kantian question; What can I know? What ought I do? What may I hope? Bolshevism, by comparison, departed from a putatively proletarian morality, or viewed cynically, from the question, how might I seize state power? while Fabianism set out from a collective question, how might society best/most effectively be organised? Even Cole, for example, wrote in a fragment:

> I know of no better political principle than Jeremy Bentham's famous Utilitarian principle of 'the greatest happiness of the greatest number' ... It does indeed (however) require interpretation in the light of the second principle – that each man [sic] must be broadly accepted as the best judge of his own happiness.[161]

Happiness was not usually seen as the primary value for the Social Democrats, indeed we might say, with Bernstein, that happiness was an end, not a premise. Resting on the cusp of modernity and of modern social theory, Social Democracy viewed the scenario in terms closer to Weber. The choices are constrained, but choices they are. Unlike Weber, they viewed socialism as one of these choices, the warring god to whom we could turn when it finally became clear that neither the Promethean Marx nor the Sisyphean Weber could adequately guide us into the new century.

Significantly, however, the Social Democrats eschewed any interest in simply rejecting Marx. In fact they seem to have been rather slow to grasp the idea that there were socialists – such as the Fabians – who were not in some way Marxists. It is equally likely that the Fabians took all socialists to be potential sympathisers. The Fabians did understand, however, better than the Social Democrats and conventional wisdom that there were real differences between their worldview and that of the Germans. For if there was to be any suggestion that Bernstein was a Fabian, there could be no such implication that Sidney Webb might be a Marxist. Webb wrote to Bernstein that the problem was not one of indifference to Marx, or of ignorance of his work, so much as that he was actually unconvinced. Bernstein had suggested that perhaps Marx was beyond Webb's ken; Sidney replied that all I can say is that I am a worse heretic than you suppose. You are charitable enough to imagine that I err only through ignorance – alas, it is more than that. Incredible as it may seem I have long since read the books you suggest, and yet stick to my opinion regarding the law of rent.[162]

Nearly forty years later Webb wrote to Kautsky, again in terms suggestive of the difference in their socialisms,

> Our work, as you will remember, has always been in the nature of analysis of the actual structure and function of social institutions... what we are concerned with is describing the institutions as they now exist without considering any theoretical origin and still more without predicting any actual result in the future.[163]

Clearly there were fundamental differences between Webb and the Social Democrats concerning both the nature of capitalism and that of socialism. The distance between Kautsky and the Webbs on Soviet communism itself is massive, because the Social Democrats did still envisage a new society where progress was made in terms of individual development. This much of Marx's legacy they did still embrace.

Viewed in this light, it becomes evident that the weakness of Fabianism lies in its ethical foundations. Bolshevism is a different kind of problem, for it has no ethics at all, save perhaps a party ethic. Fabianism, by comparison, maintains an ambivalent relationship to an ethic which is fundamentally flawed. Utilitarian ethics is completely hopeless. Any position which claims as its foundation the premise that *pleasure* ought be *maximised* is doubly decadent; because 'pleasure', like 'happiness', is an end rather than a premise, a term for a passing condition rather than a deep human aspiration, and because the quantification principle only makes this worse, introducing the calculus of mathematics where it has no place. Now the Webbs were never simply utilitarian, nor were the Fabians uniformly so, as Alan McBriar has shown.[164] Sidney Webb remains utilitarian, but focuses on the minimisation of suffering more than the maximisation of pleasure. Beatrice evidently empathises with John Stuart Mill's belief that Socrates dissatisfied is better than the animal satisfied. Neither can accurately be described as a hedonist, and yet both still work within the wake of utilitarianism. It may not be the utilitarianism of Bentham so much as that of John Stuart Mill which constrains their socialism, but the limits are still there.

Social democracy is ethically superior to both these other traditions because it reaches back through Marx to Aristotle, and while it is now widely accepted that Marx has no politics, or practical theory of changing the world, his thought does indeed contain the elements of an ethical basis which connect directly into arguments about the human condition. All of labour's utopias look both forward and back; the followers of Marx, sobered by Weber's time, alone here manage to look back, in ethics, and forward, with hope but circumspection, for they are firmly located in the present but understand something of its historicity.

5 Conclusions – beyond the goods society

Labour's utopias are different, as well as similar. The utopias of labour discussed here fail to vindicate the sense of Mattick or Cole that these were different routes to similar goals. The younger Cole would never have endorsed such a proposition in the first place, for he shared the view of the Webbs that socialists could be divided into bureaucrats (them) and anarchists (himself) or as he once put it, Sidney Webbicalists and syndicalists. Yet these different utopias do, for all that, still work within the horizons of modernity. They all alike represent discourses of modernisation. Durkheim, Webb, Shaw, Lenin, Trotsky all in different ways stand against hereditary rule, as advocates of the aristocracy of talent (their own). This again reminds us of the awesome influence of Saint-Simon, for whom the prospects of the utopia of industrialism were conditional on freeing modernity from its feudal and aristocratic accretions. Democracy was never a strong point in this, indeed our thinkers vary from the advocacy of direct democracy (Cole) to representative (Webb), and from the position of proletarian democracy (Lenin) to the repudiation of democracy as such (Shaw). The closest approximation to a politics of citizenship – rights and duties without class or functional claims – is to be found in the work of Bernstein, and to a lesser extent in Kautsky.

But if these were all modernisers, is not the project then over? This is the logic of Habermas' case in his essay on the welfare state and the exhaustion of utopian energies. Habermas views the unhappy fruition of the labouring utopia as that which takes on an institutional embodiment in the form of the welfare state. Labour's utopia is thus precisely that minimisation of labour-time which the late Marx imagined, but achieved within the space between the capitalist economy and the welfare state. The welfare state in effect takes over as labour's utopia.[1] This is a neat formula, which draws appropriate attention to the problem of the state in modernity. It also has the indirect strength of raising the question of consumerism. However much the socialist imagination has been dominated by capitalism, the two traditions have nevertheless refused to agree that the substance of utopia is provided by the image of the market. Now while the market remains the substance of the capitalist utopia and one necessary sphere of socialist utopias, it can today be argued that the real ideological locus of the capitalist utopia is not market so much as *consumption*. Marx's labouring or imagining citizen has been decisively supplanted by the individual whose sole need is to consume.[2] Consumption, mediated via markets, is widely viewed as the substance of human being. This new version of the capitalist utopia reigns supreme, as George Steiner observes in discussion of the recent events in Eastern Europe: 'American standards of dress, nourishment, locomotion, entertainment, housing are today the concrete utopia in revolutions.'[3] Trotsky's utopia emerges triumphant, but in capitalist cultural form; Trotsky, Bellamy, Lafargue are victorious, but in capitalist terms. Utopia is a hamburger.

Does socialism then simply become landed with the residual utopia of the welfare state? This is less than obvious, for there is a strong localist impulse, say, in English thinking from Morris to Cole and Laski. There have also, within Fabian ranks, been those such as Leonard Woolf for whom the logic of restricting the working day was to restrict that part of the year worked, an image closer to the utopia of André Gorz than to that of the postwar social democratic machine.[4] It would be consistent with the case argued here rather to insist that the state has its place, among other spheres of life. The welfare state is certainly part of the socialist tradition: its intellectual genesis can be found, like much else, in the work of Fourier, who, however, characteristically coupled the idea of a social minimum income with that of a sexual minimum.[5] Less promiscuous welfare hopes were also held by Ruskin. Probably it is fair to connect welfarism most directly to the Webbs. But again, this is no damning charge, unless we choose it to be. If there is refuse in the street it must be moved, whether by the state (Webb) or by the community (Cole). Socialism is a modernism, and rightly so; socialists do, for example, correctly view hygiene, health and education as worth defending. This is not as trivial a matter as it may at first seem, from the empyrean heights of theory or from the armchair comforts of postmodernism. For while markets happily colonise and corrupt all which is profitable, there remain spheres of activity where markets will not (and should not) go – child care, education, the care of the aged and so on. To argue against state intervention, against 'Fabianism' as many on the left today do is practically to vacate these spaces. Of course it can be argued that Fabianism as a practice becomes statist, paternalistic and the rest; the more central issue, surely, is the way in which all forms of mainstream political thinking become statist into the twentieth century, only more recently realising the negative effects which statism has upon the need for autonomy in everyday life. There is little sustenance beyond the emotional, then, in that kind of position which would cast Fabians as fascists and return the scope of politics to 'the people'.[6] Yet these kinds of arguments are likely to be heard more often than not, given the shrinkage of radicals away from legislation to the safer realms of interpretation.[7] While the refusal of Faustian-Trotskyist projects is to be applauded, the lapse of intellectuals into the privatised cynicism of postmodern culture is far from a happy, let alone civic, alternative. Rather we should remain Fabians – and reconsider what Fabianism had earlier meant.

Fabianism as a movement remained committed to co-operative principles, in this regard, until around the Great War, when we find, for example, Maud Pember Reeves arguing in defence of state responsibility in *Round About a Pound a Week* (1913).[8] English socialism on the whole has been more widely attracted to values of community than to the idea of the state, though there are important exceptions such as T.H. Green and the Bosanquets, for whom state was society writ large. Certainly it has been suggested, by Kitty Muggeridge, that Beatrice Webb's was the utopia of the welfare state; a further source for such a line of argument could be found in Beatrice's 1909 *Minority Report* on the poor law, which in effect advocated the idea of the modern welfare state.[9] Yet as we have seen, there are other images of socialism again in the work of Beatrice Webb – from co-operation to the constitutionalism of the 1920 blueprint and the final deceit of Soviet communism. And there were other, more emphatic voices arguing for a welfare utopia, such as those of Beveridge himself.[10]

The work of the Webbs remains compatible with welfarism because its utopia is the utopia of function. Bolshevism similarly remains compatible with welfarism because it is a labour utopia, a collectivism, a producers' utopia in the strict sense. The theme remains of some significance, for Bolshevism does not neatly disappear when its organisational form dissolves – it is a perennial dark shadow in all our social dreaming. It is only with social democracy that a sense of space emerges here, for the politics of citizenship only makes sense as a combination of rights and duties. The utopia of Cole constitutes something of a connection between Fabianism and social democracy, or at least with Bernstein, for if Kautsky represents the authentic spirit of social democracy Bernstein stands for its defensible legacy. Cole remains of great significance here if he can at last be extricated from syndicalism, which is not altogether easy. For it is not simply the case that Cole merely participated in the widespread wave of workerism which included the Industrial Workers of the World, council communism, Sorel and the young Gramsci. Cole's affinity with Rousseau was fundamental. His opposition to representation was a matter of principle, not just part of a passing enthusiasm for the slogan of direct action. More positively, however, Cole can usefully be identified as a pluralist rather than a syndicalist, as a theorist for whom any privileging of a particular social group or institution represents a constraint on humanity.[11]

If the socialist traditions have on the whole, however, become too thoroughly enmeshed with the wheels of capitalist civilisation, with the state, and with the modernist fetish of scale, then the basis of this slide is to be located in the turning away from the spirit, which it shares with capitalism. The emancipatory heritage of Marx's theory, however compromised, still viewed reason and imagination as central and defended free time in order to facilitate social self-development. Marx's was always a utopia of freedom, in this regard: Marx redefines freedom as free time, but retains the idea. This legacy was then positivised, via Bolshevism. Over Fabianism it always had a limited hold, because while Fabianism rejected the labour theory of value and what it took, as Keynes later did, to be a simple case of obsolete economics, it remained committed to a certain rendition of utilitarianism. This is the root fault in Fabianism, and not its statism or paternalism. The essential error in Fabianism here is its endorsement of that which descends from the 'pig philosophy' of Bentham. Utilitarianism is dangerous to the extent that it views the object of the good society to be that which consists of citizens who are fed, exactly a pig philosophy, a politics which identifies the needs of the individual with those of the animal.[12] But people are, after all, fed in prison camps, as are inmates in asylums, without ever having their human needs fulfilled. Human individuals need more than this, they need dignity and freedom. So long as capitalism is unable to assure these deepest hopes, socialism and its better utopias remain as sources of argument which enable us to address the human condition in modernity.

Fabianism reaches toward the spiritual, but it is constrained by its utilitarian origins and is finally swamped by the turn of events in the fifties and sixties. Both Fabianism and Social Democracy in a sense disappear into the statist political culture and the growth-governed economic logic of the postwar west. Both traditions become compromised by the postwar boom, for they fail to develop adequate answers to the question, who is to decide what now constitutes the good society? If it is those who know, then we find ourselves governed by technocrats, or worse. If it is the masses, we can perhaps anticipate nothing better than the bad eudaemonism of mass culture. Labour's utopias may each, in this process, be duly consigned to the dustbin of history. Those who wish to argue for radical utopias will find themselves recycling the more durable insights of their traditions. For the irony remains that if we really choose to go forward, then we must also agree to go back. Modernity remains unthinkable without tradition. As Durkheim wrote, that society which does not have an idea of itself will simply die.[13] The consumerist utopia offers us little more by way of spiritual sustenance than it does by way of gratification. In order to continue to live as humans, and to strive onwards, we need an idea of the society of which humans are truly capable. We need to affirm the world, with Weber, in order that it might be changed, in the spirit of Marx, as we need, with Durkheim, to have a concrete utopia of the good society in order to imagine this very project. After all its travails since the Enlightenment, through the Age of Revolutions to the epoch of holocausts, humanity deserves a better prospect than the utopia of the hamburger. The collapse of the Bolshevik experiment takes socialism back to its roots, and back to its earlier hopes. As we approach the year 2000, itself such a flashpoint in the utopian imagination, the challenge to the radicals who follow within the wake of Marxism is to reassess these traditions as well as to make sense of our immediate context, and to insist that humanity is capable of better.

Notes

INTRODUCTION

1 P. Mattick, *Rebels and Renegades*, Melbourne, Workers Literature Bureau 1946, p. 33.
2 G.D.H. Cole, 'The Webbs: Prophets of a New Order', *Current History*, November 1932, p. 143.
3 P. Bourdieu, *Homo Academicus*, Cambridge, Polity 1988, p. 256.

1 SOCIALISM, UTOPIA, SOCIAL THEORY

1 M. Berman, *All That is Solid Melts Into Air*, New York, Simon and Schuster 1982.
2 F. and F. Manuel, *Utopian Thought in the Western World*, Oxford, Blackwell 1979.
3 J.C. Davis, *Utopia and the Ideal Society*, Cambridge, University Press 1981.
4 E. Durkheim, *Socialism and Saint-Simon*, London, Routledge and Kegan Paul 1959.
5 ibid., p. 134–5.
6 P. Ricoeur, *Lectures on Ideology and Utopia*, Columbia, University Press 1986, pp. 290, 297.
7 E. Durkheim, *Socialism and Saint-Simon*, p. 137.
8 See, for example, Australian Council of Trade Unions/Trade Development Commission, *Australia Reconstructed*, Canberra, Australian Government Publishing Service 1987.
9 E. Durkheim, quoting Saint-Simon, *Socialism and Saint-Simon*, pp. 118, 139.
10 ibid., ch. 8.
11 ibid., p. 141.
12 On Fourier, see J. Beecher and J. Bienvenu eds, *The Utopian Vision of Fourier*, London, Cape 1972.
13 See R. Owen, *Report of the County of Lanark and A New View of Society*, Harmondsworth, Penguin 1970.
14 B. Taylor, *Eve and the New Jerusalem*, London, Virago 1983.
15 K. Kumar, *Utopia and Anti-Utopia in Modern Times*, Oxford, Blackwell 1986, p. 133.

16 P. Meier, *William Morris: The Marxist Dreamer*, 2 vols, Brighton, Harvester 1978.

17 E. Bloch, *The Principle of Hope*, 3 vols, Oxford, Blackwell 1986.

18 J.S. Mill, *Principles of Political Economy*, Books IV and V, Harmondsworth, Penguin 1970.

19 See generally Mary Peter Mack, *Jeremy Bentham*, New York, Collier 1963 and see G. Himmelfarb's chapter on Bentham in *Victorian Minds*, New York, Knopf 1968.

20 For Spencer, see for example, J.D.Y. Peel ed., *Herbert Spencer on Social Evolution*, Chicago, University Press 1972; for his specifically political views see Spencer, *The Man Versus the State*, Harmondsworth, Penguin 1969.

21 K. Marx, 'Excerpts from James Mill's *Elements of Political Economy*', in L. Colletti ed., *Marx – Early Writings*, Harmondsworth, Penguin 1975, p. 278.

22 See generally 'Economic and Philosophical Manuscripts', in Colletti, *Early Writings*, pp. 322–3, 345–52.

23 See A. Heller, *The Theory of Needs in Marx*, London, Allison and Busby 1976.

24 Marx and Engels, 'The German Ideology', in Marx and Engels, *Collected Works*, vol. 5, London, Lawrence and Wishart 1976, p. 47.

25 Marx, *Capital*, I, Moscow, Progress n.d., Afterword to second German edition, p. 26.

26 C. Fourier, 'Attractive Work', in Beecher, *The Utopian Vision of Fourier*, pp. 276–7.

27 Marx and Engels, 'The German Ideology', pp. 513–14.

28 Marx and Engels, 'The German Ideology', p. 393.

29 Marx, *Grundrisse*, Harmondsworth, Penguin 1973, p. 611. Elsewhere Marx casts the new division of labour as that embodied in the orchestra: *Capital* II, 1971, p. 383.

30 Marx, *Grundrisse*, p. 706.

31 ibid.

32 Marx, *Capital*, I, p. 174.

33 Marx, *Capital*, III, p. 820.

34 See generally J. Edie *et al.* eds, *Russian Philosophy*, 3 vols, New York, Quadrangle 1969; and see K. Clark, 'The City versus the Countryside in Soviet Peasant Literature of the Twenties: A Duel of utopias', in A. Gleason *et al.* eds, *Bolshevik Culture*, Bloomington, Indiana University Press 1989, pp. 175–89.

35 Marx and Engels, *The Communist Manifesto*, Peking, Foreign Languages Press, 1968, p. 36.

36 See generally T. Shanin, *Late Marx and the Russian Road*, London, Routledge 1983.

37 *The Communist Manifesto*, pp. 57–8.

38 See generally H. Lubasz, 'Marx's Initial Problematic: The Problem of Poverty', *Political Studies*, 24, 1, 1976; J. Maguire, *Marx's Theory of Politics*, Cambridge, University Press 1978.

39 *Marx – Early Writings*, p. 333.

40 Marx, 'The Civil War in France', in H. Draper, ed., *Marx and Engels. Writings on the Paris Commune*, New York, Monthly Review 1971, pp. 70–5.

41 R. Dahrendorf, *Society and Democracy in Germany*, New York, Norton 1979, p. 6.

42 Marx, 'Critique of the Gotha Program', in Marx and Engels, *Selected Works*, Moscow, Progress 1970, pp. 319–20, 327.
43 F. Engels, 'Socialism: Utopian and Scientific', in Marx and Engels, *Selected Works*, p. 424.
44 ibid., pp. 396, 399–400.
45 ibid., p. 398.
46 A. Sica, 'The Happy Fictions of Marx, Weber and Social Theory', in R. Antonio, R. Glassman eds, *A Weber–Marx Dialogue*, Kansas, University Press 1985. See also W. Hennis, *Max Weber, Essays in Reconstruction*, London, Allen and Unwin 1988.
47 On Durkheim, in this connection, see F. Pearce, *The Radical Durkheim*, London, Unwin Hyman 1989.
48 F. Feher, A. Heller, G. Markus, *Dictatorship Over Needs*, Oxford, Blackwell 1983, p. 299.
49 See L. Scaff, 'Fleeing The Iron Cage', *American Political Science Review*, 81, 3, 1987, p. 741.
50 M. Weber, 'Politics as a Vocation', in H. Gerth, C.W. Mills, *From Max Weber*, London, Routledge 1970, p. 127.
51 ibid., p. 120.
52 ibid., p. 127.
53 M. Weber, 'Science as a Vocation', *From Max Weber*, pp. 143, 153, 156.
54 M. Weber, 'Politics as a Vocation', p. 127.
55 W. Morris, 'Looking Backward', in A.L. Morton ed., *Political Writings of William Morris*, London, Lawrence and Wishart 1984, p. 249.
56 W. Morris, *A Dream of John Ball*, London, Longmans, Green 1918, pp. 39–40.

2 BOLSHEVISM

1 S. Fitzpatrick, *The Commissariat of Enlightenment*, Cambridge, University Press 1970. The section which follows relies on this account.
2 On Bogdanov, see generally K.M. Jensen, *Beyond Marx and Mach. Aleksandr Bogdanov's Philosophy of Living Experience*, Dordrecht, Reidel 1978.
3 See L.T. Sargent, *British and American Utopian Literature 1516–1975*, Boston, G.K. Hall 1979, p. 40.
4 R. Stites, 'Fantasy and Revolution. A. Bogdanov and the Origins of Bolshevik Science Fiction', in A. Bogdanov, *Red Star*, Bloomington, Indiana University Press 1984, p. 3.
5 ibid., p. 7, p. 14, and see generally Bogdanov's novels themselves, both in the same volume.
6 K.M. Jensen, *Beyond Marx and Mach*, pp. 9–10, and see more generally R.C. Williams, *The Other Bolsheviks*, Bloomington, Indiana University Press 1986.
7 V.I. Lenin, *What Is To Be Done?*, quoted by R.C. Tucker, 'Lenin's Bolshevism as a Culture in the Making', in A. Gleason *et al.* eds, *Bolshevik Culture*, Bloomington, Indiana University Press 1989, p. 28.
8 Lenin, quoted by Tucker, ibid., p. 29.
9 A. Polan, *Lenin and the End of Politics*, London, Methuen 1984.
10 Lenin, *State and Revolution*, Peking, Foreign Languages Press 1970, p. 58.

11 ibid., p. 59.
12 ibid.
13 ibid., p. 63.
14 ibid., pp. 120–1.
15 ibid., p. 121.
16 ibid., p. 122.
17 ibid., p. 50.
18 L. Trotsky, *Terrorism and Communism*, Michigan, Ann Arbor Paperbacks 1972, p. 170.
19 Lenin, *State and Revolution*, p. 101.
20 Lenin, 'Left Wing Childishness and the Petty-Bourgeois Mentality', *Collected Works*, 27, Moscow, Progress 1974, pp. 339–40.
21 ibid., p. 340.
22 ibid.
23 R.N. Berki, *Insight and Vision. The Problem of Communism in Marx's Thought*, London, Dent 1983, p. 97.
24 C.B. Macpherson, *The Life and Times of Liberal Democracy*, Oxford, University Press 1980, p. 12.
25 Lenin, 'On Co-operation', *Collected Works*, 33, Moscow, Progress 1976, p. 467.
26 ibid., p. 473.
27 ibid., p. 472.
28 ibid., p. 468.
29 ibid., p. 469.
30 ibid., pp. 470, 475.
31 ibid., pp. 470–1.
32 ibid., p. 475.
33 K. Marx, *Capital*, I, Moscow, Progress n.d., p. 305.
34 ibid., p. 309.
35 ibid., p. 312.
36 K. Kumar, *Utopia and Anti-Utopia in Modern Times*, Oxford, Blackwell 1986.
37 W.H.G. Armytage, *The Rise of the Technocrats*, London, Routledge 1965.
38 L. Trotsky, 'Perspectives of World Development', in *Europe and America: Two Speeches on Imperialism*, New York, Merit 1971, p. 33.
39 L. Trotsky, *The Revolution Betrayed*, New York, Pathfinder 1972, p. 61.
40 L. Trotsky, *Terrorism and Communism*, p. 133.
41 ibid., p. 135.
42 ibid., pp. 135–7.
43 Trotsky to Eckstein, 9.7.1911, in D. Geyer ed., *Deutsche Sozialdemokraten als Treuhänder des Russischen Parteivermögens 1910–1915*, Frankfurt, Campus 1981, p. 384.
44 Trotsky to Kautsky, 9.7.1911, 22.7.1911, ibid., pp. 406–12.
45 L. Trotsky, *Literature and Revolution*, Michigan, Ann Arbor Paperbacks 1971, p. 9, p. 11.
46 ibid., p. 14f.
47 ibid., p. 56.
48 ibid., p. 129.
49 ibid., pp. 131–2.
50 ibid., p. 201.

51 ibid., p. 229.
52 ibid., p. 230.
53 ibid., p. 231.
54 ibid., p. 241.
55 ibid., p. 250.
56 ibid., p. 251.
57 ibid., pp. 252–3.
58 ibid., p. 253.
59 ibid., p. 254.
60 ibid., p. 256.
61 P. Murphy, 'Between Romanticism and Republicanism: The Political Theory of Claude Lefort', *Thesis Eleven*, 23, 1989.
62 N. Hampson, *The Enlightenment*, Harmondsworth, Penguin 1987, pp. 204–5. See generally Burke, *Inquiry into the Sublime and the Beautiful*, London, Routledge 1958; Kant, *Critique of Judgement*, Oxford, University Press 1957.
63 See further R. Gerber, *Utopian Fantasy*, London, Routledge 1955.
64 See generally L. Trotsky, *Problems of Everyday Life*, New York, Pathfinder 1973, and *Women and the Family*, New York, Pathfinder 1970.
65 L. Trotsky, 'Family Relations Under the Soviets', *Women and the Family*, p. 57, p. 49.
66 Lenin, *Collected Works*, 15, Moscow, Progress 1973.
67 Lenin, *Collected Works*, 6, Moscow, Progress 1977, p. 378f.
68 Lenin, 'The Taylor System – Man's Enslavement By the Machine', *Collected Works*, 20, Moscow, Progress 1972, pp. 152–4.
69 On 'state capitalism', see Trotsky to Lenin, 21.1.1922, Document 749, in J.M. Meijer, ed., *The Trotsky Papers*, 2, The Hague, Mouton 1971, pp. 661–3.
70 See P. Beilharz, *Trotsky, Trotskyism and the Transition to Socialism*, London, Croom Helm 1987, ch. 7.
71 L. Trotsky, 'The New Course', in *The Challenge of the Left Opposition 1923–1925*, New York, Pathfinder 1975, p. 120.
72 R.B. Day, *Leon Trotsky and the Politics of Economic Isolation*, Cambridge, University Press 1973.
73 L. Trotsky, 'Toward Socialism or Capitalism?' in *The Challenge of the Left Opposition 1923–1925*.
74 ibid., p. 325.
75 On the strengths and limits of Gramsci's theory, see E. Laclau and C. Mouffe, *Hegemony and Socialist Strategy*, London, Verso 1985.
76 See for example L. Trotsky, *Whither England?*, New York, International 1925, p. 60.
77 N. Bukharin, *Historical Materialism, A System of Sociology*, Ann Arbor, Michigan University Press 1969; cf. A. Gramsci in Q. Hoare, G. Nowell-Smith eds, *Prison Notebooks*, New York, International 1973, pp. 419–72.
78 N. Bukharin, *Historical Materialism*, pp. 310–11.
79 N. Bukharin and E. Preobrazhensky, *The ABC of Communism*, Ann Arbor, Michigan University Press 1967, p. 70.
80 ibid., pp. 71–2.
81 ibid., p. 73.
82 ibid., p. 74.
83 ibid.
84 ibid., p. 75.

85 ibid., p. 76.
86 ibid., p. 77.
87 ibid., p. 136.
88 ibid., p. 333.
89 S.F. Cohen, *Bukharin and the Bolshevik Revolution*, New York, Vintage 1975, p. 145, p. 197.
90 ibid., ch. 6.
91 E. Halévy, *The Era of Tyrannies*, London, Allen Lane 1967.
92 N. Bukharin, *The Economics of the Transformation Period*, London, Pluto 1971, p. 160.
93 ibid., p. 161.
94 R.B. Day, 'Preobrazhensky and the Theory of the Transition Period', *Soviet Studies*, 27, 2, 1975.
95 E. Preobrazhensky, *The New Economics*, Oxford, University Press 1965, p. 3.
96 ibid., pp. 34–5.
97 ibid., p. 6.
98 E. Preobrazhensky, *From New Economic Policy to Socialism*, London, New Park 1973, p. 29.
99 ibid., p. 44.
100 ibid., p. 49.
101 ibid., p. 51
102 ibid., p. 57.
103 ibid., p. 63.
104 ibid., p. 64.
105 ibid., p. 77.
106 ibid.
107 ibid., p. 107.
108 R. Hilferding, *Finance Capital*, London, Routledge 1982.
109 M.C. Howard, J. King, *A History of Marxian Economics*, vol. 1, London, Macmillan 1989, ch. 15.
110 See R.W. Davies, 'Gorbachev's Socialism in Historical Perspective', *New Left Review*, 179, 1990.
111 J. Stalin, *Works*, 1, Moscow, Foreign Languages, 1952, pp. 336–41.
112 J. Stalin, 'The October Revolution and the Question of the Middle Strata', *Works*, 5, 1976.
113 J. Stalin, 'The Fourteenth Congress of the CPSU (B)', *Works*, 7, 1954, pp. 374–6.
114 J. Stalin, 'Concerning the Policy of Eliminating the Kulaks as a Class', *Works*, 12, 1955.
115 J. Stalin, 'Dizzy With Success', *Works*, 12.
116 B. Webb, Preface to P. Sloan, *Russia Without Illusions*, London, Frederick Muller 1938, p. viii.
117 L. Trotsky, *Whither England*, p. 81.

3 FABIANISM

1 See I. Britain, 'Two of the Nicest People if Ever There Was One', *Historical Studies*, 19/75, 1980, pp. 286–92.

2 S. Webb, 'Historic', in G.B. Shaw, *Fabian Essays*, London, Walter Scott 1989, p. 58.
3 S. Letwin, *The Pursuit of Certainty*, Cambridge, University Press 1965, pp. 328, 332, 334.
4 Webb, 'Historic', p. 31.
5 ibid., p. 56.
6 S. Webb to Burdon-Sanderson, 25.11.1897. *Letters of Beatrice Webb*, 1, Cambridge, LSEPS 1978, p. 110.
7 S. Webb to Beatrice, 16.6.1890, *Letters*, 1, p. 153.
8 S. Webb to Beatrice, 29.6.1890, ibid., p. 158.
9 Webb to Beatrice, 29.6.1890, ibid., p. 160.
10 Webb to Beatrice, 30.5.1890, ibid., p. 143.
11 S. Webb, *The London Programme*, London, Swann Sonnenschein 1891, p. 208.
12 ibid., p. 209.
13 ibid.
14 ibid., p. 210.
15 ibid., p. 212.
16 ibid., p. 213.
17 D. Wiltshire, *The Social and Political Thought of Herbert Spencer*, Oxford, University Press 1978, p. 250.
18 S. Webb, *Socialism in England*, London, Swan Sonnenschein 1890, p. 4.
19 ibid., p. 4.
20 ibid., p. 5.
21 ibid., p. 82.
22 S. Webb, *Towards Social Democracy*, London, Fabian Society 1916, p. 37.
23 S. Webb, *Socialism – True and False*, London, Fabian Tract 51 1894, p. 3.
24 ibid., p. 4.
25 ibid.
26 ibid., p. 8.
27 ibid., p. 10.
28 ibid., p. 11.
29 S. Webb, 'The Existence of Evil', Passfield Papers VI, 1, London School of Economics and Political Science, p. 34.
30 ibid., p. 35.
31 S. Webb, 'The Ethics of Existence', Passfield Papers VI, 4, London School of Economics and Political Science, p. 20.
32 ibid., p. 37.
33 ibid., p. 45.
34 ibid.
35 B. and S. Webb, *Industrial Democracy*, London 1913, published by the authors, p. 843.
36 ibid., p. 844.
37 ibid., p. 845.
38 S. Webb, 'The Economic Function of the Middle Class', Passfield Papers, VI, 20, London School of Economics and Political Science, p. 32.
39 ibid., p. 37.
40 ibid., p. 35.
41 S. Webb, 'Rome: a sermon in sociology: a lecture... at Hampstead... upon the

development of the social idea in European History'. Passfield Papers VI, 34, London School of Economics and Political Science.

42 ibid., p. 60.

43 ibid., p. 87.

44 ibid., p. 88f.

45 Webbs, in *Crusade* 3, 1912, quoted in A. McBriar, *An Edwardian Mixed Doubles*, Oxford, University Press 1987, p. 34.

46 B. and S. Webb, *The Consumers' Co-operative Movement*, London, Longmans 1921, p. 481.

47 ibid., quoting Delisle Burns, pp. 483–4.

48 B.L. Crowley, *The Self, the Individual and the Community*, Oxford, University Press 1987.

49 B. and S. Webb, *Constitution for the Socialist Commonwealth of Great Britain*, London, Longmans 1920, p. xii.

50 ibid., p. xvii.

51 ibid., p. 111.

52 S. Webb, Fabian Tract 70, cited in McBriar, *An Edwardian Mixed Doubles*, p. 161.

53 B. and S. Webb, *Constitution*, p. 196.

54 ibid., p. 350. cf. E. Durkheim, *Professional Ethics and Civil Morals*, London, Routledge, 1956.

55 B. and S. Webb, *Constitution*, p. 197.

56 ibid., p. 149.

57 ibid.

58 E. Durkheim, *The Division of Labour in Society*, London, Macmillan, 1986, p. 4.

59 ibid., p. 3.

60 S. Wolin, *Politics and Vision*, Boston, Little, Brown 1960, p. 401.

61 E. Durkheim, *Division of Labour*, p. liii and see generally G.D.H. Cole, *Guild Socialism Re-stated*, London, Parsons 1920.

62 S. Webb, *Towards Social Democracy*, p. 18.

63 See 'Beveridge Plan, memo and report of meeting with Fabian Speakers on the Plan', Nuffield, Fabian Society Papers, K31/4, 1942/1943.

64 H.G. Wells, *Faults of the Fabian*, Fabian Society Papers, B/51, Item 2.

65 See 'Beveridge Plan', Fabian Society Papers, K31/4.

66 B. and S. Webb, *The Decay of Capitalist Civilisation*, London, Fabian Society, Allen and Unwin 1923.

67 S. Webb, *Towards Social Democracy*, pp. 7, 14.

68 ibid., p. 17.

69 B. Potter, *The Co-operative Movement in Great Britain*, London, Swan Sonnenschein 1891, p. 75.

70 See more generally A. Wright, 'Fabianism and Guild Socialism: Two Views of Democracy', *International Review of Social History*, 23, 1978, pp. 224–41.

71 S. Webb, *Towards Social Democracy*, p. 36.

72 ibid., p. 39.

73 See generally C.B. Macpherson *The Life and Times of Liberal Democracy*, Oxford, University Press 1977.

74 S. Webb, *Towards Social Democracy*, p. 44.

75 B. Caine, *Destined to be Wives*, Oxford University Press 1988, pp. 209–10.

76 L. Woolf, 'Political Thought and the Webbs', in M. Cole ed., *The Webbs and their Work*, London, Frederick Muller 1949, p. 262.
77 B. Webb, *Diary*, 4, London, Virago 1985, pp. 279–80.
78 B. and S. Webb, *Soviet Communism – A New Civilization*, London, Left Book Club 1937, p. 450.
79 ibid., p. 1076.
80 ibid., p. 997. For a similar argument from a different position, see B.L. Crowley, *The Self, the Individual and the Community*, ch. 5.
81 See generally D. Caute, *The Fellow Travellers*, New York, Macmillan 1973.
82 B. and S. Webb, *Soviet Communism*, p. 998.
83 ibid., p. 999.
84 See D.E. Nord, *The Apprenticeship of Beatrice Webb*, London, Macmillan 1985.
85 S. Webb, quoted in R. Harrison, 'Sidney and Beatrice Webb', in C. Levy ed., *Socialism and the Intelligentsia 1880–1914*, London, Routledge 1987, p. 55.
86 See S. Wolin, *Politics and Vision*, p. 386.
87 R. Harrison, 'Sidney and Beatrice Webb', p. 35.
88 ibid., p. 36.
89 D.E Nord, *The Apprenticeship of Beatrice Webb*, p. 209.
90 B. Webb, *My Apprenticeship*, Cambridge, University Press 1979, Introduction.
91 D.E. Nord, *The Apprenticeship of Beatrice Webb*, p. 239.
92 B. Webb, *My Apprenticeship*, p. 239.
93 ibid., p. 166–70.
94 ibid., p. 182, 207.
95 ibid., p. 214.
96 B. Webb, *Diary*, 1, 1.2.1890, London, Virago 1985, p. 322.
97 B. Potter, *The Co-operative Movement in Great Britain*, p. 10.
98 On Owen, see for example J.F.C. Harrison, *Quest for the New Moral World*, New York, Scribners 1969.
99 B. Potter, *The Co-operative Movement*, p. 16.
100 ibid., p. 19.
101 ibid., p. 18.
102 ibid.
103 ibid., p. 26.
104 ibid., p. 28.
105 ibid., p. 35.
106 See R. Harrison, 'Sidney and Beatrice Webb', p. 68.
107 B. Potter, *The Co-operative Movement*, pp. 70–1.
108 ibid., p. 75.
109 ibid., p. 228.
110 ibid., quoting Marshall's *Principles*, Book 2, ch. 3.
111 ibid., p. 116, and see generally ch. 6.
112 ibid., p. 156.
113 ibid., p. 193.
114 B. and S. Webb, *What Syndicalism Means: An Examination of the Origin and Motives of the Movement with an Analysis of its Proposals for the Control of Industry*, supplement to *The Crusade*, August 1912, pp. 140–4.
115 ibid., p. 144.
116 ibid., p. 145.

117 ibid., p. 148.
118 ibid., p. 149.
119 ibid., p. 150.
120 ibid. As Ian Britain shows, the Webbs' attitude to work even contains moments of Morris, or at least elements of proletarian iconography in the manner of Orwell's miner. In the *Constitution* the Webbs propose that coal mining, manufacture of sewing machines or the shifting of logs might become 'truly an art' when conducted via Subject Associations à la Durkheim. B. and S. Webb *Constitution for the Socialist Commonwealth*, p. 200; I. Britain, *Fabianism and Culture*, p. 247.
121 B. and S. Webb, *What Syndicalism Means*, p. 151.
122 ibid., p. 153.
123 ibid.
124 B. Potter, *The Co-operative Movement*, p. 204.
125 B. Webb, *My Apprenticeship*, pp. 335–7.
126 B. Potter, *The Co-operative Movement*, p. 221.
127 B. and S. Webb, *Consumers' Co-operative Movement*, p. 59.
128 ibid., p. 159.
129 ibid., p. 181.
130 ibid., p. 414.
131 ibid., p. 415.
132 B. and S. Webb, *Soviet Communism*, ch. 3.
133 G.B. Shaw, cited in D. Caute, *The Fellow Travellers*, p. 78.
134 See for example F. Hearn, *Reason and Freedom in Sociological Thought*, Boston, Allen and Unwin 1985; S. Clegg, P. Boreham, G. Dow, *Class, Politics and the Economy*, London, Routledge 1986; J. Triado, 'Corporatism, Democracy and Modernity', *Thesis Eleven*, 9, 1984.
135 See generally A. Wright, *G.D.H. Cole and Socialist Democracy*, Oxford, University Press 1979.
136 G.D.H. Cole, *Self Government in Industry*, London, Bell 1918.
137 J. Vowles, 'From Corporatism to Workers' Control: The Formation of British Guild Socialism', ms, p. 61.
138 ibid., p. 74.
139 ibid., p. 195, and see generally A. Black, *Guilds and Civil Society in European Political Thought*, London, Methuen 1984.
140 G.D.H. Cole, *Self Government in Industry*, p. 122.
141 G.D.H. Cole, *Guild Socialism Re-stated*, p. 11.
142 ibid., p. 43.
143 ibid., p. 47.
144 ibid., p. 49.
145 ibid., p. 117; D. Nicholls, *The Pluralist State*, London, Macmillan 1975, P.Q. Hirst, *The Pluralist Theory of the State*, London, Routledge 1989.
146 G.D.H. Cole, *Guild Socialism Re-stated*, p. 121.
147 ibid., p. 137.
148 ibid., p. 140.
149 ibid., p. 164.
150 ibid., p. 180.
151 See generally A. Wright, *G.D.H. Cole and Socialist Democracy*.
152 ibid., p. 115.
153 ibid., p. 154.

154 ibid., p. 137.
155 W. Morris, *A Dream of John Ball*, London, Longmans 1918, pp. 39–40.
156 G.D.H. Cole, untitled ms, n.d., 'Guild socialism', *c.* 1922, Nuffield, Cole Papers, Box 1 B3/3/E, article 4, p. 7.
157 Fabian Research Department Committee on the Control of Industry, *Syndicalism*, n.d., Nuffield, Cole Papers, Box 3, B3/5/E, folder 1.
158 G.D.H. Cole, 'The Webbs: Prophets of a New Order', *Current History*, November 1932, pp. 144–5.
159 M. Holroyd, *Bernard Shaw*, vol. 1, London, Chatto and Windus 1988.
160 K. Kumar, *Utopia and Anti-Utopia in Modern Times*, Oxford, Blackwell 1986, p. 188.
161 H.G. Wells, *A Modern Utopia*, London, Chapman and Hall 1905.
162 ibid., p. 11.
163 ibid., p. 52.
164 ibid., p. 96.
165 ibid., p. 142.
166 ibid., p. 187.
167 ibid., ch. 9; pp. 263, 304.
168 ibid., p. 242.
169 H.G. Wells, *When the Sleeper Wakes*, London, Bell 1899.
170 H.G. Wells, *The New Machiavelli*, Harmondsworth, Penguin 1985, p. 112.
171 ibid., p. 114.
172 ibid., p. 154.
173 D.E. Nord, *The Apprenticeship of Beatrice Webb*, p. 239.
174 H.G. Wells, *The New Machiavelli*, p. 163.
175 ibid., p. 165.
176 H.G. Wells, *Faults of the Fabian*, p. 9.
177 ibid.
178 ibid., p. 11.
179 Fabian Archive, B 5/2.
180 K. Kumar, *Utopia and Anti-Utopia*, ch. 6.
181 G.D.H. Cole, lecture at Kingsway Hall, 4.3.1920, Nuffield, Cole Papers, B 3/5/B 4.
182 See, for example, H.G. Wells, *Russia in the Shadows*, London, Hodder and Stoughton, n.d., (1921).
183 G.B. Shaw, 'The Transition to Social Democracy', in *Fabian Essays*, p. 182.
184 G.B. Shaw, *Man and Superman. A Comedy and a Philosophy*, London, Constable 1909, p. xxxii.
185 ibid., p. 36.
186 ibid., p. 137.
187 ibid., p. 170.
188 ibid., p. 190.
189 ibid., p. 193.
190 ibid., p. 215.
191 ibid., p. 219.
192 ibid., p. 221.
193 ibid., p. 223.
194 ibid., p. 230.
195 G.B. Shaw, *Back to Methuselah. A Metabiological Pentateuch*, London, Constable 1931, p. viii.

196 ibid., p. xvi.
197 ibid., p. xx.
198 ibid., p. xlvii.
199 ibid., p. lii.
200 ibid., p. liii.
201 ibid., p. lvi.
202 ibid., p. lix.
203 ibid., p. lxxxivf.
204 G.B. Shaw, *The Intelligent Woman's Guide to Socialism, Capitalism, Sovietism and Fascism*, London, Constable 1932, ch. 4.
205 ibid., ch. 16.
206 ibid., ch. 18.
207 ibid., ch. 24.
208 ibid., ch. 42.
209 ibid., ch. 43.
210 ibid., ch. 48.
211 ibid., p. 320.
212 ibid., p. 322.
213 ibid., ch. 70.
214 ibid., p. 354.
215 ibid., p. 338.
216 ibid., ch. 76; p. 377.
217 ibid., ch. 79.
218 ibid., p. 447.
219 ibid., ch. 83.
220 ibid., p. 504.
221 G.B. Shaw, 'The Quintessence of Ibsenism', M. Holroyd ed., *Bernard Shaw – Major Critical Essays*, Harmondsworth, Penguin 1986, p. 151.
222 ibid., p. 126.
223 G.B. Shaw, *Everybody's Political What's What?*, London, Constable 1944.
224 ibid., p. 29.
225 ibid., pp. 35–6.
226 ibid., p. 38.
227 ibid., p. 40.
228 ibid., p. 42.
229 ibid., p. 57.
230 G.B. Shaw to F. Adler, 11.10.1927, Passfield Papers ll i.
231 G.B. Shaw to Adler, 14.10.1927, Passfield Papers ll i.
232 B. Webb, *Our Partnership*, London, Longmans Green 1948, p. 361.

4 SOCIAL DEMOCRACY

1 V. Lidtke, *The Alternative Culture. Socialist Labour in Imperial Germany*, Oxford, University Press 1985, cf G. Roth, *The Social Democrats in Imperial Germany*, Totowa, Bedminster 1963.
2 Marx to Engels, 7.11.1868, in *Marx–Engels Selected Correspondence*, Moscow, Progress 1975, pp. 203–4.
3 S. Macintyre, *A Proletarian Science*, Cambridge, University Press 1980, pp. 129–40; J. Rée, *Proletarian Philosophers*, Oxford, University Press 1984; A. Buick, 'Joseph Dietzgen', *Radical Philosophy*, 10, 1975, pp. 3–7.

4   J. Dietzgen, 'The Religion of Social Democracy', *Philosophical Essays*, Chicago, C.H. Kerr 1906, pp. 94–5.
5   ibid., p. 101.
6   ibid., p. 139.
7   S. Yeo, 'A New Life. The Religion of Socialism in Britain 1883–1896', *History Workshop Journal*, 4, 1977.
8   H.-J. Steinberg, 'Worker Libraries in Germany before 1914', *History Workshop Journal*, 1, 1976, and see his major study *Sozialismus und deutsche Sozialdemokratie*, Bonn, Neue Gesellschaft 1972. See also G. Haupt, 'The Role and Influence of Social Democracy in South-East Europe', in *Aspects of International Socialism 1871–1914*, Cambridge, University Press 1986.
9   A. Bebel, *Woman Under Socialism*, New York, Schocken 1971. I quote here from the volume of extracts, *Society of the Future*, Moscow, Progress 1976, pp. 19, 90.
10   ibid., pp. 25, 29.
11   ibid., pp. 48, 91.
12   ibid., p. 129.
13   ibid., pp. 126–8.
14   ibid., p. 25.
15   M. Salvadori, *Karl Kautsky*, London, New Left Books 1979; 'Reinterpreting Kautsky', *International Review of Social History*, 34/1, 1989.
16   K. Kautsky, 'William Morris', *Der Wahre Jacob*, 268, 1896, p. 231f (issue missing from IISH file).
17   K. Kautsky, 'Der Jungste Zukunftsroman', *Die Neue Zeit*, 1889, p. 268; I follow the translation of K. Bayertz, 'From Utopia to Science?', in E. Mendelsohn, H. Nowotny eds, *1984 – Science, Between Utopia and Dystopia*, Dordrecht, Reidel 1984, p. 106.
18   K. Kautsky, *Thomas More and His Utopia*, London, A.C. Black/ILP 1927, p. 1.
19   ibid., pp. 206–7.
20   ibid., p. 209.
21   ibid., p. 214.
22   K. Kautsky, *The Class Struggle*, New York, Norton 1971, pp. 133, 17, 127.
23   ibid., p. 157.
24   K. Kautsky, *The Agrarian Question*, I, Winchester, Zwan 1988, p. 30.
25   ibid., p. 97.
26   ibid., p. 101.
27   ibid., p. 104f.
28   ibid., p. 116.
29   ibid., p. 125.
30   ibid., p. 141.
31   Editors' Introduction to *The Agrarian Question*, I, p. xiii.
32   ibid., p. xvii.
33   ibid.
34   K. Kautsky, *The Agrarian Question*, II, p. 303.
35   ibid.
36   ibid., p. 325.
37   ibid., p. 329.
38   ibid., p. 339.
39   ibid., pp. 359–60.

40 ibid., pp. 362–3.
41 ibid., p. 425.
42 ibid., p. 443.
43 K. Kautsky, *The Social Revolution and the Day After the Revolution*, Chicago, Kerr 1910, p. 20.
44 ibid., p. 127.
45 ibid., p. 165.
46 ibid., p. 166.
47 ibid., pp. 166, 189.
48 K. Kautsky, *The Road to Power*, Chicago, S.R. Bloch 1909, pp. 22, 49, 50.
49 K. Kautsky, *Ethics and the Materialist Conception of History*, Chicago Kerr 1906, p. 197.
50 ibid., p. 196.
51 ibid., p. 202.
52 K. Kautsky, *The Labour Revolution*, London, Allen and Unwin 1925, p. 28.
53 S. Webb to Kautsky, 5.1.1923, Amsterdam, Kautsky Papers, IISH, DXXIII, 70.
54 K. Kautsky, *The Labour Revolution*, p. 99.
55 ibid., p. 102.
56 ibid., p. 128.
57 ibid., p. 143.
58 ibid., p. 156.
59 ibid., p. 169.
60 ibid., pp. 195–6.
61 ibid., pp. 196–7.
62 ibid., p. 201.
63 ibid., p. 203.
64 ibid., pp. 259, 224.
65 ibid., pp. 262, 283.
66 K. Kautsky, 'Demokratie und Demokratie', *Der Kampf*, xiii, 1920, p. 214.
67 K. Kautsky, *The Materialist Conception of History*, New Haven, Yale 1988, Preface.
68 See for example, K. Kautsky, *Bernstein und das Sozial Demokratische Programme*, Stuttgart, Dietz 1899, pp. 128–35.
69 K. Kautsky, 'Die Revision des Programmes der Sozialdemokratie in Oesterreich', *Die Neue Zeit*, 1901–1902, I.
70 Lenin, 'What Is To Be Done', *Collected Works*, 5, pp. 383–4; K. Kautsky, 'Die Revision', pp. 79–80.
71 K. Kautsky, 'Die Intelligenz und die Sozialdemokratie', *Die Neue Zeit*, 1894–1895, II.
72 K. Kautsky, *The Materialist Conception of History*, p. 6.
73 ibid., p. 28.
74 ibid., p. 464.
75 ibid., pp. 38–40.
76 ibid., p. 43.
77 ibid., p. 69.
78 ibid., p. 70.
79 ibid., pp. 101, 103.
80 ibid., p. 133.
81 ibid., p. 189.

82 ibid., pp. 209, 212.
83 ibid., pp. 260–1.
84 ibid., p. 262.
85 ibid., pp. 356–360, 368.
86 See generally H. Liebersohn, *Fate and Utopia in German Sociology 1870–1923*, Boston, MIT 1989.
87 K. Kautsky, *The Materialist Conception of History*, p. 397.
88 ibid., p. 399.
89 ibid., pp. 399–400.
90 ibid., pp. 410–11.
91 ibid., pp. 426, 435.
92 ibid., p. 513.
93 ibid., p. 517.
94 ibid., p. 524.
95 P. Murphy, 'Socialism and Democracy', *Thesis Eleven*, 26, 1990.
96 E. Belfort Bax, 'Our German Fabian Convert', in H. Tudor and J.M. Tudor eds, *Marxism and Social Democracy*, Cambridge, University Press 1988, pp. 61–5; H. Hirsch, *Der 'Fabier' Eduard Bernstein*, Bonn, Dietz 1977; see also R. Fletcher, *From Bernstein to Brandt*, London, Edward Arnold 1987, H. Kendall Rogers, 'Eduard Bernstein Speaks to the Fabians', *International Review of Social History*, 28, 1983, pp. 320–38, T. Meyer, *Bernstein's Konstructiver Sozialismus*, Berlin, Dietz 1977, H. Heiman and T. Meyer, *Bernstein und der Demokratische Sozialismus*, Berlin, Dietz 1978.
97 See Kendall Rogers, 'Bernstein Speaks to the Fabians'; and see Bernstein to Bebel, 20.10.1898, in H. Tudor and J.M. Tudor eds, *Marxism and Social Demo- cracy*, pp. 323–8.
98 E.B. Bax, 'Our German Fabian Convert', p. 61. See also E.B. Bax, 'The Curse of Civilisation', *The Ethics of Socialism*, London, Swann Sonnenschein n.d., for a more ambivalent view.
99 E.B. Bax, 'Our German Fabian Convert', p. 62.
100 ibid., p. 64.
101 E. Bernstein, 'Amongst the Philistines', in H. Tudor and J.M. Tudor eds, *Marxism and Social Democracy*, pp. 66–7.
102 E. Bernstein, 'Problems of Socialism', in H. Tudor and J.M. Tudor eds, *Marxism and Social Democracy*, p. 74.
103 ibid., p. 77.
104 ibid., p. 83.
105 ibid., p. 91, and see M. Weber, *Max Weber*, New Brunswick, Transaction 1988, p. 415.
106 E. Bernstein, 'Problems of Socialism', p. 94.
107 ibid., pp. 95, 97.
108 ibid., p. 105.
109 E. Bernstein, 'The Struggle of Social Democracy', in H. Tudor and J.M. Tudor eds, *Marxism and Social Democracy*, p. 151.
110 E. Bernstein, 'Statement', in H. Tudor and J.M. Tudor eds, *Marxism and Social Democracy*, pp. 193, 215.
111 Weber to Michels, 4.8.1908, quoted by L. Scaff, 'Fleeing the Iron Cage', *American Political Science Review*, 81/3, 1987, p. 744.
112 E. Bernstein, 'Critical Interlude', in H. Tudor and J.M. Tudor eds, *Marxism and Social Democracy*, p. 218.

113 ibid., pp. 220–1.
114 ibid., p. 222.
115 E. Bernstein, 'Problems of Socialism', p. 233.
116 ibid., pp. 238–43.
117 G. v. Vollmar, *Über die nächsten Aufgaben der deutschen Sozialdemokratie*, Munich, Ernst 1891.
118 The Erfurt Program is reprinted in G. Steenson, *'Not One Man! Not One Penny!' German Social Democracy 1863–1914*, Pittsburgh, University Press 1981, pp. 247–50.
119 P. Gay, *The Dilemma of Democratic Socialism*, New York, Collier 1962, p. 250.
120 E. Bernstein, *Evolutionary Socialism*, New York, Schocken 1965, pp. 49, 60–6.
121 ibid., pp. 96, 118, 124.
122 ibid., pp. 139, 141.
123 ibid., p. 143.
124 ibid., pp. 147–8.
125 ibid., p. 149.
126 ibid., p. 148, Tudor, p. 23.
127 E. Bernstein, 'Möglichkeiten Sozialismus', Bernstein Papers, IISH, E123, p. 14.
128 Luxemburg to Jogiches, 2.7.1898, in H. Tudor and J.M. Tudor eds, *Marxism and Social Democracy*, p. 225.
129 E. Bernstein, *Evolutionary Socialism*, pp. 149, 160, 164f.
130 ibid., p. 166.
131 Rosa Luxemburg, 'Social Reform or Revolution', in D. Howard ed., *Rosa Luxemburg, Selected Political Writings*, New York, Monthly Review 1971, p. 54.
132 H. Müller, *Der Klassenkampf in der deutsche Socialdemokratie*, Zurich, Verlags-Magazin 1892 and see G. Carchedi, *Class Analysis and Social Research*, Oxford, Blackwell 1987.
133 R. Luxemburg, 'Tariff Policy and Militarism', in H. Tudor and J.M. Tudor eds, *Marxism and Social Democracy*, p. 269.
134 R. Luxemburg, 'Social Reform or Revolution', p. 103.
135 E. Bernstein, 'The socialistic theory of the Bolsheviks', fragment, n.d., Bernstein Papers A123.
136 See P. Beilharz, 'The Life and Times of Social Democracy', *Thesis Eleven*, 26, 1990; N. Dennis, A.H. Halsey, *English Ethical Socialism*, Oxford, University Press 1988.
137 F. Tönnies, *Community and Association*, London, Routledge 1974.
138 See for example A. Bebel, Speech to Stuttgart Conference, in H. Tudor and J.M. Tudor eds, *Marxism and Social Democracy*, p. 302.
139 Tönnies, *Community and Association*, pp. 186–7.
140 ibid., pp. 227–8.
141 See for example U. Frevert, 'Women Workers, Workers' Wives and Social Democracy in Imperial Germany', in R. Fletcher, *From Bernstein to Brandt*.
142 V.I. Lenin, 'Speech in the Name of the RSDLP at Lafargue's Funeral', *Collected Works*, 17, p. 304.
143 Kolakowski dismisses Lafargue on the grounds of his mediocrity alone; see *Main Currents in Marxism*, 2, Oxford, University Press 1978, Ch. 6.

144 P. Lafargue, *The Evolution of Property and Social and Philosophical Studies*, London, New Park 1975, pp. 154, 155, 119.

145 ibid., pp. 99, 119, 91, 4f, 145, 167.

146 ibid., pp. 9, 208f.

147 ibid., pp. 114, 147, 104, 207, 161, 177.

148 ibid., pp. 18, 141, 177; P. Lafargue, *The Right to be Lazy*, Chicago, Kerr 1907, p. 67. In *Social and Philosophical Studies*, there appears the argument that 'Education teaches man to dispense with his intelligence', p. 148.

149 P. Lafargue, *The Evolution of Property*, p. 135 and Chapter 1.

150 P. Lafargue, *The Right to be Lazy*, p. 16.

151 ibid., p. 9.

152 ibid., p. 10.

153 ibid., pp. 16, 56, 12, 57ff.

154 ibid., pp. 24–42, 38.

155 ibid., pp. 34ff.

156 ibid., p. 44, where work is alien to human instinct. Compare Marx, in the *Grundrisse*: 'Really free working... is at the same time the most damned seriousness, the most intense exertion' (p. 611).

157 An illuminating source for background and character is F. Engels, Paul and Laura Lafargue, *Correspondence*, Moscow 1959–60, Foreign Languages Publishing House 2 vols.

158 P. Lafargue, *The Right to be Lazy*, pp. 103, 109.

159 See for example Weber to Bernstein, 1904, Bernstein Papers, D817, and see the chapters on Weber, Bernstein and Kautsky by D. Geary and J. Breuilly in W. Mommsen, J. Osterhammel, *Max Weber and his Contemporaries*, London, Allen and Unwin 1987; W. Mommsen, *Max Weber and German Politics*, Chicago, University Press 1984; and see generally M. Weber, *Max Weber*.

160 H. Liebersohn, *Fate and Utopia in German Sociology*; N. Hinton Thomas, *Nietzsche in German Politics and Society, 1890–1918*, Manchester, University Press 1983.

161 G.D.H. Cole, untitled ms, 'I know of no better political principle', Nuffield, Cole Papers, B3/3/F Box 8, folder 5, p. 1.

162 S. Webb to Bernstein, 15.10.1895, Bernstein Papers, D816.

163 S. Webb to Kautsky, 17.10.1933, Amsterdam, Kautsky Papers, IISH, DXXIII, 75.

164 A. McBriar, *Fabian Socialism and English Politics*, Cambridge, University Press 1962, pp. 149–55.

5 CONCLUSIONS – BEYOND THE GOODS SOCIETY

1 J. Habermas, 'The New Obscurity: The Crisis of The Welfare State and the Exhaustion of Utopian Energies', *Philosophy and Social Criticism*, Winter 1986.

2 N. Xenos, *Scarcity and Modernity*, London, Routledge 1989; M. Ignatieff, *The Needs of Strangers*, London, Chatto and Windus 1984; M. Walzer, *Spheres of Justice*, Oxford, Blackwell 1983; J. Seabrook, *Landscapes of Poverty*, Oxford, Blackwell 1984, *The Leisure Society*, Oxford, Blackwell 1988.

3 G. Steiner, 'In Search of Europe', *Granta 30: New Europe*, Harmondsworth, Penguin 1990, p. 130.
4 L. Woolf, *Co-operation and the Future of Industry*, London, Allen and Unwin 1918.
5 C. Fourier, in J. Beecher and J. Bienvenu eds. *The Utopian Vision of Fourier*, London, Cape 1972, pp. 55, 160.
6 P. Corrigan, D. Sayer, *The Great Arch. English State Formation as Cultural Revolution*, Oxford, Blackwell 1986.
7 Z. Bauman, *Legislators and Interpreters*, Cambridge, Polity 1987.
8 M.P. Reeves, *Round About a Pound a Week*, London, Virago 1979, ch. 16.
9 K. Muggeridge, *Beatrice Webb*, Chicago, Academy 1983, ch. 12 and see generally A. McBriar, *An Edwardian Mixed Doubles*, Oxford, University Press 1987.
10 See for example W. Beveridge, *Voluntary Action*, London, Allen and Unwin 1948; K. Williams and J. Williams eds, *A Beveridge Reader*, London, Allen and Unwin 1987.
11 See further P.Q. Hirst, *The Pluralist Theory of the State*, London, Routledge 1989.
12 See Peter Murphy, 'Socialism and Democracy', *Thesis Eleven*, 26, 1990.
13 E. Durkheim, *The Elementary Forms of the Religious Life*, London, Allen and Unwin 1976, pp. 422–3.

Bibliographical note

The fields of research covered in this study are rich in archival materials. The Passfield (Webb) papers at the London School of Economics and Political Science are invaluable, as are those of G.D.H. Cole and the Fabian Society at Nuffield College, Oxford. The most extraordinary collection of materials is to be found at the Amsterdam International Institute for Social History. Vitally useful here is the handbook by A. van der Horst and E. Koen, *Guide to the International Archives and Collections at the IISH Amsterdam*, Amsterdam, IISH 1989. (See also C. Cook, G. Pugh, *Sources in European Political History*, London, Macmillan 1987, volume one.) The Amsterdam Institute's collection includes basic bibliographies such as P. Versins, *Encyclopédie de l'Utopie, des Voyages extraordinaires et de la Science-Fiction*, Lausanne, L'age d'Homme 1972, and L.T. Sargent, *British and American Utopian Literature 1516–1975*, Boston, G.K. Hall 1979. The secondary literature on utopia is positively enormous. Apart from the major works by J.F.C. Davis and the Manuels referred to in the text, the most significant recent contribution is K. Kumar's *Utopia and Anti-Utopia in Modern Times*. Some of this more recent literature is discussed in P. Beilharz, 'Utopia and its Futures', *Thesis Eleven*, 24, 1989. An earlier body of work, too often overlooked, is that by W.H.G. Armytage, for example *The Rise of the Technocrats*, London, Routledge 1965, and *Yesterday's Tomorrows*, London, Routledge 1968. In general terms, the best encyclopedias of socialism remain M. Beer, *History of British Socialism*, new illustrated edition, Nottingham, Spokesman 1984; G.D.H. Cole's own *History of Socialist Thought*, London, Macmillan, five volumes plus supplements; L. Kolakowski's *Main Currents of Marxism*, Oxford, University Press 1978, three volumes; and T. Bottomore ed., *Dictionary of Marxist Thought*, Oxford, Blackwell 1983. A good introduction to some of the sociological problems involved in this field is P. Ricoeur, *Lectures on Ideology and Utopia*, New York, Columbia 1986. The best brief introduction to socialism presently in print is A. Wright, *Socialisms*, Oxford,

University Press 1986. The most consistently reliable work hitherto has been that of George Lichtheim. The work of David McLellan, like that of Lichtheim, can be strongly recommended. Bolshevism continues to attract scholarly attention. Leading titles on Lenin include N. Harding, *Lenin's Political Thought*, London, Macmillan 1977, 1981, two volumes; see also Harding's anthology, *Marxism in Russia, Key Documents 1879–1906*, Cambridge, University Press 1983. On Lenin, see also C. Claudin-Urondo, *Lenin and the Cultural Revolution*, Brighton, Harvester 1977, M. Liebman, *Leninism Under Lenin*, London, Merlin 1975, A. Besançon, *The Intellectual Origins of Leninism*, Oxford, Blackwell 1981, and above all, A. Polan, *Lenin and the End of Politics*, London, Methuen 1984. Important recent works on Bukharin include R.B. Day ed., *N.I. Bukharin. Selected Writings on the State and the Transition to Socialism*, Nottingham, Spokesman 1982; M. Haynes, *Nikolai Bukharin and the Transition from Capitalism to Socialism*, London, Croom Helm 1985; R. Medvedev, *Nikolai Bukharin – The Final Years*, New York, Norton 1980, and most recently K. Tarbuck, *Bukharin's Theory of Equilibrium*, London, Pluto 1989, as well as Cohen's magisterial biography. The leading authority writing on Preobrazhensky in English is Don Filtzer: see his *E.A. Preobrazhensky, The Crisis of Soviet Industrialisation*, London, Macmillan 1980, and *Soviet Workers and Stalinist Industrialisation*, London, Pluto 1986. Major earlier works include M. Lewin, *Political Undercurrents in Soviet Economic Debates*, London, Pluto 1975, and A. Erlich, *The Soviet Industrialization Debate*, Harvard, University Press 1960. Central to recent analysis, and alongside Filtzer's, is the work of Richard Day, most especially in *Leon Trotsky and the Politics of Economic Isolation*, Cambridge, University Press 1973. Trotsky is well served by the extraordinary labours of Wolfgang Lubitz in his *Trotsky Bibliography*, New York, Saur 1988. The best single volume study of Trotsky remains B. Knei-Paz, *The Social and Political Thought of Leon Trotsky*, Oxford, University Press 1978. See also I. Howe's extremely accessible Fontana Modern Master on *Trotsky*, Glasgow, Fontana 1978 and see P. Beilharz, *Trotsky, Trotskyism and the Transition to Socialism*, London, Croom Helm 1987. A valuable collection of conference papers is to be found in F. Gori ed., *Pensiero e azione politica di Lev Trockij*, Florence, Olschki 1982, two volumes. Two recent biographies are P. Broué, *Trotsky*, Paris, Fayard 1988 and T. Cliff, *Trotsky – Towards October*, London, Bookmarks 1989, both of which are attempts to supplant Deutscher's famous Trotsky trilogy, *The Prophet Armed-Unarmed-Outcast*, Oxford, University Press 1954, 1959, 1963. Words and pictures of Trotsky are available in the documentary *Trotsky* by F. Wyndham and D. King, Harmondsworth, Penguin 1972. Students in this field are also indebted to the ongoing work of the Glasgow journal *Critique*, and to the *Cahiers Léon Trotsky* (no other Bolshevik leader has a house journal outside the Soviet Union). Stalin has attracted an insightful biographer after Souvarine in R. Hingley, *Joseph Stalin, Man and Legend*, London, Hutchinson 1974. In terms of the debates around political economy, a substantial critical survey is now available in M.C. Howard and J. E. King, *A History of Marxian Economics, Volume One, 1883–1929*, London, Macmillan 1989, volume two forthcoming. The definitive history remains E.H. Carr's *A History of Soviet Russia*, London, Macmillan, fourteen volumes; an excellent short introduction can be found in Carr's *History of the Russian Revolution from Lenin to Stalin*, London, Macmillan 1979. A minor classic on the socialist opposition to Bolshevism is R.V. Daniels, *The Conscience of the Revolution*, Harvard, University Press 1960. The accounts of participants are best read together – Trotsky's *History of the Russian Revolution*, London, Sphere 1967, three volumes, say, with Sukhanov's *Russian Revolution of 1917*, New York, Harper 1962, two volumes. An early, but excellent work is W.H. Chamberlin, *The Russian Revolution*, New York, Grosset and Dunlop 1965, two volumes. For those who prefer words with pictures, an excellent book is H. Shukman ed., *The Blackwell Encyclopedia of the Russian Revolution*, Oxford, Blackwell 1988. A most valuable recent addition to the literature is R. Stites, *Revolutionary Dreams. Utopian Vision and Experimental Life in the Russian Revolution*, New York, Oxford 1989; see also his earlier study, *The Women's Liberation Movement in Russia. Feminism, Nihilism and Bolshevism, 1860–1930*, Princeton, University Press 1978. Valuable edited collections include R. Tucker, *Stalinism*, New York, Norton 1977, and A. Gleason ed., *Bolshevik Culture*, Bloomington, Indiana, University Press 1979. As well as the work of Fitzpatrick on Lunacharsky and Jensen on Bogdanov, see R.C. Walker, *The Other Bolsheviks*, Indiana, University Press 1986, and D.G. Rowley, *Millennarian Bolshevism: Empiriomonism, God-Building, Proletarian Culture*, New York, Garland 1987, for discussion of Bogdanov, Lunacharsky and also Gorky.

Fabianism is a well-worked field. Classics here include A.M. McBriar, *Fabian Socialism and English Politics*, Cambridge, University Press 1962, and *An Edwardian Mixed Doubles*, Oxford, University Press 1987, W. Wolfe, *From Radicalism to Socialism*, New Haven, Yale 1975; S. Pierson, *British Socialists – the Journey from Fantasy to Politics*, Harvard, University Press 1979, which covers *inter alia* Nietzsche and the English, and I. Britain, *Fabianism and Culture*, Cambridge, University Press 1982. The most recent of a series of instalments by way of histories of Fabianism is M. Pugh, *Educate, Agitate, Organise – 100 Years of Fabian Socialism*, London, Methuen 1984. Earlier landmark work includes that by M. Cole, *The Story of Fabian Socialism*, London, Heinemann 1961, and *Beatrice*

Webb, London, Longmans, Green 1945. I review Pugh and other recent related writings such as Pimlott's *Fabian Essays in Socialist Thought* and Durbin's *New Jerusalems* in 'Fabianism, Labourism, Social Democracy', *Thesis Eleven*, 16, 1986. Tawney has been well served by R. Terrill, *R.H. Tawney and his Times*, Harvard, University Press 1973, and more recently by A. Wright, *R.H. Tawney*, Manchester, University Press 1987; also extremely useful is J.D. Winter, *Socialism and the Challenge of War*, London, Routledge 1974. Interesting essays include F. Inglis, *Radical Earnestness, English Social Theory 1880–1980*, Oxford, Martin Robertson 1982, and N. Dennis, A.H. Halsey, *English Ethical Socialism*, Oxford, Clarendon 1988. In contrast to Tawney, the Webbs seem to continue to suffer from extremes of adulation or vitriol. For the former, see for example L. Radice, *Beatrice and Sidney Webb*, London, Macmillan 1984, or the interesting but under-theorised book by M. Nolan, *The Political Theory of Beatrice Webb*, New York, AMS 1988. For the latter, try B.L. Crowley, *The Self, the Individual and the Community*, Oxford, University Press 1987 or, in a category of its own in terms of the combination of strong criticism and insight, the work of G. Himmelfarb, for example the essay on the Webbs in *Marriage and Morals Among the Victorians*, New York, Vintage 1987. The most powerfully suggestive of recent work on the Webbs is that by R. Harrison, 'Sidney and Beatrice Webb', in C. Levy ed., *Socialism and the Intelligentsia 1880–1914*, London, Routledge 1987 (a useful volume). Alongside the work of Ian Britain, the most insightful of sympathetic criticism of the Webbs is W. Lepenies' largely overlooked study, *Between Literature and Science*, Cambridge, University Press 1988; detailed monographs on Beatrice include D. Nord, *The Apprenticeship of Beatrice Webb*, London, Macmillan 1985, and B. Caine, *Destined to be Wives*, Oxford, University Press 1988. Sidney Webb still awaits his biographer; he remains to be taken sufficiently seriously, which may be understandable, given that he is a person without Diaries. Alongside Beatrice's *Apprenticeship* (reprinted in the seventies by Cambridge and the LSE along with *Constitution* and *Methods of Social Study*), the *Letters* and Beatrice's *Diaries* remain the best way in to the Webbs. The best single study of Cole is A. Wright, *G.D.H. Cole and Socialist Democracy*, Oxford, University Press 1979; of N. Wells and J. Mackenzie, *The Time Traveller. The Life of H.G. Wells*, London, Weidenfeld and Nicholson, 1973 (see also their excellent study of *The First Fabians*, London, Quartet 1979, and see generally Norman Mackenzie's short study *Socialism*, New York, Harper 1966). Beveridge, not a Fabian but a constant presence in these arguments, has been the subject of a superb biography in J. Harris, *William Beveridge*, Oxford, University Press 1977. Bernard Shaw has been variously biographied by Harris, Pearson and others, but see now especially the trilogy by M. Holroyd, *Bernard Shaw*, in Chatto and Windus and in Penguin paperback. On Shaw, see also I. Britain, *Fabianism and Culture*, and N. Rosenblood, *Shaw: Seven Critical Essays*, Toronto, University Press 1971. On Fabianism as such, the pioneering essay by Eric Hobsbawm remains a valuable source: see 'The Fabians', in *Labouring Men*, London, Weidenfeld and Nicholson 1964. More general works which are central to the field include P. Clarke, *Liberals and Social Democrats*, Cambridge, University Press 1981; E. Barker, *Political Thought in England 1848 to 1914*, London, Butterworth 1915; R. Barker, *Political Ideas in Modern Britain*, London, Methuen 1978; W.H. Greenleaf, *The British Political Tradition*, London, Methuen, volumes one and two, 1983; M. Freeden, *The New Liberalism* and *Liberalism Divided*, Oxford, University Press 1978 and 1986; S. Collini, *Liberalism and Sociology*, Cambridge, University Press 1979; Collini, D. Winch, J. Burrow, *That Noble Science of Politics*, Cambridge, University Press 1983; Burrow, *Evolution and Society*, Cambridge, University Press 1970. Recent works on labour and labour thinking include R. Price, *Labour in British Society*, London, Croom Helm 1986; G. Foote, *The Labour Party's Political Thought*, London, Croom Helm 1985, and P. Hirst ed., *The Pluralist Theory of the State*, London, Routledge 1989. The best general way to seek an inroad into Fabianism is via the *Fabian Tracts*, in most larger libraries, or see the selection in S. Alexander, *Womens' Fabian Tracts*, London, Routledge 1988. Those possessed of less time might find the following, model essays useful: Cole, 'The Webbs: Prophets of a New Order', *Current History*, November 1932; Cole, 'Beatrice Webb as an Economist', *Economic Journal*, December 1943; L. Woolf, 'Beatrice Webb', *Economic Journal*, June 1943. An older, but fascinating collection is M. Cole ed., *The Webbs and Their Work*, London, Frederick Muller 1949. A useful comparison of two traditions is A. Wright, 'Fabianism and Guild Socialism', *International Review of Social History*, 23, 1978. Earlier thinkers are well covered in B. Taylor, *Eve and the New Jerusalem*, London, Virago 1983; J.F.C. Davis, *Utopia and the Ideal Society*, Cambridge, University Press 1981 which covers, among others, John Bellers; T. Keynon, *Utopian Communism and Political Thought in Early Modern England*, London, Frances Pinter 1989; A. Black, *Guilds and Civil Society*, London, Methuen 1984; Holbrook Jackson, *The 1890's*, London, Cresset 1988, and *The Rise and Fall of Nineteenth Century Idealism*, New York, Citadel 1969; A. Menger, *The Right to the Whole Produce of Labour*, London, Macmillan 1899; E. Halévy, *The Growth of Philosophic Radicalism*, London, Faber 1928; N. Thompson, *The Peoples' Science. The Popular Political Economy of Exploitation and Crisis*, Cambridge, University Press 1984, and especially *The Market and its Critics*, London, Routledge 1988; E. Hynes, *The Edwardian Turn of Mind*, Princeton,

University Press 1968; W. Hulse, *Revolutionists in London*, Oxford, University Press 1970; A. Ulam, *The Foundations of English Socialism*, New York, Octagon 1964; A.L. Morton, *The English Utopia*, London, Lawrence and Wishart 1952. Ruskin has been well essayed in P. Anthony, *John Ruskin's Labour*, Cambridge, University Press 1983, and J.D. Rosenberg *The Darkening Glass*, Columbia, University Press 1961. P. and J.D. Rosenberg have also published two vital studies of Carlyle. See respectively *The Seventh Hero*, Harvard, University Press 1974, and *Carlyle and the Burden of History*, Oxford, University Press 1985. Morris has been copiously studied by Edward Thompson, in *William Morris – From Romantic to Revolutionary*, London, Merlin 1977 and by Paul Meier, *William Morris: The Marxist Dreamer*, Brighton, Harvester 1978, two volumes. A wonderful introduction to Morris in the Oxford Modern Masters series is Peter Stansky's *William Morris*, Oxford, University Press 1983. Two extremely helpful readers on the English romantics are P. Keating ed., *The Victorian Prophets*, Glasgow, Fontana 1981, and E. Jay and R. Jay, *Critics of Capitalism. Victorian Reactions to 'Political Economy'*, Cambridge, University Press 1986. Useful readers for Ruskin and Morris are the Penguins edited by Kenneth Clark and Asa Briggs, respectively.

German Social Democracy is probably the least well-worked of the traditions discussed here, at least so far as publication in the English language is concerned. Recent exceptions include R. Fletcher, *Revisionism and Empire*, London, Allen and Unwin 1984, and ed., *From Bernstein to Brandt*, London, Edward Arnold 1987; H. Tudor and J.M. Tudor, *Marxism and Social Democracy*, Cambridge, University Press 1988; V. Lidtke, *The Alternative Culture. Socialist Labour in Imperial Germany*, Oxford, University Press 1985, and R. Evans, *The German Working Class 1888–1933*, London, Croom Helm 1982, as well as G. Eley and D. Blackbourn, *The Peculiarities of German History*, Oxford, University Press 1984. Two reliable recent histories are G. Steenson, *Not One Man! Not One Penny! German Social Democracy 1863–1914*, Pittsburgh, University Press 1981, and S. Miller, H. Pothoff, *A History of German Social Democracy*, New York, Berg 1986. Central earlier works include G. Roth, *The Social Democrats in Imperial Germany*, Totowa, Bedminster 1963, and C. Schorske, *German Social Democracy, 1905–1917*, Harvard, University Press 1955. Significant recent theoretical work also includes that of A. Hussain and K. Tribe, *Marxism and the Agrarian Question*, London, Macmillan 1983, and *Paths of Development in Capitalist Agriculture*, London, Macmillan 1984. On Rosa Luxemburg, see J.P. Nettl, *Rosa Luxemburg*, Oxford, University Press 1966, two volumes and more recently the essays by N. Geras, *The Legacy of Rosa Luxemburg*, London, New Left Books 1976. On Bernstein, see especially P. Gay's timeless work, *The Dilemma of Democratic Socialism*, New York, Collier 1962. Bernstein's other available works in English include *Ferdinand Lassalle as a Social Reformer*, London, Swan Sonnenschein, 1893, *Cromwell and Communism*, Nottingham, Spokesman 1980, and *My Years of Exile*, London, Parsons 1921. Kautsky's memoirs are in *Erinnerungen und Erörterungen*, The Hague, Mouton 1960. Fine biographies of Kautsky include G. Steenson, *Karl Kautsky 1854–1938: Marxism in the Classical Years*, Pittsburgh 1978; M. Salvadori, *Karl Kautsky and the Social Revolution*, London, New Left Books 1979, and R. Geary, *Karl Kautsky*, Manchester, University Press, 1987. Also extremely interesting are the documents collected in D. Geyer ed., *Kautsky's Russisches Dossier*, Frankfurt, Campus 1981, and G. Haupt ed., *Karl Kautsky und die Sozialdemokratie Südosteuropas. Korrespondenz 1883–1938*, Frankfurt, Campus 1986 (and see Haupt's significant posthumous collection, *Aspects of International Socialism 1871–1914*, Cambridge, University Press 1986). A Kautsky bibliography is available in W. Blumenberg, *Karl Kautsky's Literarisches Werk*, The Hague, Mouton 1960. Arguably still the best way to get some sense of what classical social democracy stood for is to read Kautsky's extraordinary journal, *Die Neue Zeit*, a cultural institution which has apparently yet to attract its own historian, at least in English (but see A. Hall, *Scandal, Sensation and Social Democracy – the SPD Press and Wilhelmine Germany 1890–1914*, Cambridge, University Press 1977). Connections of interest in *Die Neue Zeit* are manifold; Trotsky, for example, was a contributor 1906–9. Among contemporary journals covering the broad field of this book, see *International Review of Social History*; *History Workshop Journal*; *History of Political Thought*; *Victorian Studies*; and *Social History*. There are various other period sources, such as the Austro-Marxist journal *Der Kampf*. On Austro-Marxism itself, see T. Bottomore, P. Goode eds, *Austro-Marxism*, Oxford, University Press 1978; M. Blum, *The Austro-Marxists*, Kentucky, University Press 1985; A. Rabinbach, *The Crisis of Austrian Socialism*, Chicago, University Press 1983. Among other leading German materials, see H.-J. Steinberg, *Sozialismus und deutsche Sozialdemocratie*, Bonn, Neue Gesellschaft 1972, T. Meyer, *Bernstein's Konstructiver Sozialismus*, Berlin, Dietz 1977; Meyer and H. Heimann, *Bernstein und der Demokratische Sozialismus*, Berlin, Dietz 1978. Two vital source books are Bernstein ed., *Dokumente des Sozialismus*, Berlin, Sozialistiche Monatshefte 1902–5, reprint Sauer and Auvermann 1968, and F. Osterroth, D. Schuster, *Chronik der deutschen Sozialdemokratie*, Dietz 1963, new edition 1975–8. A useful brief introduction to the philosophical context is J. Roberts, *German Philosophy*, Cambridge, Polity 1988, and see H. Schnädelbach, *Philosophy in Germany 1831–1933*, Cambridge, University

Press 1984. On the German Social Democrats, feminism and Nietzsche, see N. Hinton Thomas, *Nietzsche in German Politics and Society 1890–1918*, Manchester, University Press 1983, and see for example the period writings of L. Braun, *Selected Writings on Feminism and Socialism*, Indiana, University Press 1987. On the Russian context, see B.G. Rosenthal, *Nietzsche in Russia*, Princeton, University Press 1976, and A. Vucinich, *Social Theory in Tsarist Russia*, Chicago, University Press 1976 as well as the various writings of A. Walicki.

On the fascinating issue of national Bolshevism and national socialism, see O.E. Schuddekopf, *Linke Leute von rechts*, Berlin, Kohlhammer 1960. On the French see *inter alia* the interesting volume *Marxism and the French Left* by Tony Judt, Oxford, University Press 1986. See also J. Roth, *The Cult of Violence. Sorel and the Sorelians*, Berkeley, California 1980 or L. Portis, *Sorel*, London, Pluto 1980. A good introduction to British syndicalism is B. Holton, *British Syndicalism 1900–1914*, London, Pluto 1976. On the Italians, see D. Roberts, 'The Italian Syndicalists from Marxism to Fascism', PhD, UCLA at Berkeley 1971, and *The Syndicalist Tradition and Italian Fascism*, Manchester, University Press 1979. For de Man, see P. Dodge, *A Documentary Study of Hendrik de Man, Socialist Critic of Marxism*, Princeton, University Press 1979. A major essay here is D. Pels, 'Henrik de Man and the Ideology of Planism', *International Review of Social History*, 32, 1987. A useful survey collection is D. Geary ed., *Labour and Social Movements in Europe Before 1914*, New York, Berg 1989. The best general text on the Comintern is F. Claudin, *The Communist Movement*, London, Peregrine 1975. Antonio Gramsci remains a fascinating figure in this context, and one who continues to attract scholarly attention. A fine point of entry is Alastair Davidson, *Antonio Gramsci – Towards an Intellectual Biography*, London, Merlin 1977. A stimulating small study is James Joll's Fontana Modern Master, *Gramsci*, Glasgow, Fontana 1977. Central insights into Gramsci's biography and theory are available in his own *Selections from the Prison Notebooks*, New York, International 1971, *Letters from Prison*, London, Cape 1975 and 'The Southern Question', in L. Marks ed., *The Modern Prince and Other Writings*, New York, International 1957. Gramsci has been extended into contemporary radical social theory by E. Laclau and C. Mouffe, *Hegemony and Socialist Strategy*, London, Verso 1985. A resumé of some of these arguments is presented in crystalline prose in 'Socialist Strategy – Where Next?' *Marxism Today*, January 1981. Some of Gramsci's context is sketched by R. Bellamy in *Modern Italian Social Theory*, Cambridge, Polity 1987.

The theoretical culture on which this book draws is the pluralistic kind of socialism and radical critique exemplified in essay form in the English language by the pages of the journal *Thesis Eleven*. The idea of the necessity of utopianism in modernity owes much to the work of Agnes Heller. See especially her 'Philosophy of History and the Idea of Socialism', in *A Theory of History*, London, Routledge 1982, and *A Radical Philosophy*, Oxford, Blackwell 1984. The problem of Jacobinism with reference to the Bolshevik tradition has best been addressed by Ferenc Fehér, for example in *The Frozen Revolution: An Essay on Jacobinism*, Cambridge, University Press 1987. The radical critique of Marxism was pioneered by Cornelius Castoriadis: see his collected *Political and Social Writings*, Minnesota, University Press 1989, two volumes, volume three forthcoming, or my review, 'Castoriadis: Political and Social Writings', *Thesis Eleven*, 24, 1989. Castoriadis' leading theoretical work is *The Imaginary Institution of Society*, Cambridge, Polity 1987; the category 'imaginary', which can in some senses be rendered in rough equivalent as 'project' or 'utopia' has influenced my thinking profoundly. In this context one should also consult the work of Claude Lefort, for example in *The Political Forms of Modern Society*, Cambridge, Polity 1986. Finally, the writings of Alain Touraine offer a profound insight into the sociology of the labour movement; see especially Touraine, Wieviorka and Dubet, *The Workers' Movement*, Cambridge, University Press 1987. The best brief introduction to Touraine's sociology is the essay 'Is Sociology Still the Study of Society?' *Thesis Eleven*, 24, 1989. Introductory vignettes of these theorists can be found in my edited collection, *Social Theory – A Guide to Central Thinkers*, Sydney, Allen and Unwin 1991. The affinities and symmetries between parts of these recent traditions and those in English radicalism are only now becoming evident: see, for example R. Plant, A. Vincent, *Philosophy, Politics and Citizenship*, Oxford, Blackwell 1986, or my essay, 'Theories of History: Agnes Heller and R.G. Collingwood', in J. Burnheim ed., *Essays for Agnes Heller*, Dordrecht, Reidel 1991. An excellent paper here is S. Collini, 'Sociology and Idealism in Britain 1880–1920', *Archives Européennes de Sociologie*, 19, 1978; there remains a great need for more work of this kind, and for more synthetic and comparative analysis. For Marshall, the best essay to read remains his own *Citizenship and Social Class*, Cambridge, University Press 1950, an essay which possesses some affinities with the argument of Fehér and Heller in their leading paper, 'Class, Democracy, Modernity', *Eastern Left, Western Left*, Cambridge, Polity 1986. As regards the classics themselves, the best reading apart from the texts includes M. Berman, *All That Is Solid Melts Into Air*, New York, Simon and Schuster 1983; R.N. Berki, *Insight and Vision. The Problem of Communism in Marx's Thought*, London, Dent 1983; and see the bench-mark study by S.S. Prawer, *Karl Marx and World Literature*, Oxford, University Press 1978. Pathbreaking recent Weber scholarship includes L. Scaff, *Fleeing the Iron Cage*, Berkeley, California University Press 1989 and W. Mommsen, *The Political and Social Theory of Max Weber*, Cambridge, Polity 1989. Still one of the best sources is Marianne Weber, *Max Weber, A Biography*, new edition, New Brunswick, Transaction 1988. A new interpretation of Durkheim is available in F. Pearce, *The Radical Durkheim*, London, Allen and Unwin 1989. Turning back to the Enlightenment, a brilliant short introduction is E. Cassirer, *Rousseau, Kant, Goethe*, Princeton, University Press 1945, and see his *Philosophy of the Enlightenment*, Princeton, University Press 1951. More recent introductions include R. Anchor, *The Enlightenment*, Berkeley, California University Press 1969, and N. Hampson, *The Enlightenment*, Harmondsworth, Penguin 1987. The various writings of Peter Gay and Judith Shklar here, like those of Lichtheim on socialism, are invariably stimulating and insightful. One brilliant study of Rousseau is J. Starobinski, *Jean-Jacques Rousseau. Transparency and Obstruction*, Chicago, University Press 1988. Those new to Rousseau could just as well read *Reveries of a Solitary Walker* or the *Confessions*. On Hegel, see Charles Taylor's *Hegel*, Cambridge, University Press 1975 and L. Dickey, *Hegel*, Cambridge, University Press 1987. A recent addition to the Hegel literature in English is the translation of his introductory *Propadeutic*, but there is no easy way in to Hegel. A major recent work of interpretation is D. Howard, *From Marx to Kant*, Albany, State University Press 1985. A massive work of scholarship which crosses many of these concerns is R. Wuthnow, *Communities of Discourse*, Harvard, University Press 1989. Wallerstein says of it in review that it is in fact three books, one each on the Reformation, Enlightenment, and European socialism. Finally, there are various book length essays which might provide the interested reader with some sense of some of the problems involved in our traditions. They include B. Crick, *In Defence of Politics*, in various Penguin editions, J. Dunn, *The Politics of Socialism*, Cambridge, University Press 1984, M. Ignatieff, *The Needs of Strangers*, London, Chatto 1984, P. Hirst, *Law, Socialism and Democracy*, London, Allen and Unwin 1986, B. Hindess, *Politics and Class Analysis*, Oxford, Blackwell 1987, J. Seabrook, for example in *Landscapes of Poverty*, Oxford, Blackwell 1984 or *The Leisure Society*, Oxford, Blackwell 1988, Z. Bauman, *Legislators and Interpreters*, Cambridge, Polity 1987, and N. Xenos, *Scarcity and Modernity*, London, Routledge 1989. A fascinating essay which casts back to the sixteenth century, and then into the third millennium is S. Toulmin, *Cosmopolis*, New York, Free Press 1989. Now read on.

Index